Beccles Clerical Society
June 29/43.

# REDEMPTION AND REVELATION

# REDEMPTION AND REVELATION

## In the Actuality of History

BY

## H. WHEELER ROBINSON

M.A., D.D.

LATE PRINCIPAL OF REGENT'S PARK COLLEGE,
OXFORD

London
NISBET & CO. LTD.
22 BERNERS STREET, W.1

*First published April 1942*
*Reprinted January 1943*

MADE AND PRINTED IN GREAT BRITAIN BY
UNWIN BROTHERS LIMITED, LONDON AND WOKING

# GENERAL INTRODUCTION

THE Editors of this series are convinced that the Christian Church as a whole is confronted with a great though largely silent crisis, and also with an unparalleled opportunity. They have a common mind concerning the way in which this crisis and opportunity should be met. The time has gone by when "apologetics" could be of any great value. Something more is needed than a defence of propositions already accepted on authority, for the present spiritual crisis is essentially a questioning of authority if not a revolt against it. It may be predicted that the number of people who are content simply to rest their religion on the authority of the Bible or the Church is steadily diminishing, and with the growing effectiveness of popular education will continue to diminish. We shall not therefore meet the need, if we have rightly diagnosed it, by dissertations, however learned, on the interpretation of the Bible or the history of Christian doctrine. Nothing less is required than a candid, courageous and well-informed effort to think out anew, in the light of modern knowledge, the foundation affirmations of our common Christianity. This is the aim of every writer in this series.

A further agreement is, we hope, characteristic of the books which will be published in the series. The authors have a common mind not only with regard to the problem but also with regard to the starting-point of reconstruction. They desire to lay stress upon the value and validity of religious experience and to develop their theology on the basis of the religious consciousness. In so doing they claim to be in harmony with modern thought. The massive achievements of the nineteenth and twentieth centuries have been built up on the method of observation and experiment, on experience, not on abstract *a priori* reasoning. Our contention is that the moral and spiritual experience of mankind has the right to be considered, and demands to be understood.

Many distinguished thinkers might be quoted in support of the assertion that philosophers are now prepared in a greater measure than formerly to consider religious experience as among the most significant of their data. One of the greatest has said, "There is nothing more real than what comes in religion. To compare facts such as these with what is given to us in outward existence would be to trifle with the subject. The man who demands a reality more solid than that of the religious consciousness, seeks he does not know what."[1] Nor does this estimate of religious experience come only from idealist thinkers. A philosopher who writes from the standpoint of mathematics and natural science has expressed the same thought in even more forcible language. "The fact of religious vision, and its history of persistent expansion, is our one ground for optimism. Apart from it, human life is a flash of occasional enjoyments lighting up a mass of pain and misery, a bagatelle of transient experience."[2]

The conviction that religious experience is to be taken as the starting-point of theological reconstruction does not, of course, imply that we are absolved from the labour of thought. On the contrary, it should serve as the stimulus to thought. No experience can be taken at its face value; it must be criticized and interpreted. Just as natural science could not exist without experience and

[1] F. H. Bradley, *Appearance and Reality*, p. 449.
[2] A. N. Whitehead, *Science and the Modern World*, p. 275.

the thought concerning experience, so theology cannot exist without the religious consciousness and reflection upon it. Nor do we mean by "experience" anything less than the whole experience of the human race, so far as it has shared in the Christian consciousness. As Mazzini finely said, "Tradition and conscience are the two wings given to the human soul to reach the truth."

It has been the aim of the writers and the Editors of the series to produce studies of the main aspects of Christianity which will be intelligible and interesting to the general reader and at the same time may be worthy of the attention of the specialist. After all, in religion we are dealing with a subject-matter which is open to all and the plan of the works does not require that they shall delve very deeply into questions of minute scholarship. We have had the ambition to produce volumes which might find a useful place on the shelves of the clergyman and minister, and no less on those of the intelligent layman. Perhaps we may have done something to bridge the gulf which too often separates the pulpit from the pew.

Naturally, the plan of our series has led us to give the utmost freedom to the authors of the books to work out their own lines of thought, and our part has been strictly confined to the invitation to contribute, and to suggestions concerning the mode of presentation. We hope that the series will contribute something useful to the great debate on religion which is proceeding in secret in the mind of our age, and we humbly pray that their endeavours and ours may be blessed by the Spirit of Truth for the building up of Christ's Universal Church.

# PREFACE

THIS book is the third of a "trilogy" which has largely covered my working life as a teacher and preacher of the Christian faith. The first of the three, *The Christian Doctrine of Man*, published in 1911,[1] was dominated by an initial interest in the psychology of religion, and was approached through an academic thesis on "The Psychological Terms of the Hebrews".[2] The second, *The Christian Experience of the Holy Spirit*, represented the extension of this psychological emphasis to its philosophical and theological background, and was published in 1928.[3] The third, *Redemption and Revelation*, now offered to the reader, concentrates on the media of revelation and especially the redemptive act of the Cross, as based in the actuality of history. Psychology, philosophy and history each make an essential contribution to theology, and I see now, as I could not have seen at the beginning, that there is a unity underlying these three books deeper than that of conscious purpose. The "pragmatic" method of their production has probably served to keep them closer to life than a more "academic" attempt to deal systematically with these great themes of theology. Some amount of repetition is unavoidable, in the use of such a method, and more especially because some sections of this book (as will be indicated in this preface) were written in their original

[1] By T. & T. Clark, Edinburgh.
[2] This was not published at the time, but its general results were reproduced in an essay on "Hebrew Psychology in relation to Pauline Anthropology" (*Mansfield College Essays, 1909*) and in another on "Hebrew Psychology" (in *The People and the Book*, ed. by A. S. Peake, 1925).
[3] By Nisbet & Co., London.

form for particular occasions. But such repetition may help to clarify the general statement.

On the subject of the first of these books, *The Christian Doctrine of Man*, I found a distinct lacuna in our theological literature. The continued circulation of that book (since 1911) encourages me to think that it has done something to fill the gap. On the work of the Holy Spirit, there were many books, but none of them seemed to me to be at once sufficiently "realistic" in the treatment and sufficiently constructive in aim, especially in relation to the Doctrine of the Holy Trinity. On the present subject, English theology has a considerable number of books, some of them classical, which make real contributions to the subject. I should have hesitated to enter upon this well-trodden ground, had I not felt that the actuality of history supplied a line of approach to which sufficient attention has not been paid.

The keynote of the present book is implied in its title. The revelation made by the Gospel is that of a redemption; the redemption does not consist simply in a revelation which influences men to lead a new life; the revelation produces this (subjective) change of attitude and conduct because it reveals an (objective) redemption which God has independently wrought in Christ, which is completed in the actual transformation taking place in Christian lives.

This "old-fashioned" view of the Cross is here based primarily on the Hebrew realism out of which the new faith grew, a realism which underlies the whole Biblical conception of a revelation through history. One great way of interpreting Christ's death is through the conception of sacrifice, as an offering to God. But sacrifice must not be confused with the very different juristic conception of penal substitution. I believe that this conception does enter (amongst others) into the theology of St. Paul, as does to a smaller degree the sacrificial conception. Penal substitution is one way of expressing the objective character of redemption, but it is inadequate, if only because the conception of God as "righteous" is not the whole truth about Him. God is a just judge, but He is far more.

As regards the form in which the argument of this book is presented, viz. the approach through the axioms of a philosophy of history, I was led to this by what were for a long time detached studies of both redemption and revelation. I found them both converging on the conception of the "actuality" of history. By this I mean the aspect of human life which sees it as the realistic achievement of eternal values in the unique category of time. The Christian theist finds all good already in God, the ultimate home of all human values. But he is also committed to finding moral and spiritual "reality" in the working out of human lives, whether for good or for evil. Only on this basis can moral responsibility be maintained. That which is done on earth counts eternally in heaven. Conversely, the purpose of heaven must ultimately be worked out on earth. In the actuality of human life the divine purpose finds a new and unique category of achievement, reached through the exercise of human freedom. The abuse of that freedom which human history displays is beyond man's power to atone; it requires the divine "redemption", and the actuality of that redemption in Christ supplies the supreme revelation of God, which itself becomes the cardinal factor in changing the hearts and lives of men.

Several chapters or sections of this book have previously been printed. The Introduction ("The Meaning of History") and Chapter II ("The Ministry of Error") appeared in abbreviated form in *Religion and Life* (1940 and 1936) and I have to thank the Editor, Dr. J. W. Langdale, for permission to use them here, as also Mr. John Murray for his readiness to allow the reprinting of Chapter I ("The

Validity of Christian Experience"), which originally appeared in the volume called *The Future of Christianity*, edited by Sir James Marchant (1927). I am grateful also to Messrs. Cassell and Co. for similar permission to use Chapter XIV, § 3 ("Personality and the Life Beyond"), which first appeared in 1925, in the volume called *Life after Death*, also edited by Sir James Marchant. Dr. Whitley, former Editor of *The Baptist Quarterly*, kindly allows me to reprint Chapter IX ("History and Revelation"), first printed there in 1934. Part of Chapter VIII ("The Prophetic Consciousness of Israel") was published in the *Zeitschrift für die alttestamentliche Wissenschaft* (1923); owing to the war, I have not been able to ask the present Editor for permission to re-publish, but have every reason to think that he would have granted it. The section of Chapter XIV called "The Kenosis of the Spirit" is based on an article printed in *The Expository Times* in August, 1924, of which the Editors kindly allowed me to make further use.

My friend and former colleague, the Rev. A. J. D. Farrer, has continued to give me valuable help by reading the typescript, and by making many acute criticisms, which have led me to re-write certain sections. Another friend, my present colleague, the Rev. E. A. Payne, has read the proof-sheets, giving patient and unsparing attention to corrections of detail. Parts of the book have been read as detached papers to the Society for Old Testament Study, the Oxford Society of Historical Theology, the Origen Society, and the London Society for the Study of Religion, and I am indebted to the members of these Societies for many useful comments and criticisms.

H. WHEELER ROBINSON

OXFORD,

*Christmas, 1941.*

# CONTENTS

|   |   | PAGE |
|---|---|---|
| GENERAL INTRODUCTION | . . . . . . . | v |
| PREFACE | . . . . . . . . . . . | ix |
| SUMMARY OF THE ARGUMENT | . . . . . . | xvii |
| INTRODUCTION: THE MEANING OF HISTORY: . . . | xxv |
| (axioms of a Christian interpretation) | |
| 1. The Creative Activity | . . . . . . | xxvi |
| 2. The Actuality of History | . . . . . | xxx |
| 3. History Creative of "Values" | . . . . . | xxxv |
| 4. The Subjective Factor | . . . . . | xxxviii |
| 5. The Temporal within the Eternal | . . . . | xli |

## PART I

# THE ACTUALITY OF HISTORY

## CHAPTER I

| THE VALIDITY OF CHRISTIAN EXPERIENCE | . . . . | 3 |
|---|---|---|
| 1. The Appeal to Experience | . . . . . | 3 |
| 2. The Divine Activity | . . . . . . | 8 |
| 3. The Tests of Reality | . . . . . . | 10 |
| 4. The Unity of Experience | . . . . . | 14 |
| 5. The Moral Conditions | . . . . . | 17 |

## CHAPTER II

| THE MINISTRY OF ERROR | . . . . . . . | 21 |
|---|---|---|
| 1. The Development of Religion as involving Error | . | 25 |
| 2. Particular Contributions of Error to Religion | . | 28 |
| 3. The Good Will as the only Absolute Good | . . | 34 |

*Contents*

## CHAPTER III

PAGE

THE SYMBOLISM OF LANGUAGE . . . . . . . . 39

   1. The Psychology of Language . . . . . . 41

   2. Language intermediate between Thought and Life . 42

   3. Adequacy of the Theological Vocabulary . . . 48

## CHAPTER IV

THE ACTUALITY OF GOOD AND EVIL . . . . . . . 57

   1. The Actuality of the Event . . . . . . 57

   2. The Good and Evil Volitions . . . . . . 60

   3. The Social Origin and Divine Source of Morality . . 67

   4. The Worth of History to God . . . . . . 70

## CHAPTER V

THE DIVINE INITIATIVE . . . . . . . . . 73

   1. The Purpose of God . . . . . . . . 74

   2. The Contingency of History . . . . . . 77

   3. The Significance of Israel's History . . . . . 87

## PART II

# THE MEDIA OF REVELATION

## CHAPTER VI

THE PRINCIPLE OF MEDIATION . . . . . . . . 95

   1. The Variety of Media . . . . . . . . 97

   2. The Interrelation of Faith and Worship . . . 100

   3. Sacramental Mediation . . . . . . . 103

   4. Relation of the Media to the Idea of God . . . 107

   5. Basis for the Classification of Religions . . . 111

## CHAPTER VII

PAGE

THE PHYSICAL MEDIA . . . . . . . . . . 114

    1. Divination . . . . . . . . . . 115

    2. Nature and Miracle . . . . . . . . 118

    3. The Limitations of Nature-Worship . . . . 126

## CHAPTER VIII

THE PSYCHICAL MEDIA . . . . . . . . . . 131

    1. Dreams . . . . . . . . . . . . 131

    2. Ecstasy and Possession . . . . . . . 134

    3. The Prophetic Consciousness of Israel . . . . 138

## CHAPTER IX

HISTORY AND REVELATION . . . . . . . . . 158

    1. The Activity of God in History . . . . . 159

    2. The Prophet in History . . . . . . . 162

    3. The Actuality of History as Revelation . . . . 166

    4. The Authority of Revelation in History . . . . 170

## CHAPTER X

THE CHRISTIAN REVELATION . . . . . . . . 177

    1. The Actuality of the Historical Data . . . . 182

    2. The Godward Significance of the History . . . 185

    3. The Manward Significance of the History . . . 189

## PART III

# THE FACT OF REDEMPTION

## CHAPTER XI

THE REDEEMER . . . . . . . . . . . 197

    1. The Suffering Messiah . . . . . . . . 197

    2. The Risen Lord . . . . . . . . . . 200

## CHAPTER XI (*continued*)

PAGE

THE REDEEMER (*continued*)

3. The Pre-existent Christ . . . . . . . 202

4. The Son of God . . . . . . . . . 203

5. The Logos . . . . . . . . . . 205

6. The God-man . . . . . . . . . 207

## CHAPTER XII

THE MEANING OF REDEMPTION . . . . . . . 219

1. The Metaphor . . . . . . . . . 219

2. Redemption in the Old Testament . . . . . 220

3. Redemption in the New Testament . . . . 228

4. Redemption from what? . . . . . . . 235

## CHAPTER XIII

THE REDEMPTIVE SUFFERING . . . . . . . 245

1. The Redeemer's Victory . . . . . . . 245

2. The Redeemer's Sacrifice . . . . . . . 249

3. The Redeemer as Representative . . . . . 257

4. The Divine Redemption . . . . . . . 262

## CHAPTER XIV

THE REDEEMED . . . . . . . . . . . 281

1. The Ideal Life . . . . . . . . . 281

2. The Kenosis of the Spirit . . . . . . . 290

3. Personality and the Life Beyond . . . . . 297

INDEX: (A) Names . . . . . . . . . . 313

(B) Scripture References . . . . . . . 316

(C) Subjects . . . . . . . . . . 317

# THE ARGUMENT OF THIS BOOK

THE *Introduction* indicates some of the (philosophical) pre-suppositions involved in a Christian interpretation of history. History is under the control of God, yet so as to allow to man a genuinely creative activity. The resultant actuality of events constitutes a category *sui generis*, gradually working out its own values. Yet these claim an authority which cannot be derived from history. The psychical factor is able to transform the meaning of the physical event, so justifying the place given to faith by religion. History, though a process in time, is conceived as belonging to an eternal order of which it forms a constituent part.

## PART I

In Chapter I, the validity of Christian experience in general is defended against the criticism that it is "subjective" and therefore illusory. It is claimed that that experience is just as much entitled to supply data for belief in objective reality as any other part of our experience, such as that based on our perceptions of the natural world. It is recognized that a subjective factor is essentially involved in the creation of the spiritual "fact" out of the mere "event", but this unity of experience is treated as an essential feature of the whole process by which man advances in the knowledge of God, and by which the spiritual order gathers up into itself the present conditions of space and time.

In Chapter II, the same charge of "subjectivity" is faced in one of its particular applications, viz. that the course of history shows man to have been repeatedly influenced, even in his pursuit and attainment of the true, by illusions which he has had subsequently to renounce. This ministry of error in the service of truth is fully admitted, but it is claimed that it is a necessary and inevitable part of the pedagogic process, reflecting no dishonour on the providence of God and no shade of uncertainty on the acquisition of truth, though this must always for man be partial and imperfect.

In Chapter III, an objection of another kind is met, viz. that our human language, and the thought with which it is bound up, are inadequate to enable us to pass beyond the borders of our human experience, and that we are therefore condemned to agnosticism. But language is admittedly symbolic even in dealing successfully with matters of present experience; there is, therefore, nothing illogical in claiming that it may also be used symbolically yet effectively of that which lies beyond present experience. Whether such an extension is valid will depend on the degree to which we accept the "higher anthropomorphism" and believe in the spiritual kinship of God the Creator and man His creature. If there is no common ground, *cadit quaestio*; if there is, even to a very partial and limited degree, then human language and human thought are sufficient to warrant inference as to the unseen, indeed for us to claim that the eternal is already revealed in the temporal, and that the temporal enters into the eternal.

In Chapter IV, the meaning of "actuality" indicated in the Introduction is developed in relation to the distinction between thinking and doing, and that between a volition and its execution. In a world of spiritual beings, actuality belongs to the volition as well as to the external event. The actuality of evil is not less "real" than that of the good, and challenges the purpose of God. The actuality of good always finds that good already existent in the purpose of God.

In Chapter V, history in general is said to reveal something of the divine purpose. Because that history is what it is, God the Creator must become God the Redeemer. Neither Nature nor human history can be regarded as purposeless, since they both issue in "values". The contingency of history is simply one aspect of its actuality. In human life, as in Nature, God works from within, as well as from without. The apparent irrelevancy of historical events to spiritual truth has helped to make "mysticism" attractive, or, from another standpoint, to throw the emphasis on the teaching, rather than on the work, of Jesus. But historical events are the inevitable "body" to the "soul" of truth, and are not necessarily external to it. We may admit a certain relativity in the truth so mediated, yet this does not invalidate it, but provides a moral challenge. Israel's history, which illustrates these general principles, also constitutes a redemptive approach to the Christian data, and shows us that human personality (as seen in the prophet) can provide the supreme contact between God and man.

## PART II

In Chapter VI, it is claimed that a religion is characterized by its principle of mediation, the way in which God is conceived to make contact with man, and man to approach God. The media which can be employed are very various, but certain dominant types, physical, psychical and historical, can be seen clearly, especially in the religion of Israel. Individual faith must find sustenance and expression in social worship, and worship acquires its fixed institutions which tend to persist, even when the community has outgrown them, or needs to re-interpret them. The "sacraments" of religion illustrate this variety of interpretation and range from the simplest to the most subtle forms of man's communion with powers beyond himself. The kind of media employed will always influence the idea of God, and even mysticism must employ an inheritance of ideas derived from the media of the mystic's environment. Religions can be classified by their media, or by their relation to the principle of mediation.

In Chapter VII, the use of physical objects as religious media is considered, such as the world-wide phenomena of divination, ranging from the casting of the sacred lot to the observation of the movements of birds or stars. The miraculous "sign" or "portent" has always a contemporary background of its own, derived from the view held of nature in general. The ancient world recognized order in nature but was without our more abstract and generalizing conception of "laws of nature", and this must be taken into account in any consideration of "miracle", always a relative term. "Miracle" of some kind is essential to a religion of revelation, such as that of the Bible. It can be adequately defended only when the order of nature is seen to be part, but only part, of the more comprehensive *personal* relations of God with man. Nature as a whole is rightly regarded as a (partial) revelation of God. On the other hand, a religion that is founded on any form of nature-worship is inevitably limited in its higher developments, and has to be supplemented from other sources to meet the advancing spiritual needs of man. This is illustrated from Mithraism, the chief rival of Christianity in the third century A.D.

In Chapter VIII, the use of psychical media is illustrated from the phenomena of dreams, ecstasy (properly involving the absence of the soul from the body as in Shamanism) and spirit-possession (in which the external powers temporarily occupy the human personality, as in the Delphic oracle). This leads to a more detailed examination of the prophetic consciousness in Israel, the supreme point of contact between God and man to be found in history, outside the Christian belief in the Incarnation.

In Chapter IX, the nature and place of revelation in religion is viewed in general, from a historical standpoint. It is claimed that God is active in history, which constitutes His chief means of revelation. The prophetic personality occupies a central place both for Israel and for Islam. The modern conception of history as a purposive unity goes back to Israel. The authority of an historical revelation must be ultimately intrinsic and we cannot eliminate the subjective factor in the reception and interpretation of the evidence, by positing an external authority. Every revelation will necessarily bear the marks and limitations of its historical period, but this does not mean that the eternal is not revealed, because achieved, in the temporal.

In Chapter X, the Christian revelation is considered, especially in its Protestant evangelical form. It is seen to rest on the actuality of historical data which are essential to it. But not less essential is the personal response of faith; event and faith are always interrelated in the religious "fact". This history has a Godward significance, since the deeds of man must concern God, and also because the sins of men demand the redemptive activity of God, if history is ever to be the record of the achievement of His purpose in creating man. On the other hand, this redemptive activity of God itself constitutes His supreme revelation to man; the love of God is known through what Christ has done to redeem man. The fact of redemption therefore becomes of supreme importance.

## PART III

In Chapter XI, there is a rapid survey of the doctrine of the Person of the Redeemer, as suggested by some of the most characteristic descriptions of Him, viz. as the suffering Messiah, the Risen Lord, the Son of God, the Logos. It is suggested that the modern approach must lie through our conception of personality as a unity, rather than through the ancient contrast of two "natures". Our human achievement of personality is always imperfect, even apart from the limitations of "finite" being. Yet it supplies the highest category by which we can conceive the being of God, in whom we think of it as perfectly realized. Such ascription can be justified only if there is real kinship between human and divine personality, and that kinship opens up the possibility of a divine Incarnation, that of the God-Man, Jesus Christ. In Him we have to do with the redemptive personality of God.

In Chapter XII, the Biblical meaning of the term "redemption" is discussed, in order to bring out its original significance of "ransoming" from captivity or other evil, and to show its extension into the idea of "salvation" in general. This raises the important question, "redemption from what?" when applied to the work of the Redeemer. After brief reference to the historical doctrine of a ransom paid to the Devil, there is a review of those evils from which the modern man seeks deliverance, the permanent evils that endure for the race beneath the transient forms which they assume from time to time (such as those of ancient demonology). It is argued that there is need for both an individual and a racial redemption, and this not only from the power, but also from the guilt, of sin.

In Chapter XIII, the redemptive work of Christ is considered first as a *victory* of good over evil, His cross effecting an actual transformation of the consequences of evil into good. Secondly, the redemptive suffering of Christ is viewed as a *sacrifice*, and the chief sacrificial references in the New Testament are interpreted in the light of the Old Testament sacrifices. The continued and widespread use of this metaphor (and its present popularity) shows its utility and value, though it does not yield an adequate doctrine of atonement. Thirdly, the sense in which Christ can be considered man's *representative* is discussed, and emphasis is here laid on His full achievement of human personality. But it is further argued that divine redemption involves the carrying back of Christ's suffering on the Cross to the *suffering of God* Himself. The Holy God does not react to human sin simply in the wrath of retribution, but also in the "patience" by which the "eternal" consequences of sin are transformed into the sufferings of divine grace. Of this, the "temporal" sufferings of Christ are the visible part. Thus God bears the burden of human guilt and so redeems man from it. The partial value of the historic metaphors ("ransom", "sacrifice", "satisfaction", etc.) is recognized, but it is claimed that we cannot (without "transactionalism") base the doctrine of redemption on anything short of divine passibility, a conception which is Biblically and philosophically justified. The divine forgiveness must be costly to God Himself. The final redemption of the world will consist in such transformation of the meaning of human history as makes it into a divine victory (seen in miniature as actually won on the Cross). By "cross-bearing", men take their necessary place in the redemptive work of Christ.

In Chapter XIV, the life of those who are redeemed by Christ is shown to be based on His redemptive work, which supplies a new motive for "sanctification". The personal response of faith involves entrance into a new relation to other men. Our participation in this victory is by "faith-mysticism", which is the real kernel within any protective shell of 'corporate personality', ancient or modern. The redeemed life is throughout dependent on the work of the Holy Spirit, the active presence of God in the believer. This can be only by a self-emptying, or "kenosis", of the Holy Spirit, comparable, and in fact continuous, with the work of the Incarnation. Finally, the future life is considered as a fuller stage in the achievement of personality, both individual and social, and by its very nature always progressive. Eternal life begins here but is consummated hereafter.

# INTRODUCTION

## THE MEANING OF HISTORY

BUT has history a meaning? In these perplexing days, when so many landmarks, spiritual as well as material, are being destroyed, the thoughts of men are often summed up in Matthew Arnold's well-known lines in *Dover Beach:*—

> "we are here as on a darkling plain
> Swept with confused alarms of struggle and flight,
> Where ignorant armies clash by night."

We are no longer sure that history spells progress. We see what were regarded as established values challenged and apparently overthrown. The confusion of the present throws doubt upon the conclusions of the past.

It is clear enough that we can interpret history only when we rise above it. Alongside of Arnold's "darkling plain" we may set the famous simile of Lucretius.[1] Above the tumult of the warring legions, with all their confusion of detail, there is some spot on the high hills from which

[1] *De Rerum Natura*, II, 323–32 :—

> "praeterea magnae legiones cum loca cursu
> camporum complent belli simulacra cientes,
> fulgor ibi ad caelum se tollit totaque circum
> aere renidescit tellus supterque virum vi
> excitur pedibus sonitus clamoreque montes
> icti reiectant voces ad sidera mundi
> et circumvolitant equites mediosque repente
> tramittunt valido quatientes impetu campos.
> et tamen est quidam locus altis montibus unde
> stare videntur et in campis consistere fulgor."

they are blended into the unity of one flashing point. The
Christian interpretation of history finds its view-point on
the hill of Calvary. But the paths leading up to it were
those trodden by the prophets and apocalyptists of the
Old Testament. These men were unique in the ancient
world in tracing the ordered purpose of God in the happenings of history. The peculiar quality of a historical revelation depends on such interpretation. The Christian view
of the world completes what they began. To argue any
formulation of it here is beyond our scope. But it may
be worth while to ask, by way of introduction to this book,
what are its axioms. There are at least five characteristics
of history which the Christian interpretation of it claims
to discern, and on which the truth of the Christian faith
ultimately depends. These "axioms" are (1) the creative
activity of history, (2) its actuality, (3) its values, (4) its
subjective factor, and the transformation of meaning which
can result from this, and (5) the inclusion of its temporal
events within an eternal order.

§ 1. *Creative Activity.* Since the Christian faith pre-
supposes moral responsibility, there must be some degree
of freedom in the moral choice exercised by man. This is
not the place to discuss the thorny question of human
freedom, the reality of which may be challenged on either
a materialistic or idealistic basis. At any rate, we may say
that the moral view of history is fundamental for the
Christian interpretation of it. This does not mean, as we
shall see (§ 3), that the moral standards of any particular
stage are necessarily final or complete, nor does it mean
unmotived or unlimited freedom. The moral choices of a
rational being are not unmotived, and motive depends on
character, which has a relatively fixed quality. But freedom
is not one element in a chain of sequences; it is the quality
of personality acting as a whole and above the level of

psychological analysis.[1] The freedom possessed by a moral agent is certainly limited both by his previous history and by his immediate environment. An act of volition is highly complex, and even if we could analyse all its factors there would remain the something more which belongs to it as the self-expression of a living being. It is that something more which concerns us when we consider the behaviour of moral agents and their interplay in history. It is in regard to this something more that a moral agent judges himself, in terms of blame or credit, and is so judged by his fellows, whether they be his contemporaries or the future historians who gather up the *records* of the past and compile that "continuous, methodical *record*" which is what we mean by history in the narrower and stricter sense. Here we shall use the term "history" for the process itself, as well as for the record of it.

If, now, we think of this conscious possession of creative capacity which underlies morally responsible action and distinguishes man from the order of nature, we can see that such a characteristic has important religious, as well as moral, consequences. In the Bible, as is well known, the knowledge of God is intimately bound up with obedience to God, so intimately indeed that we can say in fact that if a man does not will to do the will of God, he shall not know of the teaching whether it be of God. The emphasis of the Bible falls distinctly on volition, both in the Old Testament and the New, and the obedient will is the doorway to any real knowledge of God. We can hardly over-emphasize this point, both for the Christian faith itself and for the interpretation of history according to Christian standards. According to the Bible the knowledge of God is unattainable by any intellectual argument, and

---

[1] Cf. *The Christian Doctrine of Man*, by H. Wheeler Robinson, pp. 292 ff., for the conception of a closed psychological circle which is within the total personality to which freedom belongs.

in fact the Bible religion never builds on such a foundation.
It demands obedience, and promises growing knowledge
through obedience. It suggests that the living God can be
known only in terms of life and not in terms of thought.
*Life* is in fact a category of knowledge of a new order, and
one which is ultimately more important than any category
belonging to the intellect.[1] It brings man into as close a
fellowship with God as is possible for a creature living
under marked limitations. But he is not only a creature;
he is also in his own way a creator. He creates the little
world in which he lives within the limitations prescribed
for him by his heredity and environment. In exercising
the creative function which is assigned to him as a moral
agent he is potentially capable of entering into a real
fellowship with God the Creator, and such fellowship is
mediated, not by any abstract knowledge, but by an
activity which is in miniature like that of God, however
limited its scope.[2] When man goes forth to his work and
to his labour until the evening he does not only take his
place in that great creative panorama which the 104th
Psalm pictures; he enters into a sphere of creative activity
all his own, a microcosm to God's macrocosm.

If we try to estimate the relation of this creative capacity
to the work of the divine Creator, we are again entering a
very difficult and controversial realm, and no attempt will
here be made to discuss the problems.[3] But it may fairly
be said that the Christian faith, following the pattern set

---

[1] Cf. F. R. Tennant in the *Encyclopaedia of Religion and Ethics*, IX,
200: "the world is not rationalizable without remainder: 'reality is richer
than thought', as Lotze often remarks."

[2] Cf. John Macmurray, *The Clue to History*, p. 33: "What is characteristic of the Hebrew conception of God is that God is primarily a worker.
. . . Nothing could express more succinctly the essence of the Hebrew
conception of God in its full religious integrity, than the statement attri-
buted to Jesus, 'My father worketh hitherto and I work'."

[3] I have tried to deal with some of these in *Suffering, Human and Divine*,
Cc. VI–VIII.

in the Bible, asserts divine control without admitting prejudice to moral responsibility. No doubt, at certain times and in certain stages of the development of doctrine, the emphasis has fallen more on one side than on the other, as the history of Augustinianism versus Pelagianism or of Calvinism versus Arminianism amply demonstrates. But, on the whole, the normal Christian view is that, whatever the divine control which religious faith demands, room must be found for the real exercise of a creative freedom through man. Let us admit frankly that we cannot frame any formula which would justify this, though we can point to the fact that the surrender made by personal faith in God and the growth in grace of a saintly personality do suggest the possibility of a real freedom co-existing within a spiritual control. It may be that our difficulty in framing any formula is due to the fact already indicated, that the living God is to be known in categories of life and not simply of thought. At any rate we have to think of a continued exercise of God's creative power through the creative freedom of moral agents. Admittedly this is a new level of creative activity on God's part, since, as we have seen, it involves the continuous education of the moral agent, and his growth in grace. We can hardly put it more strikingly than did Thomas Traherne, who said that when God had done all He could by the exercise of His own liberty, then He did more by creating man's.[1]

In our judgment of history, then, we must give full scope to this conception of it as the record of a creative work of God, highly complicated through the intervention of human agents, exercising their moral liberty. This will account for the slowness of the movement or the obscuration of the divine purpose in it. In spite of them, history is creating something *sui generis*, which is not to be reduced to the mere evolution of physical forces (with a psychical

[1] *Centuries of Meditations*, IV, 46.

accompaniment) or to be translated wholly into terms of intellect, without highly important residua.

§ 2. *The Actuality of History.* History is properly "the continuous methodical record" of events. We need a word to describe the quality or status of the event as that which has "taken place" once for all. We can hardly find a better term than "actuality", for it avoids, or rather postpones, the philosophical problems attaching to any use of the term "reality", whilst claiming for the event a clear distinction from the mere conception of it. True, the conception is itself a psychical event, which may or may not find expression in a related physical event. But our knowledge of all psychical events (other than those within our own consciousness) is indirect and mediated. We depend for that knowledge on the spoken or written "word", or we infer it from what we regard as the consequences of such events. A good deal of St. Augustine's inner development might have been inferred from his general theological writings; but we are brought much nearer to the inner "events" of his life by his autobiographical *Confessions.* His attraction to Cicero's "Hortensius" or his disappointment with the Manichaean teacher, Faustus, are just as much "events" as his physical movements from Thagaste to Carthage, Rome, Milan and Hippo. All these events, psychical or physical, "happened" and possess the quality of "once-for-allness" (Einmaligkeit). Once done they cannot be undone, and only in imagination can we travel back along the line of this actuality. They are irrevocable because they are irreversible, and many a proverb of the "spilt milk" kind reminds us of this often tragic aspect of life.

Another aspect of this actuality of the event is that it clarifies the ideas of the agent and of his contemporaries. Before the inner decision is taken, or the outer act is done,

there may be a number of possibilities more or less undefined. The man who is about to make some decision may
be drawn this way and that; but once he has made it, with
any fixity of purpose, and still more when he has registered
his decision in the visible act, all the possibilities save one
are excluded, and a new situation must be envisaged, with
the new factor of *this* event. The papal ambitions of
Gregory the Seventh were limited only by the known
world, and his methods were in principle no more restrained
than those of a modern dictator; the "event" of his ex-
communication of Henry the Fourth of Germany shook
the imperial throne to its foundations. But the diplomatic
penitence of the king, standing barefooted for three days
before the gates of the castle of Canossa, was a not less
decisive event, since it restored political power to Henry,
before it passed into history as the most famous incident
of the conflict between Church and Empire. Such an event
obviously sums up the past and clarifies the future, when
it takes place on the stage of world history. But the same
truth holds of some trivial incident in a humble cottage,
which may mark the turning-point in domestic fortunes.
The visible deed, and—to a less degree—the spoken word
may clarify a situation for evil or for good to the agent
or speaker himself. as nothing else could—to say nothing
of what they reveal to others. Bacon's aphorism illustrates
the point: "Reading maketh a Full Man; Conference a
Ready Man; and Writing an Exact Man." The reduction
of thought to its exact literary form always tends to
clarify it; we escape from the penumbra of vague groping
and know what we know; we discover how "woolly" our
thinking has been through the very effort to give it sharp
outline. So it is with every other kind of deed; the definition entailed by the actuality of the event always clarifies
the situation.

The chief reason why the actuality of the event means

so much more than the conception of it is that the conscious act of a moral agent requires the exercise of volition.
It is a richer and fuller expression of personality than
purely intellectual activity can ever be. Of course, intellectual activity may be itself the product of volition of
an intense kind and is so far itself an "event". But we are
not thinking now of the student or the statesman revolving
high theses of philosophy or politics as part of his life-
work. We are simply contrasting the idea—perhaps involuntary—of something to be done and the actual doing
of it, perhaps at the cost of a resolute effort of will. There
is far more of the man in the deed than in the thought of
the deed.[1] Thought is always an abstraction from life and
life is always more concrete than its analysis by thought.
Something of this we may see in the "symbolic" acts of
Hebrew prophets, which are much more than dramatic
illustrations of the spoken word. They are products of
that instinctive realism of the Hebrew, which made him
strive for some fuller expression of his thought than even
the spoken word—with all its contemporary objectivity—
could supply. The breaking of earthenware by Jeremiah
achieved something more than could a verbal metaphor
of the destruction of the city, since it liberated more of
the prophetic personality and so mediated more of the
divine activity. This is a most important element in
the sacramental principle and in the central Christian
fact of the Incarnation, as we shall see at a later
stage of the argument. Both are more than the expression of a thought, because they have the actuality of the
event.

What has already been said illustrates and leads up to
the assertion that in the actuality of the event we have a
new category, a unique articulation of spiritual fact which

[1] Cf. A. C. Bradley, *Oxford Lectures on Poetry*, p. 203: "the soul that
remains interior is not the whole soul."

cannot be reduced to any intellectual formula.[1] But though we cannot define it by anything less than itself—it has the very texture of life—we can parallel it to some degree from the realm of art. The creation of the beauty of a picture or the majesty of a statue or the satisfying symmetry of great music all add a new quality to the conception of the artist or sculptor or composer. Probably the very process of artistic creation has itself further developed the conception,[2] but this is not what is here meant. The creation of something objective both clarifies the creator's own thought and expresses it to others, and initiates for that which is created an independent history of its own. The particular qualities of the medium—whether words, paint, marble, or musical sound—create new means of expression as they impose new limitations, but again this is not what is here meant. The hidden and potential beauty of the artist's thought is *actualized* in concrete particularity, and enters into a new category.

Art, indeed, is more than an illustration and should perhaps be rather described as a co-existent expression of the spiritual. Here we cannot do better than borrow Newman's classical description of music.[3]

"Let us take another instance, of an outward and earthly form, or economy, under which great wonders unknown seem to be typified; I mean musical sounds, as they are exhibited most perfectly in instrumental harmony. There are seven notes in the scale; make them fourteen; yet what a slender outfit for so vast an enterprise! What science brings so much out of so little? Out of what poor elements does some great master in it create his new

---

[1] Cf. the remark of Santayana, from his very different philosophical standpoint, that "*actuality* has extraordinary ontological privileges" (*The Realm of Spirit*, p. 49).

[2] Cf. E. A. Poe's instructive analysis of the creation of his poem, "The Raven", in "The Philosophy of Composition" (*Poems and Essays*).

[3] *Oxford University Sermons*, pp. 346–47.

c

world! Shall we say that all this exuberant inventiveness
is a mere ingenuity or trick of art, like some game or
fashion of the day, without reality, without meaning?
We may do so; and then, perhaps, we shall also account
the science of theology to be a matter of words; yet, as
there is a divinity in the theology of the Church, which
those who feel cannot communicate, so is there also in the
wonderful creation of sublimity and beauty of which I
am speaking. To many men the very names which the
science employs are utterly incomprehensible. To speak
of an idea or a subject seems to be fanciful or trifling, to
speak of the views which it opens upon us to be childish
extravagance; yet is it possible that that inexhaustible
evolution and disposition of notes, so rich yet so simple,
so intricate yet so regulated, so various yet so majestic,
should be a mere sound, which is gone and perishes?
Can it be that those mysterious stirrings of heart and keen
emotions, and strange yearnings after we know not what,
and awful impressions from we know not whence, should
be wrought in us by what is unsubstantial, and comes and
goes, and begins and ends in itself? It is not so; it cannot
be. No; they have escaped from some higher sphere; they
are the outpourings of eternal harmony in the medium of
created sound; they are echoes from our Home; they are
the voice of Angels, or the Magnificat of Saints, or the
living laws of Divine Governance, or the Divine Attributes;
something are they besides themselves, which we cannot
compass, which we cannot utter—though mortal man, and
he perhaps not otherwise distinguished above his fellows,
has the gift of eliciting them.''

If, in Newman's phrase, music is "an outward and
earthly form or economy" expressing something greater
than itself,[1] how much more is it true of that which music

---

[1] Browning's well-known line about the use of the chord by the musician
will recur to many readers:—"That out of three sounds he frame, not a
fourth sound, but a star" (*Abt Vogler*, vii).

creates in us—"those mysterious stirrings of heart and keen emotions, and strange yearnings after we know not what, and awful impressions from we know not whence", which are part of our very life? Christian theology, too much influenced by Greek thought, has never done full justice to the Hebraic emphasis in Biblical revelation, the realism of the concrete event. This emphasis makes life itself, rather than the analysis of it, the true revelation of God. The actuality of history, up to and including the Incarnation, is God's supreme medium of utterance to man.

§ 3. *History Creative of "Values"*. One of the marked features of history is the emergence of spiritual values within it. This is not to be ascribed to a number of arbitrary interventions from without in a process essentially alien to them. All the evidence goes to show that these values, whether aesthetic, intellectual, moral or religious, are integrally related to the whole process in which they gradually appear. Even at the higher levels of their development, when they have acquired ample and independent recognition in the life of a community, their appreciation requires a certain degree of individual education. At lower levels we can often discern the point at which civilization first became conscious of them, as with the classical standards of Greek art and philosophy, Hebrew morality and religion. But, even so, there are usually sufficient data to show a long preparation for such emergence. Thus human history so far exhibits a similar process to that of biology, where the functions of higher organisms can often be traced back to rudimentary beginnings.

Let us take, as a concrete example of this universal principle, some of the recognised features of architecture, such as the Greek lintel, the Roman round arch, and the pointed arch which is known as "Gothic". These can each be regarded as methods "of solving the first problem of architecture, how to build a roof over a given space".[1] In Egypt, and derivatively in Greece, the flat roof with its lintel was supported on stone columns. The different kinds of Greek, and consequently of Roman, columns—Doric, Ionic, Corinthian—are all elaborations of the obvious methods of supporting a flat roof on wooden poles which came from earlier days. The systematic development of the arch comes from the Romans (who borrowed from the Etruscans), though the arch itself goes back (in Egypt) to 3000 B.C.[2] It was the arch which made possible the vaulted roof, but the further difficulty of cross-vaulting in the late Norman period led to the invention of the pointed arch so that material might be economized "by the skilful distribution of masses at the points where arch-thrusts were concentrated, and by the disposition of arches so that the thrust of one was met and annihilated by that of another".[3] Thus the most distinctive features of these great types of architecture were all evolved in the course of meeting a utilitarian need—that of roof-making. The severe dignity and grace of a Greek portico, the massive solidity of a Roman arcade, the soaring roof of a Gothic nave, are "values" slowly evolved from simple necessities.

The same principle holds of the development of moral relations. The ethical demands of the New Testament are rooted and grounded in the social conceptions of the great Hebrew prophets, and these themselves go back to the social life of nomadic clans, whose very existence depended on the social unity of the group. Justice and mercy—the twin pillars of Hebrew as of Christian morality

[1] E. A. Greening Lamborn, *The Story of Architecture in Oxford Stone*, p. 15.

[2] J. H. Breasted, *A History of Egypt* (1912), fig. 47, opposite to p. 100.

[3] E. A. Greening Lamborn, *op. cit.*, p. 56.

—are raised on the foundations of the desert life of Israel. By recognizing such *origins*, we are not foreclosing the issue as to the ultimate *source* of morality, we are thinking only of the process by which man has grown into the knowledge of something greater than himself and his individual interests. Through struggle and conflict, under the pressure of the sheer necessities of life, the spirit of man has reached out to qualities of living not less divine, through their ultimate source in the Spirit of God, because they were "discovered" by man in the process of his own history. The loftiest idealism is cradled in the crudities of a primitive realism.

Even when we turn to the highest values of all, those of religion, we discover that there is no escape from history save through history. The mystic claims immediacy of access to the divine. But the specific content of his experience is always supplied by values which, whether consciously or unconsciously, he draws from history. The fierce simplicity of the formula of Islam—"There is no God but Allah, and Muhammad is His prophet"—is explicable only in the light of a long development of Semitic religion and the personal fortunes of a particular Arab. The œcumenical creeds of Christendom that gather the reverence of the centuries conceal within their closely wrought and subtle phraseology the strife and conflict, noble or ignoble, of men of like passions with ourselves. Again, let us remind ourselves that all this does not decide the question of their truth or falsity. It simply declares the law that the knowledge of truth must be born of travail. If God has indeed revealed Himself to man, this is the method which He has seen fit to adopt. Our greatest spiritual possessions and our loftiest faith have had such a lineage as this. History is creative of its own values, and from the mouth of its own children it hears its blessing or curse.

If we are prepared to accept such a view of these values, it would seem to follow that their authority over us must be intrinsic. They have demonstrated their authority by being what they are. They have survived by proving their ability to command and hold the loyalty of the soul of man. This does not mean that every generation or every individual must start out anew on a series of experiments, scrapping the values already attained. There is a place and a necessary place for authority, even if it be only the authority of antiquity. There is a *consensus gentium* which should win our respect and attention, even though it cannot be the ultimate foundation of values. There are classical achievements in art which become norms for posterity, philosophical interpretations of the universe which are accepted as typical "patterns", national histories which broadly support moral principles.[1] Above all these there is the existence of a Christian society which witnesses, however imperfectly, to the Gospel of Christ. But neither academy nor university nor state nor Church can be more than secondary authorities, in comparison with the ultimate authority of God, as He is revealed in the values created by the history He has controlled. On His behalf, they make their intrinsic appeal to us, and win from us the intuitive response of the whole personality in faith. For it is they that give the real content to our conceptions of God.

§ 4. *The Subjective Factor and the Resultant Transformation of Meaning.* To those who have been accustomed to accept conventional standards as ultimate (e.g. "The Ten Commandments") or have been trained to defer to a corporate authority (e.g. the Roman Catholic Church), it may seem that the interpretation of history so far indicated

---

[1] E.g., the futility of substituting force for fellowship as the basis of empire.

lands us in excessive subjectivity. If the values are
guaranteed only by their intrinsic worth, our own recognition of that worth becomes the decisive factor. But, as
is widely argued, does not the peculiar quality of our
recognition of them require an authority beyond itself, an
authority disclosing itself by "revelation" through appointed
organs?

The proper answer to this question is not so simple as
it appears to many. We cannot thus divide our experience
sharply between "subjective" and "objective" factors. Both
are involved in the simplest perception. The history of
philosophy seems to show that if we start with a dualism
of subject and object we shall never build a bridge across
the gulf. But there is no need to start with such a dualism.[1] The unity of consciousness already embraces a
duality of reference.

I should not have discovered myself, but for my "not-
self". I should not perceive any "object" apart from an
activity of myself as subject. Science necessarily abstracts
from this unity and considers only the universal, but its
apparent "objectivity" in complete detachment from an
individual subject is delusive; even the scientific observer
has his personal equation. We may regard the authority
of the Church as itself an abstraction from that totality of
experience amid which it was born, with whatever divine
sanction. The Church declares the truth which, it asserts,
has been divinely revealed to it. The declaration is
legitimate only so long as it is admitted that the authority
of the Church must itself depend on the prior recognition
of that authority by its members.

The only escape from this "argument in a circle" is to
recognize the duality of the life recorded by history,
corresponding to the duality of individual experience.

[1] The first chapter of *Psychological Principles*, by James Ward (1920)
is a good corrective of this tendency.

We must avoid making a false antithesis between subject and object, and avoid over-emphasizing either the subjective or objective factor. The last-named risk is particularly noticeable in the religious realm. It may reasonably be held, for example, that Protestantism has tended to over-emphasize the subjective side of religious experience, whilst Catholicism has over-emphasized the objective. Or, we may make the contrast in somewhat different terms, and say that Protestantism is too individualistic and Catholicism too corporate. Whether or not this judgment is true, the fact remains that the religious conviction of the individual is at some point and in some degree as essential to the birth of true religion as the social guarantee is essential to his education and correction.

Here, however, our concern is to do justice to the subjective factor in the interpretation of historical events. From the very outset, the meaning of an event is conditioned by the attitude towards it of those whom it concerns. We cannot think of "meaning" otherwise than as meaning for someone—meaning conditioned and modified by *his* particular attitude and outlook.[1] This affects those who report the event and provide the raw material of history, as well as all those—whether writers or readers of history— who are called to interpret the whole series of events to which it belongs. We have only to read several newspaper reports of the same event to have this familiar fact brought home forcibly to us. There is no such thing as a complete objectivity of perception, record, or interpretation.

This fact has a most important bearing on the subject of this book. If there is no objective fixity in the interpretation of the event, but its meaning so varies with the

---

[1] That an event happened at some remote period has no value for us till we attach a meaning to it, and this meaning may provide (*a*) the mental picture of the past, as that which has been, (*b*) the cause of certain phenomena which still affect us, (*c*) a symbol chosen, with whatever warrant. to represent some value, which it helps to interpret.

varying attitude of those whom it concerns, then the "fact" constituted by event *plus* meaning is itself not unalterably fixed. The meaning of an event may be one thing to its contemporaries, and quite another to their successors. To a man reviewing his own past, that past will have different meanings, and so different values, at differing periods of his life. A transformation of attitude may profoundly alter, not the bare event (which is, however, always an abstraction), but the total "fact" of an interpreted event. The necessity to earn a living at a time when other youths are still at school or the University is sometimes bitterly resented by an ambitious boy; yet he may eventually see that the experience so won has been a better equipment for his life's work than anything more academic could have been. So it is with the longer and larger retrospects of history. The conquest of England by the Normans in 1066 must have seemed to the conquered an unmitigated disaster. Yet a modern historian can write, "the completeness of William's despotism in England was a blessing in disguise[1] . . . the foundations were laid for the construction of a free and a well-governed state."[2]

The actuality of history therefore remains, but does not rule out the possibility of a "transvaluation" of the events of history. Something of this inevitable "impressionism" is suggested by Taine's epigram "The chief person in a picture is the light in which everything is bathed".[3] To the significance of this for the doctrine of redemption as well as for the doctrine of revelation, we shall return at a later point.

§ 5. *The Temporal within the Eternal.* All this has

[1] The same phrase is used by G. M. Trevelyan of the Wars of the Roses (*History of England*, p. 263).
[2] H. A. L. Fisher, *A History of Europe*, pp. 212, 214.
[3] Quoted by John Rothenstein, *Nineteenth Century Painting*, p. 157.

served to bring us to the crowning problem of our subject,
as indeed of all other subjects—the relation of time to
eternity, which is the ultimate philosophical problem.
The particular aspects of it which here concern us can be
framed in three dualities, which would have to be resolved
into transparent unities in order to meet all our difficulties.
The dualities are that (*a*) history must vindicate God, and
yet is inadequate within itself to do this, (*b*) the values of
history which, as we have seen, require a temporal order
for their actualization, also require an eternal order for
their interpretation and justification, (*c*) the temporal
must be so taken up into the eternal, that its *process*, as
well as its product, has meaning and value for God.

(*a*) If a man is to labour wholeheartedly and unselfishly
for the welfare of others, economic, æsthetic, moral or
religious, he must believe in his cause.  He must believe
not only that what he does is worth doing, but also that
it can be done and that it will be done.  In other words,
he must believe that the universe (whatever his philosophy
of it) is backing his individual effort, and that history
(written large or small) will vindicate his loyalty.  It is
difficult to conceive any sustained devotion to any cause
which does not implicitly or explicitly involve this faith.
A man will fling down his own life that the cause may win
without him, as did the men of Thermopylæ, but it must
win.  Even if he is convinced at last that victory is
beyond his horizon, he must still hold the spiritual
supremacy of the cause to be involved in its essential
worthwhileness.  Somewhere and somehow, *magna est
veritas et praevalet.*[1]

Such a conviction seems an essential part of personal
loyalty and devotion to any of the values of our experience.
But it is, of course, no guarantee of its own validity.
That will depend on its relation to the universe and the

[1] So the true reading (not *praevalebit*) of 1 Esdras iv. 41.

ultimate nature of the universe: "if God is for us, who is against us?" Nor can the conviction of ultimate success prescribe the time or manner of it. That will depend both on the many factors in the history and on the relation of the human purpose to the divine. There is in particular the inclusion of many individual purposes in "the will of God", so that the ultimate outcome may not be in the exact line of any one of them, but "a resultant of forces", gathering them up into itself. A man can never be sure that his single purpose exhausts God's in a given situation. The will of God may be accomplished by the very clash of opposed loyalties. Joshua at Jericho, on the eve of his Palestinian campaign, had the vision of an armed figure which he instinctively challenged, "Art thou for us or for our adversaries?" At once came the answer, "Nay; but as captain of the host of the Lord am I now come." Such a vision of something, or rather someone, superior to the forces arrayed on both sides of any human issue is essential to a right view of history.

But, however natural and true the demand that history shall vindicate God by its final result, such a vindication cannot take the form simply of some final achievement of values in the actual course of history. As Berdyaev remarks "the perfect state is impossible within history itself; it can only be realized outside its framework".[1] Even if history were to show, as admittedly it does not, steady progress towards such an earthly goal, there would remain the problem of the fate of all the generations except the last. "Such a consummation, celebrated by the future elect among the graves of their ancestors, can hardly rally our enthusiasm for the religion of progress."[2] Nature's carelessness of the single life may find justification if it issues in something higher than itself, but hardly otherwise. The emergence of man can be regarded as

---

[1] *The Meaning of History*, p. 197.  [2] Berdyaev, *op. cit.*, p. 190.

justifying the travail of nature only if man himself be reserved for a destiny beyond and above history. His values are so bound up with an individual consciousness that we cannot be satisfied with the extinction of his individuality[1] without other fruit than a succession of other individuals for an indefinite period. To explain and justify history, we must look beyond history.

(*b*) This brings us to the second pair of contrasted demands which history makes upon our thought. We have already seen (§ 3) that the values of spiritual life are worked out and "discovered" by man through the actuality of history. Without this practical contact with the sheer necessities of life, there can be little reality in our conception of these values. In fact, our struggle to reach some temporal goal—however limited and finally incomplete in itself—is an essential element in the appropriation of eternal "values". The schoolboy's prize is the incentive to a discipline that will remain his when the coveted book is flung aside. Loyalty needs its flag, though it does not perish when the flag is torn down. We can hardly know our own sincerity until we have found an altar at which to sacrifice something for its sake. As soon as we try to abstract the values from their concrete embodiment, we evacuate them of all reality and become sentimentalists. The spiritual must always be embodied to be known and faithfully served; the eternal must clothe itself in temporal form to enter effectively within our horizon. "The Christian theologian is not afraid of the paradox that absolute truths of religion are bound up with contingent truths of history."[2]

Yet it is not less true that the interpretation of these values requires their reference to an eternal order. Beauty and truth and goodness cannot be wholly explained on

---

[1] This point is developed in Chapter XIV, § 3.
[2] C. H. Dodd, in *The Study of Theology* (ed. K. E. Kirk), p. 222.

any humanistic theory of them.   They exert their fascination and authority over us just because they are not
ultimately our own creation.   Their objectivity is far
more real than any response we make to them.   "We love,
because He first loved us."   The higher zest of life consists
in this perpetual and exhaustless process of discovery.
Just as a true teacher keeps fresh only by new excursions
into the realms of undiscovered truth, and is always
conscious of the narrow limits of his knowledge, so the
pupil is continually being surprised, on his own lower level,
that the teacher "knew it all before".

The beauty of the rose or of the sunset, which the
simple mind accepts as "objectively" present in the flower
or the sky, may be explained by biological or physical
analysis as something else, physiological or meteorological.
Yet behind and above these legitimate explanations at
lower levels of meaning, there remains the revelation of
something which we *discover* rather than create, something
which is spiritual as well as material.   Most clearly of all,
religious faith depends upon the reality of a divine initiative.   The sufficient reason why no form of humanism
will ever permanently yield religious values is that such
humanism gives the initiative to man, and by making him
independent of God, robs religion of its vital breath,
which is trust in the living God.   So soon as we rationalize
these different values to the point of explaining them
wholly from within our human history, we deprive them
of their most essential quality, which requires their
derivation from an eternal order.

(*c*) The remaining question is that of the relation of
time and eternity within our human experience.   How
can an event in time be also above time?   This is what
we virtually claim when we relate our human values to a
divine order and posit such an order as their only adequate
explanation.   There is a way of doing this which reduces

the temporal to a mere shadow of the eternal, and this way has a great tradition behind it—the Platonic. But it is not the way to which our emphasis on the actuality of history commits us. From that standpoint, it would be more natural to say that eternity is the projection of time than that time is the shadow of eternity—provided that we regard "projection" as interpretative, and not constitutive. To correlate time and eternity adequately is obviously a task beyond our powers, and possible only for God. Every element in our experience will pass beyond our reach as it passes beyond our temporal horizon. We cannot yet know as we are known. But we can claim to know God *at the point at which He chooses to make contact with us,* and under the embodiment which He accepts. This is the principle of the Incarnation and the axiom of a true Christian epistemology. The actuality of history is not a shadow of eternity, but the partial revelation of its reality. We should fully recognize that the distinction between time and eternity is important for the interpretation of the temporal order. "It was the greatness, not the littleness, of the Greeks that made them feel that history and the Time process had a tragedy at the heart."[1] But it is also important to claim that the only Christian resolution of this tragedy is for the temporal to be taken up into the eternal as an integral and constitutive part of it.

For the Christian theologian, his supreme value—the Person and Work of Jesus Christ—stands within the time process, not at the end of it. That should constitute no difficulty. As Mr. H. G. Wood has said,[2] it is biological prepossession that is partly responsible for our reluctance to ascribe finality to what seems a particular stage in a process. So far as that stage is made the vehicle of an

[1] F. H. Brabant, *Time and Eternity in Christian Thought,* p. 33.
[2] *Christianity and the Nature of History,* p. 155.

actualization of the eternal, it may constitute the ultimate standard just as much as if it came at the end of the process. The values created by a great composer of music are not dependent on his place in the time-series. The embodiment of the spiritual in history stands or falls by what it is, not by where it comes. The real difficulty— and the more frankly we face it the better—is how to evaluate a dynamic process in terms of an already existent eternal order. We cannot be content to say that the process simply repeats imperfectly and slowly something that already is, without adding anything to it. That would contradict our own consciousness of creative activity and of moral responsibility. When the enlightened conscience has to make a moral decision, the very heart of the matter is that the decision *does* make a difference. But neither can we be content to say that our co-operation with the purpose of God in making the right decision lies outside His activity. This would make Him a limited God, invoking human allies in the establishment of His kingdom. The deepest conviction of the saint is that he is entering into a realm that already exists for God, and that his own greatest achievement takes the form of a surrender, through which God can act.[1] Perhaps only in such intimate personal experience, rather than through any metaphysical formula, can we hope to come near the truth. What the human experience adds to God's un-limited wealth of being and purpose must lie in the actuality of expression. But this actuality, if it be conceived as due to a freedom exercised *within*, and not simply parallel to, the activity of God, constitutes a new category, which can claim its place as a positive enrichment of the created universe. It is higher in value than the expression of divine activity in sun and moon and stars and all the

---

[1] See 2 Cor. ii. 14, for St. Paul's conception of himself as a prisoner led captive in the triumphal procession of Christ through history.

immensities of Nature, just because it depends on the exercise of finite but real freedom.

This, then, is the point of view from which we shall approach the great Christian doctrines of redemption and revelation. They are taken together in this book because they are here regarded as different aspects of the actuality of history. That which man has done, as well as that which man is, must be "redeemed". The final meaning of it all must vindicate God, and no phase of history must leave a blot in God's 'scutcheon. But such a redemption will itself constitute the supreme revelation of God. History will be seen as a vast redemptive and therefore revealing process. Extension in time will become a higher parallel to extension in space, and both will find their ultimate unity, as man his peace, in the will of God.

# PART I

# THE ACTUALITY OF HISTORY

I. THE VALIDITY OF CHRISTIAN EXPERIENCE

II. THE MINISTRY OF ERROR

III. THE SYMBOLISM OF LANGUAGE

IV. THE ACTUALITY OF GOOD AND EVIL

V. THE DIVINE INITIATIVE

B

# CHAPTER I

## THE VALIDITY OF CHRISTIAN EXPERIENCE

WE all know that the term "experience" is capable of great abuse. As an esoteric court of appeal, it can be the buttress of fanaticism. As an unanalysed congeries of emotions, it can be the excuse for an unhealthy dualism between the heart and the brain. As inclusive of all the phenomena of consciousness, it can be made to yield almost any conclusion we like, and can become the solvent of positive views about anything. In this book[1] the appeal to the Christian consciousness is taken in its widest sense, in the belief that the over-emphasis of one type is likely to be corrected in the light of other types. Christian experience is taken to provide data, rather than to prove dogma, and the data must be submitted to the critical analysis of reason. On the other hand, it is maintained that these data have at least as much right to be considered as those of any other branch of experience, and that they warrant positive conclusions as fully as do those employed by the physicist or biologist, though belonging to a different level of reality, and necessarily involving different methods.

§ 1. *The Appeal to Experience.* Obviously, our first step must be to establish the validity of this appeal, which has been characteristic of the theology of the nineteenth and early twentieth century, notwithstanding such reactions from it as may be seen at present in neo-Thomism and Barthianism. Specially in evidence

[1] Here the "General Introduction" prefixed to this series may usefully be consulted.

3

have been the eager collection and comparison of data
from the widest ranges of the religious consciousness,
and the consequent rise of a new science, the psychology of religion, which has created a whole library of
good, bad, and indifferent books since this century began.
It may be seen, again, in the concern of philosophic
theology with human personality and its values as of
central interest and supreme importance. A further
proof lies in the fact that the outstanding theologians of
the last century, the men who mark the line of its most
potent theological influence upon the present, are beyond
question Schleiermacher and Ritschl, both of whom made
this appeal. It is the common ground of men so remote
in their conclusions as Dr. W. R. Inge and Baron von
Hügel; the former can sum up his *Confessio Fidei* by
the formula, "true faith is belief in the reality of absolute
values",[1] the latter his discussion of "Religion and Reality"
by saying of our ascription to the supreme Reality of
"what we ourselves possess that is richest in content,
that is best known to us, and that is most perfect within
our own little yet real experience", that "we have done
what we could".[2]

In making this appeal, theology is simply interpretative
of the common religious consciousness of the present day,
the fundamental consciousness (for the Christian) of an
experienced fellowship with God through Christ. We are
sometimes in danger of unduly magnifying the differences
of doctrine amongst Christians. These differences are by

[1] *Outspoken Essays*, II, p. 35.
[2] *Essays and Addresses on the Philosophy of Religion*, First Series, p. 50.
Newman's well-known criticism of "Liberalism" (*Apologia*, Note A) may
be accepted as a clear statement of the issue. "Liberalism then is the
mistake of subjecting to human judgment those revealed doctrines which
are in their nature beyond and independent of it, and of claiming to
determine on intrinsic grounds the truth and value of propositions which
rest for their reception simply on the external authority of the Divine
Word."

no means unimportant. But they will be found to attach chiefly to the *mediation* of divine activity, as through the sacraments or the ministry. On both sides of this mediation, in the doctrine of the divine Person with whom we have fellowship, and the human response within that fellowship, there is much more of common ground than we sometimes admit. We might put to a number of representatives of different Christian communities the practical question, "What must I do to be saved?" and there would be wide differences in the form and emphasis of the answers. Yet even in those which stressed the necessity for some sort of external authority, whether Church or Bible, the tendency would probably be to a pragmatic test of the validity of that authority.[1] "Trust what the Church or the Bible tells you—and see if the experience of your obedience does not confirm you in that obedience." This emphasis would be still more marked, if we went on to put the further question about religious certitude, "How can I know that I am saved?" It would not misrepresent the general trend of such answers to both questions to say that (apart from the claim for a particular discipline or mediating authority, as a tutor to bring us to Christ) they would probably make a triple appeal to Christian experience, viz. (1) the intrinsic worth and trustworthiness of the religious values, (2) their sufficient sanction in and through Christ, (3) the experience of divine activity through Christ (which involves a doctrine of the Holy Spirit). This is the victory that has so far overcome the world—our faith that God has really given Himself to us in Christ. We can give reasons for this confidence, but our "assents" are always deeper than our formal and logical reasons, and therefore the ultimate argument will always be some form of the appeal to an experience.

[1] These remarks are based on an actual experiment of this kind.

This, of course, has always been true. Wherever there has been vital religion, there has been the implicit or explicit appeal to experience. Beneath the changing formulation of doctrine, and beneath the slower changes of the Church's institutions, there is something more permanent, to which we come nearest in the great devotional books. We cannot "date" a mystical experience of this kind: "Say, Fool of Love, if thy Beloved no longer cared for thee, what wouldst thou do?" "I should love Him still," he replied. "Else must I die; seeing that to cease to love is death and love is life."[1] Such an experience is not "immediate" in the strict sense of being unmediated—there is no absolutely unmediated experience—but relatively to the religion of creeds and institutions the mystical claim to immediacy may be allowed.

One generation or school will find in such experience the witness of the Spirit, and another faith in absolute values, and both are justified. In any case, it is something incomparable and unique, and it is the very thing we are apt to miss when we study a system from without.[2] The "modernist" who prides himself on having broken loose from the authority of Church or Bible may easily forget that within the nurture and protection of that authority there was known the warmth of a vital experience of God, which we have hardly learnt to sustain without it. The point is that "experience" is not something to be placed in bare antithesis to the external authority of Church or Bible. Whatever false claims may have been urged or are urged still on their behalf, they mediated and

---

[1] *The Book of the Lover and the Beloved*, by Ramon Lull (Eng. Tr. by E. Allison Peers), p. 35. Cf. Rom. ix. 3; 1 John iv. 16: "where love is, God is"—even when He is silent. It is not, of course, suggested that such an experience as Lull's is that of the "average" Christian.

[2] Cf. Lord Acton's *Letters*, I, p. 60: "the deepest historians . . . do not know how to think or to feel as men do who live in the grasp of the various systems." This pregnant sentence is quoted again, in its context, in Chap. II, § 2.

still mediate a religious experience. However natural may be the growth of human personality into the Christian experience of fellowship with God, it will always depend on the shaping and stimulating influence of social tradition, of which every evangelistic appeal and every form of religious education is a new application. Those, therefore, who claim for Bible and Church a *de jure* authority can at least point to a *de facto* necessity as the basis of their doctrine.

In the formulation of this doctrine, however, we must not overlook the facts which the study of the origins of both the Bible and the Church is always bringing before us. Historical study of the Bible compels us to look beyond a literature to a history, and within that history to the religious consciousness of individual men. Every doctrine of Scriptural revelation turns at last on our interpretation of the prophetic consciousness of the Old Testament and the apostolic consciousness of the New— in other words on facts of religious experience. It is not otherwise with the authority of the Church. The polity which expresses that authority can be traced as a slow development, in close relation with the geographical and social conditions of the early centuries. The doctrinal decisions of Church councils can be shewn to have been influenced by ecclesiastical diplomacies and personal predilections, as well as by reaction to surrounding philosophies and religions. All this does not necessarily prevent us from recognizing a divine direction of the Church and an authoritative utterance through it, any more than similar phenomena prevent us from acknowledging the inspiration of Scripture. But it does compel us to recognize also that the authority of the Church is ultimately a specialized form of the authority of experience.[1]

---

[1] By "authority of experience" I do not mean to suggest that the "experienced" is independent of someone "experiencing" and therefore

In other words, the authority of both Bible and Church is derived from the interpretation of divine activity in human experience, and experience is the more inclusive category. It is, of course, only as we thus co-ordinate and include the whole of Christian experience through all the generations that we can reach objective standards, and escape from the waywardness of individualism. Whatever delegated and derived authority may be properly recognized, the ultimate authority for the modern mind that has learnt to criticize its own assumptions must be something *intrinsic*, something that philosophy will call "values" and theology the activity of the Spirit of God. Where God is present, He is active, and where He is active, He needs no testimonial of character. There is no novelty in this appeal to the intrinsic character of experience. It is, for example, found in Butler's cogent sentence, "Things and actions are what they are, and the consequences of them will be what they will be."[1] The novelty, such as it is, lies in the fearless confidence that a reconstruction of Christian thought on the basis of experience will give us back all that is necessary for religion and all that is true for theology, in the older appeals to derived authorities.

§ 2. *The Divine Activity.* It would be a mistake to

interpreting it. (See the useful contrast of "ed" and "ing" in Lloyd Morgan's *Emergent Evolution*, p. 39). The ultimate authority in religion is God as known in our experience of His activity; but this activity (within our consciousness) takes the form of a fellowship, to which man contributes, even though God contributes far more. That which is thus "experienced" is the ultimate compelling fact, the basis of personal conviction; the authority exercised over us by this experience is that of intrinsic worth or value. If it be objected that this is an argument in a circle, since the value is a value for *me*, the reply must be along the lines of the Introduction, § 4. It is of course implied that the individual experience is correlated with the collective experience of the race and criticized by it. This collective experience is partly articulated in the Bible and in the Church, which are therefore authoritative in their own degrees.

[1] Sermon VII, "Upon the Character of Balaam", last paragraph.

suppose that this new emphasis on experience is simply an apologetic device, to which we have been driven by the criticism of the origins of Bible and Church. Necessity is the mother of invention, but invention may be the discovery of truth. Just as modern philosophy is driven back on a criticism of experience for its epistemology, its science of knowledge, so is modern theology. Philosophy discovers that the dualism which began with Descartes[1] creates insuperable difficulties, and that it is necessary to get back to a duality within the unity of experience as something "given". Theology discovers its foundation in an actual experience of fellowship with God, as not less something "given". It is significant that this is admitted even by Ritschl, the typical example and pioneer of alienation from metaphysical construction in theology, for he says "in religion the thought of God is given".[2] This is not to be construed as a warrant for holding any particular dogma to be a direct revelation. In grace, as in nature, there are secondary causes, and most of us will admit that "our schemes of value, whether scientific or metaphysical, take symbolical shapes when we try to make them principles of action or even objects of contemplation".[3] But we are justified in saying that for Christian theology the "given" is that which we interpret as the real presence of God through the Spirit of Christ active in Christian experience, and that this "given" affords a valid knowledge of God within the limitations of human experience. The last clause must be emphasized. Just as any theory of the Incarnation which does justice to the historical data must have some principle of "Kenosis" (in the broadest sense of the term), so there is a

[1] Cf. Ward, *Psychological Principles*, p. 12 f.; von Hügel, *Essays and Addresses*, First Series, p. 51.

[2] *Die christliche Lehre von der Rechtfertigung und Versöhnung*, III, p. 17 (Eng. Tr., "Justification and Reconciliation", p. 17).

[3] Inge, *Outspoken Essays*, II, p. 15.

necessary "Kenosis" or "self-emptying" of the Holy Spirit involved in any and every indwelling of man.[1] We certainly cannot ignore the claim of Christian experience to be a new creation in which God is active in ways beyond those of His activity in human experience in general. But if that activity is to be within the realm of conscious life, it must take some such form as the New Testament doctrine of the Holy Spirit, a mingling of Spirit with spirit, a fellowship of God and man. That is conceivable only because God in His grace accepts the limitations of our personality as the sphere of His activity. In regard to the Incarnation, it is our faith that the personality was sinless, but a personality which is not sinless involves a further and deeper act of grace. Only as we study the full significance of this primary fact of Christian experience can we see the full evidence for the continuity of God's ways and for the revelation of His character. The divine drama of history which the Bible sets forth in the making of a people, the inspiration of prophets, the discipline of exile, the death on the Cross, is seen to be still in its fifth act, the coming of the Kingdom of God. Through them all His Spirit is active; in them all He "empties Himself" in differing degrees.

§ 3. *The Tests of Reality.* The chief contemporary criticism[2] of religious experience is condensed in the question, "Is religion an illusion?" Many factors have contributed to the present formulation of the question, but most prominent amongst them has been the study of origins, and particularly, in our own time, the study of the psychological origins of religious experience. It is

[1] See "The Kenosis of the Spirit", *Expository Times*, August 1924, pp. 488–93, by H. Wheeler Robinson; also Chapter XIV, § 2 of the present book.

[2] To refute this criticism, of course, does not exclude the recognition of the *ministry* of illusion, with which Chapter II deals.

sometimes difficult to be patient with the naïve assumption of so many writers that an account of the genesis of anything is *ipso facto* a philosophy of its ultimate origin or "source".[1] But it will prove worth while to have passed through a long period of unrest and uncertainty, if it compels us to make sure of our foundations. Many current criticisms of religion drawn from psychology will prove as ineffective as many criticisms of the Bible in the last generation drawn from science; they will prove to be not necessarily wrong in themselves but perverse in their application, and the re-statement of the nature of a religious experience will be the sounder because it has had to shew their perversity by a clearer presentation of itself.

Such a partial, but misapplied, truth may be seen in the claim that every religious conception has had a prior history, and bears upon it the stamp of the particular mind (and generation) of him who conceives it, so that it is only a "projection" of that mind. We may reply simply, but sufficiently, "The real question at issue is not, Is the idea of God a projection, but is it *only* a projection? If the phrase may be allowed, Does the projection *hit* anything?"[2] Even if we agreed to recognize "that religion reflects the fundamental life-experiences of man and that the driving impulses in these experiences are the most elemental instincts, such as food and sex",[3] we should still be bound to consider without prejudice the possible truth of the faith so reached. In such consideration, our task would not be to construct an elaborate argument for the being of God, as an inference from such

---

[1] More careful use of terms, here as elsewhere, would clear up many misconceptions. By "origin" we should denote the full history of anything as explanatory of its existence; by "genesis" its beginning, which is a mere phase or episode of that history; by "source" we may suggest the timeless reality, to which our explanation must go back, if it is to be complete.

[2] *The Gospel and the Modern Mind*, by W. R. Matthews, p. 90.

[3] *The Psychology of Religious Experience*, by E. S. Ames, p. 50.

experience; it would rather be to maintain something already given in that experience, according to the interpretation of religion itself. The answer to the challenge is, in fact, precisely similar to that which might be made, and in philosophy has often been made, to the doubt of the existence of an external world. We have not so much to prove that something may exist, as to remove the objections to retaining our intuitive and instinctive belief that it exists.[1] We have, then, to sustain the thesis that "The claim to trans-human validity continues upon the whole as present, operative, clear, in the religious intimations, as it continues present, operative, clear, in the intimations of the reality of an external world."[2]

At first sight, the ordinary man would say that it could not be sustained. He has grown up into the acceptance of a world of "real" objects, independent of his own thinking about them. He forgets, or has never considered, the obscure and tentative gropings of the infant, the gradual adjustment to its environment, the immense cumulative effect of habit and routine and social tradition. But let him ask himself how he becomes sure of the "reality" of any object external to himself, as distinct from, say, its presentation to him in a dream, and he will be surprised to find how subtle and complex the obvious can be. Why am I convinced of the "reality" of the birch-tree which grows opposite to my study window? Not because I can go out into the garden, and touch the trunk, for again I have *in a dream* made that tactual test of an object that seemed illusory to sight alone. My real reasons for accepting the evidence of my eyes at the present moment are chiefly three. The perception is persistent; the tree remains there, and is never gone "as a

---

[1] von Hügel, *op. cit.*, p. 44, to which essay this section is deeply indebted. His whole discussion of "Religion and Illusion, and Religion and Reality" is the best treatment of the subject known to me.

[2] *Op. cit.*, p. 44.

dream when one awaketh". The perception is congruous with those that accompany it; the tree appears in a garden, and is not seen growing in the sky, as it might by some trick of aeroplane picture-writing. The perception is confirmed by general agreement; others see it as well as I, and I have no need to hurry in alarm to an oculist. Persistence, congruity and agreement—these are the foundations of my acceptance of an external world. But in what respect are they wanting to the testimonies of the religious consciousness? It is the persistence of a moral or religious impression which alone secures its often unwilling acceptance as authoritative. It is the congruity of its results with the whole experience of life—the pragmatic test, "by their fruits"—with which no religious faith can for long dispense. As for the confirmation of "agreement", the practical universality of a religious consciousness of some kind or other is one of the most striking features of human experience—so that scepticism, not faith, is that which needs explanation, and may prove at last to be the actual illusion.

It might fairly be claimed that if we were relatively as accustomed to the objects of faith as to those of sight, they would be not less "real" to us than these; indeed to many men of deep religious experience the unseen world has become far more "real" than the seen, though most of us are at the infantile stage in these things. We must also remember the far greater complexity and subtlety of the spiritual world with which the religious consciousness has to do. At its highest levels, the "values" of personality are not objects that can be seen or handled. Truth and beauty and goodness live in the delicate and elusive reactions of spirit with spirit. God, the supreme Spirit, cannot be conceived as an object amongst other objects. His relation to us, for any adequate theistic conception, must be all-embracing and all-inclusive. His activity is

not that of a "piecemeal" supernaturalism;[1] He is to be
conceived as the home and source of all that makes our
true life. "We love, because He first loved us." The
values of personality imply and reveal Him. They imply
Him, because their compelling authority, their mysterious
fascination, their "otherness" and inexhaustible wealth,
are all inexplicable unless they exist already in super-
abundant fulness, and the values of personality can exist
only in and for personality, in and for Spirit great enough
to include Personality in its attributes. They reveal God,
because they are the very content of His nature, because
where they are, He is, not simply as a remote Bestower,
but as an active spiritual Presence. "In the cases of these
Intelligible Orders we have already something more or
less religious."[2] Again and again, the attempt has been
made to explain them on the human level, or to give them
a religious value without God, and the attempts have
always failed. But when the implicit logic of these values
is recognized, and they are taken up into the religious
consciousness, they obtain their noblest sanction, as God
obtains in and through them His most adequate revelation,
which is always life, and the whole of life. Our deepest
need is to see *God* steadily and see Him throughout all
life.

§ 4. *The Unity of Experience.* Within this great realm
of spiritual realities creating the values recognized by the
human consciousness as authoritative, the specifically
religious values which gather round the Person of Christ
occupy a primary place. The historical facts to which
Christian faith is directed do not simply provide the nuclei

---

[1] James, *Varieties of Religious Experience*, p. 520. The statements
made above are perhaps too condensed, but they are expounded in subsequent chapters; see, for example, Chapter XIV, § 2, "The Kenosis of the
Spirit," for the application to Christian experience.

[2] von Hügel, *op. cit.*, p. 56.

of these values, as when Jesus is made the great example of true religion, nor are they simply a means to an end, as when the Incarnation is presented as a revelation of God, designed to produce a moral and religious influence on man. Christianity is a historical religion in a sense deeper than this. God's entrance into history is redemptive actualization as well as revelation; it belongs to His very nature to share our sorrows and bear our sins, and He would not be the God and Father of our Lord Jesus Christ if He had not done this. Nor is the manner of His doing it accidental or arbitrary. "For in Christianity human nature is regarded as becoming not a passing disguise, but a permanent organ of the divine. . . . Man was, it teaches, from the first in the image of God, and the Son is eternally an element in the Godhead. That is, the union of God and man belongs to the very essence of both the one and the other."[1] To these words of a Christian philosopher, we may add those of a Christian theologian: "All genuine religion, especially Christianity, is revelational, evidential, factual—this also within the range of sense-and-spirit, and can never become a system of pure ideas or of entirely extra-historical realities."[2] But the recognition of this essential truth brings into view the peculiar difficulty of every appeal to religious experience as the basis of theological reconstruction. Christian experience is dependent on a historic revelation, yet it essentially consists in a personal response to God, known to be actively present in the personal consciousness. The consequence is that such experience is always entangled with historical data, themselves legitimately open to criticism, so that an element of uncertainty often creeps into it; on the other hand, when these data are ignored or minimized, Christian faith easily loses its specifically

---

[1] *Problems in the Relation of God and Man*, by C. C. J. Webb, p. 240.
[2] von Hügel, *op. cit.*, p. 269.

Christian character. "The religious experience without the vision of history would be empty, the historical event without the religious experience blind."[1] Here, then, are two elements in the Christian experience which seem to base it on feet of mingled iron and clay (the *respective* strength or weakness being defined according to the predilections of the analyst). In contrast with this entanglement, the simple appeal to the authority of either Church or Bible seems to have a peculiar cogency, and has always a plausible simplicity.

But it may prove that the truth lies deeper. If and when God does enter into our experience, there will always be something we can understand, and always something that passes understanding. Both the psychology of religion and historical criticism are legitimate sciences and must be given full scope and receive full attention. But the Christian experience is the unity of God's active presence, that unity which the familiar benediction describes: "The grace of the Lord Jesus Christ, and the love of God, and the communion of the Holy Spirit", the unity of access through Christ in one Spirit unto the Father.[2] We are dealing with a spiritual experience, and it is of the very nature of spirit to reach a unity by inclusion. There is an entanglement of body and soul, which leaves unsolved problems to both physiology and psychology, yet offers a working unity of experience. There is an apparently closed circle of psychical activities which leaves no place for human freedom, yet personality takes this closed circle up into its exercise of freedom.[3] So we may think of that greater unity wrought by the Spirit of

[1] Robert Winkler, in *Das Geistproblem*, p. 32, an admirably condensed statement of the modern approach through experience.

[2] 2 Cor. xiii. 14; Eph. ii. 18.

[3] See Introduction, § 1, and cf. Wobbermin's use of the same figure of the closed circle for the problem here before us, in his *Systematische Theologie*, I, pp. 405 ff.

God, when He takes of the things of Christ and makes them the living tokens of His presence to faith. It is, indeed, the problem of the Incarnation itself repeated in the experience of the believer. The duality of natures is not a dualism. There could be no such unity of man and God in the Person of Christ, or in the experience of His disciples, if there were not spiritual kinship between man and God; but there could be no such fellowship as Christian experience postulates if God were not other than, and infinitely more than, man, and had not made His partial "otherness" accessible and operative through the historical revelation of the Incarnation.[1] History is actual, and its actuality is part of its eternal meaning. No philosophy is adequate for Christian theology which does not make room for this reality. The "Jesus of history" is one with the "Christ of experience" because history is spiritual, and the Lord—the risen Lord of the New Testament faith—is the Spirit. The unity which faith affirmed in the New Testament times is affirmed by the faith of Christian life to-day, on the ground of an experience wrought through the Spirit.

§ 5. *The Moral Conditions.* A further aspect of this complex unity of Christian experience may be seen in the moral demands of faith, the kind of character needed in order to *know*. Here we may trace the historic influence of the Old Testament foundation for the New Testament faith. The "guest-psalms", for example, the fifteenth and twenty-fourth, describe the character of the man who

[1] This is the familiar issue between immanence and transcendence, neither of which can be ignored or minimized with impunity. Barthianism has over-emphasized transcendence in reaction from idealistic or humanistic types of religion which dwelt too exclusively on immanence. The Christian theologian will always have to wrestle with the task of explaining how the transcendent God can be known through His immanence, which is the essential problem for any doctrine of the Incarnation, or for any philosophy of the relation of time and eternity.

C

would claim sanctuary in Yahweh's house in terms drawn from the teaching of the great prophets. The demands of those prophets are continued in the teaching of Jesus; *the character of God is known only as it is shared,* and there is no salvation without such knowledge of God. In that cardinal truth lie in germ many subsequent problems of Christian theology, such as the relation of justification and sanctification, or of regeneration and conversion, or of divine grace and human freedom. There is no before and after in these deep realms; we can speak at most of different aspects of the unity of experience, and call them by different names, according to our angle of approach. Both ethics and theology have their legitimate contributions to make, and are left facing each other with their inevitable problems; but the interpreted unity of experience subtly harmonizes their contrasts.

With these more theoretical problems we are not here concerned, but there is a practical problem that has to be faced by most of us. The earnest seeker after God who has come to cry in sincerity, "O that I knew where I might find Him!" is frequently led to expect and to seek an answer in terms too exclusively intellectual. He labours to construct a "belief" where the only satisfying thing is a "faith", a personal trust and obedience making essentially moral demands. There is some excuse for this misconception in the limitations of the English language, for unfortunately there is no cognate verb corresponding with the noun "faith", and the reader, sometimes even the preacher, fails to recognize that "Believe on the Lord Jesus Christ" really says, "Have *faith* in Him", i.e. "Trust Him". The result of such misconception is not only that the battle for faith is often waged with but a part of our resources, but that the issue itself seems unfair. Truth is disguised in this or that intellectual garment; faith is made to depend on our acceptance of some doctrine which needs a scholar's training for its understanding.

The practical solution of the problem is obvious to those who have found their way through doubt to a genuine Christian faith, and it has repeatedly found illustration in the lives of such men. The example of Horace Bushnell will serve to shew this; it is stated by himself in a passage known to be autobiographic:—

" . . . there comes up suddenly the question, 'Is there, then, no truth that I do believe? Yes, there is this one, now that I think of it: there is a distinction of right and wrong that I never doubted, and I see not how I can; I am even quite sure of it.' Then forthwith starts up the question, 'Have I, then, ever taken the principle of right for my law; I have done right things as men speak; have I ever thrown my life out on the principle to become all it requires of me? No, I have not, consciously I have not. Ah! then, here is something for me to do! No matter what becomes of my questions—nothing ought to become of them if I cannot take a first principle so inevitably true, and live in it.' The very suggestion seems to be a kind of revelation; it is even a relief to feel the conviction it brings. 'Here, then,' he says, 'will I begin. If there is a God, as I rather hope there is, and very dimly believe, He is a right God. If I have lost Him in wrong, perhaps I shall find Him in right.' "[1]

We may go further than to point out the practical necessity of some such path, if the moral content of faith is to be known. The moral challenge concealed in the apparent disguise of truth becomes another proof of divine discipline. If the aim of the Christian revelation is not simply or chiefly to impart knowledge, but far more to develop character, to qualify men for a fellowship with God that does not rest on what others have said about Him, but on what He is in Himself, then intellectual

[1] *Life and Letters of Horace Bushnell*, ed. of 1880, pp. 57–59.

difficulties form a necessary part of our training. There is no more impressive statement of this important truth than that of Robert Browning in that highly illuminating poem, "A Death in the Desert". We see the aged apostle, John, as the last link with the Jesus of history. He has committed to writing his testimony, but there are new conditions for those who never knew Jesus in His earthly life. The task and test of life is the learning love, and the proofs must shift to make the test valid and effective and man's progress real. The point for each generation to consider is whether the *present* evidence of faith is adequate, not whether the evidence that satisfied a past generation is still as effective for ourselves. So when we face our modern question whether religion be not projection from the mind of man, we are but learning the wisdom of God:—

> "Building new barriers as the old decay,
>   Saving us from evasion of life's proof,
>   Putting the question over, 'Does God love,
>   And will ye hold that truth against the world?'"

# CHAPTER II

## THE MINISTRY OF ERROR

IN the previous chapter, the point reached was that truth often presents itself to us in disguise and that its recognition in such conditions forms a moral test and a discipline of character. Only as we practise truth must we expect to be able to recognize it, in spite of its disguise. But one form of this disguise of truth consists in its relativity, which means that it is frequently accompanied by partial error. Such error, accepted as part of the truth by us, would seem to be a constant condition of our progress into truth. It is like the "scaffolding of fiction within the child's mind; deprive it of the scaffolding and it will never grow".[1] This is what Lord Acton meant by his reference to "the mysterious property of the mind by which error ministers to truth and truth slowly but irrevocably prevails".[2] From this standpoint we can better appreciate the force of Lessing's well-known epigram:—

"If God held in His right hand all truth, and in His left only the ever-active impulse to search for truth, even with the condition that I must for ever err, and said to me 'Choose!' I should humbly bow before His left hand and say, 'Father, give! Pure truth belongs to Thee alone!'"[3]

[1] R. G. Collingwood, *Speculum Mentis*, p. 125.
[2] *The Study of History*, pp. 54, 55. In his "Note (73)" he gives a striking list of testimonies to both sides of this statement.
[3] *Sämmtliche Schriften*, XI (2) 401: English as quoted in the *Encyclopaedia of Religion and Ethics*, VII, p. 894.

This chapter is not concerned with the philosophical questions as to the criteria of truth[1] or with the psychological problems of error.[2]   We have not to ask, therefore, whether appearance is linked to reality by correspondence, or causality, or pragmatic creation, or some form of idealistic identity, nor have we to ask how the illusory appearance is mistaken for reality, so giving rise to error. Our present concern is with the place taken and the service rendered by error in regard to religion.   Obviously, any dogmatic assertion of what is truth and what is error in contemporary religion would be especially out of place in such a subject, and the illustrations (numerous because of the pragmatic approach) are chosen as inoffensively and as broadly as possible.   There is plenty of material in the history of religions to illustrate errors now universally regarded as such.   The problem before us is quite distinct from that of moral evil, which has received so much fuller discussion, though error probably occupies a much larger place in life.   Nothing said here must be taken as blurring the absoluteness of the distinction between moral good and evil (see Chapter IV).

Error in general has been defined by G. F. Stout as "mere appearance which also appears to be real.   The essence of all mere appearance is that it is a feature of an object which belongs to it only in virtue of the psychical conditions under which it is apprehended."[3]   If we accept this definition, and apply it to our special form of error, we may say that error in religion is the ascription to God

---

[1] See Chapter I.

[2] In a suggestive article by Professor Gilbert Murray ("Vice and Illusion: the psychology of vice": *Philosophy*, XI, 43, July 1936, pp. 259–70), he analyses three "bad habits", viz. those of drink and drugs, sexual excesses and gambling, and finds selfishness and illusion to be fundamental.   The claim that virtue is knowledge is unfounded.   Faith helps and faith often rests on illusion.   It is always difficult to convey the whole truth, and some are helped by their illusions, especially when these are unselfish.

[3] *Personal Idealism*, ed. by  H. Sturt, p. 31.

of that which belongs only to man's imperfect perception of truth. Perhaps all religious error is ultimately a wrong kind of anthropomorphism, the wrongness being relative to the man and his generation. But examples are better than any attempt at definition. John Wesley[1] says that "the giving up witchcraft is, in effect, giving up the Bible". Now, even if we are to admit that the belief in witchcraft was at one stage inseparable from the growth of religion, few would allow that John Wesley's Gospel really did depend on such a belief, or that such a belief in his time did contribute to the growth of his personal religion or that of anybody else. It was a fossil-survival, or at most a living parasite on it. With such beliefs, when they are clearly wrong and clearly unhelpful, this discussion is not concerned. But the conversion of Mary Slessor, the missionary to Calabar, may illustrate the kind of error which does minister to religion. An old Scots-woman of Dundee used to gather a few girls round her hearth to talk to them about salvation.

" 'Do ye see that fire?' she exclaimed suddenly. 'If ye were to put your hand into the lowes it would be gey sair. It would burn ye. But if ye dinna repent and believe on the Lord Jesus Christ your soul will burn in the lowin' bleezin' fire for ever and ever.' "

Few of us would defend such a belief in such a form and application; but it frightened Mary into the kingdom, where she was the more useful because she grew out of that belief, and never herself tried to win others by the same method.[2] To such a person, at such a stage, the error did minister to her religious growth.

Of course, it is not possible to analyse error, considered simply in itself, into the harmful and helpful varieties of it. We have always to consider it in relation to its

---

[1] *Journal*, May 25, 1768.
[2] *Mary Slessor*, by W. P. Livingstone, p. 3.

historical or personal setting before we can do this. We cannot say of sand that it is either harmful or helpful to a motor-car till we know what use is made of it; it might be thrown into the engine to wreck it, or scattered on a slippery road to enable its wheels to grip. All that concerns us at the moment is the utility of error to the progress of religion.

We must, however, notice the previous question—can error have utility at all? John Morley, in his well-known book, *On Compromise* (ed. of 1886), denies this: "erroneous opinion or belief", he says, "in itself and as such, can never be useful" (p. 56), though "errors in opinion and motive . . . are inevitable elements in human growth" (p. 83). He is arguing chiefly against the position of a supposedly enlightened minority which is content to leave the majority in error for their own good. With that application of his argument there need be no quarrel; the position could hardly be taken by a genuine lover of truth. But Morley himself admits in regard to error (1) "the possible expediency of leaving it temporarily undisturbed" (p. 60), and (2) the abundant instances in history in which it "has seemed to be a stepping-stone to truth" (p. 75), though he would explain these away by reference to the truth latent in the error. Do not such admissions really point beyond themselves, and can such hard and fast distinctions of truth and error ever be more than pure theory, unrelated to the life we know and share? In that life, error at any given moment is inseparable from truth. Where is the absolute standard by which such contemporary distinction can be made? But if there be none that obtains universal recognition, it is pure assumption to say that no man can be helped by that which seems to us to be error, especially as it may be the stepping-stone for him into our own alleged truth. Morley's argument, however sound as a rebuke of cynical indifference to truth, seems to ignore the service to man's historical development rendered by all those religious ideas and institutions which a subsequent generation may come to call error.

§ 1. *The Development of Religion as involving Error.* If we accept the principle of historical development at all, we must admit the universality of error. Historical development implies degrees of truth at successive stages of the development. But degrees of truth are only the other side of degrees of error, and partial truth may itself mislead by its mere partiality. Even if a religion claims to start with a deposit of absolute truth given through Moses or Christ or Muhammad, the truth given must be historically apprehended. It is significant that the followers of all three have found it necessary to formulate a theory of oral tradition, to adjust the fixity of the "absolute" truth to the developing needs of successive generations. But partially apprehended truth means partial error. John Robinson's farewell words to the Pilgrim Fathers of the *Mayflower* are often quoted, though not always correctly; he was very confident, reports Winslow, "the Lord had more truth and light yet to break forth out of His holy Word". That was a prospective admonition to keep an open mind as to new and truer interpretations of Scripture; but obviously it has a retrospective application, and implies error in the past, when it becomes past. For all who interpret the Bible historically, it suggests that error will be mingled with truth all along the line of its growth. We cannot, for example, dismiss Jephthah's vow in the manner of a minister to whom as a boy I once referred it; "it teaches us", he said, "not to make rash vows". We must face the issue that what was wrong for a subsequent age was right for Jephthah from the standpoint of his age, and that even his sacrifice of his daughter illustrates the ministry of error to religion.

The relativity of truth in its historical growth may be illustrated by the *lex talionis*. In the Sermon on the Mount, Jesus condemns it without any qualification: "Ye have heard that it was said, An eye for an eye, and a tooth for a tooth; but I say unto you, Resist not him that is evil: but whosoever smiteth thee on thy right cheek, turn to him the other also."[1] That carries us back to the Book of the Covenant,[2] from which the *lex talionis* is quoted, a document probably belonging to the early days of the Hebrew monarchy. But, in that very law there is a great advance in social morality over the unrestrained blood-revenge of the desert, itself reflected in Lamech's barbaric song:—

> "For I kill a man for a wound to me,
>     And a boy for a scar.
> For Cain takes vengeance seven times,
>     But Lamech seventy times and seven!"[3]

In many instances the development consists not in the gradual restraint of an evil, such as that of unrestricted revenge, but in the gradual liberation of a truth from some accompanying error, which served as its matrix. An example may be found in the sense of corporate personality which extends so widely in the ancient world, and is illustrated in the Old Testament by the fate of Achan's family. The growth of the idea of individual responsibility which may be seen in Jeremiah and Ezekiel ultimately led to the rejection of the old idea of the group; yet the group idea itself expressed, however imperfectly, that sense of social solidarity which our modern individualism has had to re-discover for itself. Indeed, it may be said that all our conceptions of truth have this accompaniment of error. Error is like the alloy in Browning's figure of the ring which he applies to the story of the "Ring and

[1] Matt. v. 38, 39.          [2] Exod. xxi. 24,
[3] Gen. iv. 23, 24, tr. by Skinner.

the Book"; the pure gold of fact in the ancient story is worked up by the alloy of his imaginative construction of the events into a finer shape and a fuller beauty. The alloy of error is an inevitable and constant factor in the whole process of development of truth, theoretical or practical, if only because of the very nature of the time-process.

Another aspect of our many-sided theme is seen in the disparate development of religion and ethics. We need not consider the frequent existence of a high grade of religion in association with a low grade of morality. The great line of development seen in the Bible has so associated religion and ethics that we almost instinctively measure the worth of a religion by its ethical products. But the converse combination does concern us—that of a relatively low complex of religious ideas in association with a relatively high grade of morality. Here we readily recognize the practical worth of the religious attitude as a whole, even though it seems to us bound up with erroneous ideas of religion; we admit that the spirit is right though the form of its conception may be wrong. The Osiris myth of ancient Egypt is clearly the personification of a nature-cult derived from the Nile; yet that myth is the cradle of a great ethical development, and Osiris, in the course of many centuries, becomes the great moral judge of men. The companion myth of the Sun-god is even more obviously rooted in primitive conceptions of nature; yet we know to what lofty heights of religious faith the worship of Aton could bring a Pharaoh, making his hymn the basis of the 104th Psalm. We are not likely to accept the faith of Muhammad that the angel Gabriel dictated to him the suras of the Kur'an; yet we cannot doubt the ethical truth of the 80th sura, where the prophet acknowledges the divine rebuke for his rough treatment of a blind man seeking instruction, whilst he was engaged in conversation with one of the chiefs of the Kureisch. Or, let us think of the story of Yuan Chwang, a pilgrim to Indian Buddhist shrines in the seventh Christian century. Pirates boarded his vessel in the Ganges, and proposed to sacrifice him to their goddess Dinga. As he lay on the altar, he prayed that he might be re-born in heaven and learn the Truth. Then, having perfected himself in wisdom, he desired—"Let me return and be born here below that I may instruct and convert these men, and cause them to give up their evil deeds, and practise themselves in doing good." The story fitly ends with a sudden storm, of which he was unconscious, which so alarmed the pirates that they did him reverence and became his disciples—which illustrates the ministry of error to morality as well as religion.[1]

§ 2. *Particular Contributions of Error to Religion.* So far we have merely illustrated the universal presence of error as a concomitant of growth into religious and moral truth. We have now to consider more precisely the kind of service rendered by error to religion and morality. Three aspects of this may be distinguished, viz. the sharpening of the intellectual apprehension and definition of truth, the moral discipline and social progress through conflict with error, and the pedagogic value of beneficent illusion.

Lord Acton once wrote, in a letter to Mary Gladstone,

"My life is spent in endless striving to make out the inner point of view, the *raison d'être*, the secret of fascination for powerful minds, of systems of religion and philosophy, and of politics, the offspring of the others, and one finds that the deepest historians know how to display their origin and their defects, but do not know how to think or feel as men do who live in the grasp of the various systems."[2]

[1] *Hibbert Journal*, Oct. 1914.     [2] *Letters of Lord Acton*, p. 60.

That applies equally to the work of the teacher and preacher of a religion. He must himself feel the force and strength of the error he would replace by the truth he himself holds. A good illustration of this is supplied by George Fox;[1]

"One morning, as I was sitting by the fire, a great cloud came over me, and a temptation beset me; but I sat still. And it was said, 'All things come by nature'; and the elements and stars came over me, so that I was in a manner quite clouded with it. But as I sat still, and silent, the people of the house perceived nothing. And as I sat still under it, and let it alone, a living hope arose in me, and a true voice, which said, 'There *is* a living God who made all things.' And immediately the cloud and temptation vanished away, and life arose over it all; my heart was glad, and I praised the living God. After some time, I met with some people who had a notion that there was no God, but that all things came by nature. I had a great dispute with them and overturned them, and made some of them confess that there is a living God. Then I saw that it was good that I had gone through that exercise."

In the whole development of doctrine, it is a commonplace to note how much the heretics have contributed to that which afterwards was recognized as truth; the prophets of Israel are amongst the most obvious examples. But heresy has contributed to truth in less direct ways, even whilst remaining heresy in the subsequent judgment of men. Whatever the Christian theologian of to-day may think of the Chalcedonian definition and of its positive contribution to a Christology, it is clear that the clash with views there rejected did define the issue and so far advance the truth. Even a theologian of such broad sympathies as Schleiermacher recognizes the great value of negative definition in the pursuit of truth. In an early section of *Der christliche Glaube* (par. 22), he describes

[1] *Journal*, I, p. 26 (eighth edition, 1901).

four heresies—the Docetic and the Ebionite, the Manichaean
and the Pelagian—as virtually exhaustive of the possibilities, and as forming limiting ideas in regard to Christology.  The first pair, the Docetic and the Ebionite,
represent the exclusive emphasis on the divine and on
the human respectively in the Person of Christ; the second
pair, the Manichaean and the Pelagian, represent human
nature either as beyond salvation or as able to save itself;
a true statement of the Christian faith must avoid all
these extremes which rule out either a Saviour or salvation.
The positive value of a faith is seen by the negatives that
would take away its foundations.

The second contribution of error worthy of notice is
through the struggle which it forces on truth both to
discover and to maintain itself.  The value of this moral
discipline is clearly independent of the precise issues:—

> "Rightly to be great,
> Is not to stir without great argument,
> But greatly to find quarrel in a straw,
> When honour's at the stake."[1]

It is sufficient, so far as moral discipline goes, that men
should stand for that which they hold to be truth against
that which they hold to be error, even though their
judgment of the truth or error be eventually disproved.
But, clearly, the assimilation of truth, the effort and
struggle to make it ours, are essential to all progress in
religious truth.  This is the law of life which the biologist
finds working everywhere.[2]  The same law surely holds
of life on its higher levels.  It is recognized in the New
Testament, when Paul says to the Corinthians,[3] "There

---

[1] Shakespeare, *Hamlet*, IV. 4.
[2] J. H. Bradley, *Parade of the Living*, pp. 251, 258. "It is only when
organisms must struggle against heavy odds to gain comfort that they
succeed in bettering themselves. . . . No great evolutionary advance has
ever come under an easy environment."
[3] 1 Cor. xi. 19.

must be also heresies among you, that they which are approved may be made manifest among you." Aquinas comments on this passage[1] that this gain to the faithful is not to be reckoned to the credit of heretics since it is far from their intention. But it *is* a gain to the faithful, as we may see again and again in the history of the Church—in its ancient clash with Gnosticism, or in the Counter-Reformation within Catholicism which was provoked by the Reformation.

It must not be thought, however, that the moral discipline of the individual or the group comes simply through the clash of parties or institutions in Church or State. This might serve merely to buttress prejudice or to arouse the worst passions of men. No small part of the moral discipline comes through the disguise of error through which the truth must be recognized. We have already referred to Browning's "A Death in the Desert", where it is suggested that the certainty of truth in the first disciples of Jesus has been replaced by the challenge of subsequent uncertainty in order that truth might be sought and loved for its own sake, and maintained by a personal struggle which guarantees its quality, in order that

"truth, deadened of its absolute blaze,
Might need love's eye to pierce the o'er-stretched doubt.
. . . . . .
God's gift was that man should conceive of truth
And yearn to gain it, catching at mistake,
As midway help till he reach fact indeed."

The quotation just made introduces a third aspect of the contribution of error to religion, viz. that there may be a pedagogic value in error, a beneficent illusion. Frederic William Robertson has a notable sermon on "The Illusiveness of Life", based on Abraham's unfulfilled

[1] *Summae Theologicae Secunda Secundae,* Q. XI, Art. III.

expectation of the possession of Canaan.  He illustrates
the illusiveness of life by the way in which we are deceived
by our senses in regard to the distance, shape and colour
of objects, the anticipations of life unfulfilled in its course,
the eschatological hopes of the Church.  Yet, he argues,
by such things we are led on step by step, as the school-
boy by the prize he seeks, into the real gain of knowledge.
Moreover, there is a deeper reward in the process than in
the imagined goal, and in that which we become beyond
all that we hoped to get.  We are reminded of the closing
proposition of Spinoza's *Ethics*, viz. "Beatitudo non est
virtutis præmium, sed ipsa virtus."

Perhaps there could be no simpler illustration of the
pedagogic value of error than that supplied by idolatry.
A second century writer, Maximus of Tyre,[1] wisely distinguishes between those who do not, and those who do,
need images, according to their powers of mental realization.  The image, he says, is like the copy traced by the
teacher of writing, which the child's hand follows under
the teacher's until memory enables him to dispense with
this aid.  With this sympathetic attitude, we may fitly
compare the act of Stephen Grellet, that charming combination of French aristocrat and American Quaker.  He
was visiting a convent in Naples, and noticed a number
of the girls kneeling before a Madonna, nominally
engaged in their devotions, but actually laughing to one
another.  A little later, he had an opportunity of addressing them, and the first thing he did was to rebuke them
for their irreverence.[2]  There is something spiritually fine
in that rebuke from a Quaker for the failure to be
reverent towards what to him was an idol.  He recognized
the worth of devotion even in a form he condemned; he
admitted the truth of beneficent illusion.  It is a truth,

[1] VIII, 2, in ed. of F. Dübner, 1877; cf. E. Bevan, *Holy Images*, p. 71.
[2] *Memoirs of Stephen Grellet* (B. Seebohm), II, p. 48.

even though we agree with Dayananda Sarasvati spending his vigil in the temple of Siva, and saying to his father, "I feel it impossible to reconcile the idea of an omnipotent living God with this idol, which allows the mice to run over his body, and thus suffers himself to be polluted without the slightest protest."[1] The error which one man rejects may be another's present stage of truth.

The fact of beneficent illusion is not less apparent when we take long perspectives of the history of religion. Mythology has been the foster-nurse of religion, as alchemy of chemistry and astrology of astronomy. Plato in the *Republic* argues for the use of fiction in persuading men to accept that which is good for them, though beyond their power of comprehension in its purer shape (III, 414 ff.). Whatever we may think of the difficulty and danger of the deliberate use of deception, there can be no question that *life* does deceive us, and often for our good, as well as for our hurt. The cry of the prophet Jeremiah, "O Lord, thou hast deceived me, and I was deceived" (xx. 7), is echoed by the cry of dereliction from the Cross of Christ in its deepest agony. Yet through Jeremiah's experience of divine deception came some of the greatest spiritual truths of Israel and the richest development of its lyrics, whilst the desolation of the Cross, with its unfulfilled hope, has become the central point of the Christian contact with God.

Such life-experiences as these remind us how far removed are we of the western world from the *Maya* of the eastern. To us the world in which we live is a real world, even though its apprehension is subjectively conditioned by error; the illusion of life is a necessary element of a process in which something is actually achieved. But to the Vedantist the sole reality of the world of phenomena is

[1] J. N. Farquhar, *Primer of Hinduism*, p. 161.

D

that of a dream, from which deliverance comes when the sleeper awakes. There is a significant story of the saintly Markandeya, rewarded by the promise of whatever he asks. His request is, "to look upon the Magic through which the world with its guardian gods imagines a distinction in being". So one evening there arises a great wind and a great flood, reducing the seeming cosmos to chaos. At last he sees Krishna as a babe, who absorbs him like a gnat by drawing a breath. Then from *within the god* he sees cosmos once more, time displayed as though it were real, till the child's breath expels him once more into chaos. A moment after and chaos itself disappears, and Markandeya is back in his familiar place in that world of illusory cosmos which he has seen from within the god. So a dream within a dream has revealed the truth of things, and that dream within a dream is Maya.[1] But those whom the Bible has taught to regard life as the actuality of will, rather than the illusion of thought, can think of its partial illusions as stepping-stones from the reality of the soul to the reality of its God.

§ 3. *The Good Will as the only Absolute Good.* If then error be omnipresent in our religious thought and life and inseparable from contemporary truth, and yet may serve, in its own manner, as a twin ministrant with truth to man's growth in religion and morality, what conclusions may we draw from this ministry? The constitution of life as we find it, the conditions under which we must necessarily live, do not suggest that the attainment of intellectual truth is the primary end of religion. The liberating knowledge of truth which the New Testament offers is itself very far from being an intellectual attainment; it goes back to that knowledge of God in the Old Testament which is an attitude of the will more than an

[1] L. D. Barnett, *The Heart of India*, pp. 65 f.

effort of the intellect. We are here to be and to do rather than to know, and our knowledge is subordinated to our being and doing. The differences of intellectual truth possessed by religion at its higher levels are reduced to a small measure in comparison with all their common difference from the truth as it is to God; yet most of us feel that there is a fundamental difference between right and wrong in act and deed that sets us on God's side or against Him. This I take to be the deep meaning of Wittgenstein's profound aphorism: "We are conscious that even if all *possible* intellectual questions are answered, our problems of life still remain untouched. Certainly, no further question then remains, and in this very fact is the answer. The solution of the problem of life is seen in the disappearance of this problem."[1]

Such a view as this links up our argument with the "actuality" of history as emphasized from the outset. The admission that the attainment of intellectual truth is not the primary end of religion does not exonerate us from seeking truth, and fighting for truth, however relative. To do this is not simply a matter of social obligation, which can be delegated to others as professional combatants; it is the essential condition and test of individual growth in intellectual truth, which always must condition individual growth in religion. This bears directly on the practical question of propaganda and missions. Can a man be sincere in his religious faith if he does not seek to impart it, at least in what he regards as its essentials, to other men?

As with the individual life, so with the race—"the battle, that solves every doubt". As John Stuart Mill says, in his *Liberty* (ed 3, p. 86):—"Truth, in the great practical concerns of life, is so much a question of the reconciling and combining of opposites, that very

---

[1] *Tractatus Logico-Philosophicus*, p. 186.

few have minds sufficiently capacious and impartial to make the adjustment with an approach to correctness, and it has to be made by the rough process of a struggle between combatants fighting under hostile banners." Who shall be confident, in any such conflict, that God's truth is not greater than that of either side, not in the sense of being their synthesis, so much as of requiring both in their very clash to accomplish His purpose? Such a conclusion, however, is not intended in the Hegelian sense. The Hegelian synthesis of opposites—truth, error, higher truth—does not suit that way of looking at life which this chapter has suggested; we should still be left asking questions about the value of the whole process, and still be left to explain how error, as well as moral evil, could appear at all in such a scheme of things. But though Kant does leave us with many problems, his fundamental emphasis on the good will as our contact with ultimate reality leaves room for the recognition of intellectual error as the minister of religion.

The chief aim of the present chapter has been to emphasize one feature in the actuality of history which is often ignored or evaded. To prevent the drawing of wrong conclusions from such an emphasis, some of them may here be summarily indicated.

(a) As was said at the outset, there is no intention to confuse the relation of error to truth with the conflict of evil and good in the moral realm. Here the distinction is absolute in quality, for it springs from man's use of his freedom within the limits permitted to it. There can be no reconciliation of moral evil with the purpose of God; for moral evil nothing avails but a divine redemption. Error, however, is something which springs not from man's will, but from the necessary conditions under which it is exercised. We repent of our sins; we regret our errors—a very different attitude.

(*b*) The existence of error, like the existence of moral evil, is a problem for theism, though of a different kind, and requiring a different solution.[1] It has its tragic features, which should not be overlooked; men miss the truth through no fault of their own, but simply by being where they are, in geography or history. If life on earth were all, and death meant its final limit, the injustice to individuals might seem irreconcilable with either the goodness or power of God. But if there is life beyond death, admitting of further opportunity and development, the apparent injustice is removed, and the ministry of present error can operate in the service of that ultimate truth which is the gift of the highest goodness.

(*c*) Our full recognition of the relativity of the truth possessed in human experience is no denial of the possession of absolute truth by God. When we judge the truth and error seen in the thought and lives of other men, as we cannot avoid doing, honesty demands full loyalty to our own convictions, and humility inspires the acknowledgement that, at best, we are only a further stage on the long journey we, as well as they, must take. "Subjectively" a man is right when he acts in accordance with his convictions of truth, though "objectively" his conduct may be wrong when seen from the standpoint of a fuller knowledge of the truth.

(*d*) From this relativity of truth and error, it by no means follows that what a man thinks does not matter, since he is to be judged not by it, but by his conduct in relation to it. Religions, for example, are by no means

---

[1] Dr. W. R. Matthews asks me whether error, as well as sin, does not need to be included in the doctrine of redemption which underlies this book (see, especially, Chap. XIII). I should agree so far as to say that the *meaning* of error must ultimately be transformed, as it is when it becomes a stage in individual progress towards eternal life. But the problem seems to me to belong to creation, rather than to redemption. Error is a *necessary* limitation of finite beings; sin is a wilful and unnecessary challenge to the purpose of God.

equal in their power to "save" men, even though a lower
religion faithfully followed may place a man higher than
the highest religion to which he gives but superficial heed.
Ignorance, as well as sin, has to be combated by fuller
knowledge and "Ignorance is a more ultimate fact in our
lives than error".[1] The advantage of knowledge and truth
over ignorance and error is that they give man his moral
opportunity on a higher level, with ampler resources for
moral good, *provided he wills to use them*. "The only
absolute good is the good will."

[1] A. E. Taylor, *The Faith of a Moralist*, I, p. 377.

# CHAPTER III

## THE SYMBOLISM OF LANGUAGE

WE have seen that the error mingled with truth in the content of our religious knowledge does not cancel it out, or justify general scepticism or even agnosticism, but actually ministers to the development of that knowledge. But now another difficulty ought to be faced with equal frankness, which arises from the form, rather than the content, of that knowledge. Is the instrument we are bound to employ, the instrument of human language, adequate for the purpose to which it is here put? Since, moreover, as we shall see, articulate thought depends on the use of language, can that thought ever rise to a true apprehension of a realm of reality lying beyond our present range of experience? Within that range language is admittedly symbolic; how can a symbol of some fragment of human experience apply to divine activity?

These are questions which must have haunted all of us who try to think out the meaning of things. How often we want to express a genuine element in our consciousness, such as sympathy with a sufferer, and find no words at our command! In rarer moments, also, there may come the sudden consciousness of "reality" beyond us, breaking in upon us, such as the inexpressible beauty of Nature in some choice spot, or some act of generosity or courage that thrills us, or some awareness, it may be, whilst we are praying, that an unseen presence is close at hand. We cannot put any of these experiences into words, and so our thought of them lacks clear articulation, yet the reality of that which is known is for us beyond question. Even the poetic genius can do no more by his choice of verbal symbols than to awaken or clarify the memory of such experiences in those who have already had them. In theology we do well to remember the warning given by one of the greatest and most daring pioneers of theological speculation:—

"Let every one, then, who cares for truth be little concerned about words and language, seeing that in every nation there prevails a different usage of speech; but let him rather direct his attention to the meaning conveyed by the words, than to the nature of the words that convey the meaning . . . there are certain things the meaning of which cannot be unfolded at all by any words of human language, but which are made known more through simple apprehension than by any properties of words."[1]

The warning is the more impressive because it comes from the compiler of the *Hexapla*, the last man to be careless about the use of words. He would indeed have us to aim first at verbal exactitude, but then to recognize that we are only at the threshold of theology.

Origen's caveat takes us to the heart of the subject of this chapter, which is the relation of the theological vocabulary to the realities which it professedly describes. The title, "The Symbolism of Language", is meant to indicate that we are not concerned with that symbolism of the order of *nature* which appealed so strongly to Origen himself, nor to the symbolic *objects* which human hands have created, whether the fetish, the amulet, the idol or the work of art, nor again to the symbolic *acts* which take so large a place in the ritual of religion, from the gestures of the savage, through the symbolic acts of Hebrew

[1] Origen, *De Principiis*, IV. i. 27; Eng. trs. by F. Crombie in *Ante-Nicene Christian Library*.

prophets, up to the most profound Christian sacramentalism. All these could be regarded as indirect forms of
language,[1] but our concern is with human speech itself
and its adequacy to express extra-human reality. We
shall consider first very briefly the general psychology of
language, so far as it bears on the subject, then the intermediate place which language holds between thought and
life, finally and chiefly the adequacy of its "symbolism"
of spiritual reality. We take *sumbolon* to mean a purely
arbitrary sign or token of something other, as the beacon-
fire was a *sumbolon* of the capture of Troy,[2] or the
coinage of the ideal city a *sumbolon* "for purposes of
exchange".[3]

§ 1. *The Psychology of Language.*[4] A great deal has
been written on the psychology of language and on some
points there is still much controversy. But the majority
of psychologists would probably agree that language begins
with gestures and vocal utterances which are purely
emotional. These expressions of emotion are naturally
associated with particular occasions, such as in the cry of
terror. In course of time they derive specific meaning
from this association, and the cry aroused by danger
becomes a warning against it. In the primitive society
they are interpreted by common sympathy and they are
also stimulated by the tendency to imitation which plays
so great a part in the development of social custom.
When once intelligible meaning has been linked to par-

---

[1] Another extension of the subject would be the "symbolism" of modern
physical theories, such as that of the electron: "no one has even seen an
electron, or has the remotest conception as to what it would look like"
(Jeans, *The Mysterious Universe*, 1930 ed., p. 41).

[2] Aeschylus, *Agam.* 8.

[3] Plato, *Republic*, II, 371 B.

[4] The résumé here given is necessarily very condensed; for a full discussion, see W. M. Urban's *Language and Reality* (1939), Pt. I. See also,
J. Ward, *Psychological Principles*, pp. 286 ff.

ticular sounds, the tradition of the society will supply the matrix in which the individual grows up.  Thus we get the possibility of something which we can call language. Children, as we know, grow slowly into the capacity to differentiate sounds and to apply them to objects, under the influence of their particular environment.  The differences of dialect in different groups illustrate this social origin of language.  There is a sense, of course, in which "thought" of a vague kind may be said to exist before language.  But thinking in the full sense becomes possible only by the sharper discrimination of meaning which language supplies.  Here the most important step forward is the birth of the generic image, which is set free by language through the use of the class name.  The generic image has been compared with the product of composite photography; from a number of more or less similar impressions a resultant emerges which combines their chief similarities.  For example, from a number of particular men, the class name "man" is formed.  In this process, however, we must not think of the individual as purely passive.  In the formation of the concept which underlies the generic image selective interest is, of course, active.  When once the generic image is provided with a name, individual thinking is able to proceed with its further analysis of experience.

§ 2. *Language intermediate between Thought and Life.* It will be seen therefore that language occupies a middle place between thinking and living.  Its rudiments are evoked by some conscious reaction to life and the growth of intelligence is dependent on the use of language.  On the other hand, intelligence is always projecting itself on life and by its growing experience continually, if unconsciously, modifying its own use of language. Such modification inevitably reacts on the process of actual thinking. So there is a constant give and take between thinking and living, by way of language.

We may compare language with our paper currency— valueless in itself, yet so intimately linked to our conceptions of value that we ordinarily estimate the value of anything material in terms of "pounds". Yet, as we know, there is nothing absolute in such value. The purchasing value of the pound can vary greatly, and our standard is constantly open to new definition in terms of the actual goods the pound can purchase. So is it with language. Words in themselves mean nothing until they are referred to life, and few inferences are likely to be more misleading than those based on etymology unchecked by actual usage.

Life is continually moving beyond the vocabulary which was evolved to describe it, continually putting new wine into old wineskins. Let us take some examples of this. The Christian community of the first century had to express the new moral quality of its life and so adopted the word *agapé*. It may be that, as Moulton and Milligan say,[1] "In its redemption from use as a mere successor to the archaic *erōs*, Alexandrian Jews of 1/B.C. seem to have led the way", but, at any rate, *agapé* became a characteristically Christian word, with a characteristically Christian content. Again, in more specialized fields, the poet and the philosopher and the scientist are constantly modifying the old vocabulary to express their new ideas, or coining new terms. Thus the adjective "incarnadine", meaning properly "flesh-coloured", has been given the meaning "blood-coloured" by Shakespeare's use of it as a verb in the words

> "—this my hand will rather
> The multitudinous seas incarnadine,
> Making the green—one red."[2]

[1] *The Vocabulary of the Greek Testament*, s.v.    [2] *Macbeth* II, ii.

When Whitehead tells us that "The ultimate facts of immediate actual experience are actual entities, prehensions and nexūs",[1] each of the three terms employed is given a special meaning within his "Philosophy of Organism", and convey little meaning apart from their context. He might almost as well have written x, y and z.    In 1818, Pelletier and Caventou called attention to the green colouring material of plant-life, and invented for it the new word "chlorophyll".[2]    The combination of the two Greek words for "green" and "leaf" tells us nothing new, but the connotation which biology gives to the new term justifies the statement that it now denotes "the most wonderful substance in our world".

These examples will serve to remind us of the continuous modification of language to meet the new needs of thought and life in our social relations.    But there is also a continuous modification of vocabulary in our individual development.    The word "history", for example, means one thing to the school-boy, for whom it is a school lesson from a text-book, another to the ordinary citizen, for whom it is a more or less uncertain congeries of newspaper references and vague memories of what he learnt at school, and yet another for the professional student of it, who thinks in terms of the documents belonging to the period in question.

Thus, both in the history of the language and in the life of the individual, word-signs are never capable of permanent definition, and we cannot treat them as if they were the fixed symbols of an algebraic equation.    It is convenient and indeed necessary for ordinary intercourse that we should treat them as though they were recognized quantities, as though, in fact, the name were the thing. But as soon as we pass to their more exact use, as in science or philosophy, more precise definition becomes

---

[1] *Process and Reality*, p. 26.          [2] Sir A. E. Shipley, *Life*, p. 28.

necessary. It is this more precise usage that makes scientific or philosophical books difficult for the ordinary reader, who is content with rough approximations. It is also useful to remember that the language of ordinary speech is only one means of expression, even though it is the most important. To Helen Keller, for example, blind, deaf and dumb, a series of touches by her teacher's fingers acquired the meaning of that flow of water which she felt with her other hand; thus she entered a world of meaning expressed in the language of touch.[1] It has been pointed out by Mr. J. W. N. Sullivan, in his well-known study of Beethoven, that the great composer "was exceptionally insensitive to language as an instrument for the expression of his thoughts and feelings,"[2] and the clumsiness of his letter-writing amply supports this statement. On the other hand, Beethoven is the admitted master of the expression of great experiences through the medium of musical sound. We speak, for example, of the Third Symphony as interpreting the conflict between "heroism" and "fate". We could not translate that interpretation into ordinary language; it is *sui generis* because of its means of expression, the only one in which the genius of Beethoven was able to utter itself. For him, as for all who respond to his music, this becomes a true language, however different from that of ordinary speech. If it lacks the articulation of words, and the intellectual grasp of ideas, it opens up vast emotional experiences, beyond the power of words to arouse, and goes far to justify the proud boast which Browning puts into the mouth of Abt Vogler:—

"The rest may reason and welcome: 'tis we musicians know."

Each art, in fact, necessarily accepts the limitations

[1] *The Story of My Life* by Helen Keller, p. 23.
[2] P. 122 of 1937 ed.

and advantages of its own medium of expression. All the arts depend on what they suggest, as well as on what they represent. "The Sublime in Art is the power to suggest, to evoke round the thing represented, luminous circles, that grow vaster and vaster still . . . to lay bare the canopy of Heaven above the head of the gazer or the abysses of Hell beneath his feet."[1] But each art has, through its particular medium, initial advantages or disadvantages. Painting concentrates and objectifies the artist's conception within a single field of vision, with all the aid to the imagination which outline and colour provide, so that the painted portrait may reveal the actual man, as the most faithful biography would fail to do. But poetry opens up wider possibilities, even of visual imagery. Sir Claude Phillips, whose words have just been quoted, writes on "What the Brush cannot paint,"[2] and selects, as his example of this, that which he calls "the most exquisite passage in all literature", viz. the lines beginning, "How sweet the moonlight sleeps upon this bank!"[3]

Perhaps of all the arts, that of poetry comes nearest, in combined effect, to the adequate expression of unseen spiritual reality. It may lack the more direct and uni-

[1] Sir Claude Phillips, *Emotion in Art*, p. 177.    [2] *Op. cit.*, pp. 35-50.

[3] Shakespeare, *Merchant of Venice*, V. 1:—

> "How sweet the moonlight sleeps upon this bank!
> Here will we sit, and let the sounds of music
> Creep in our ears; soft stillness and the night,
> Become the touches of sweet harmony.
> Sit, Jessica. Look how the floor of heaven
> Is thick inlaid with patines of bright gold:
> There's not the smallest orb which thou behold'st,
> But in his motion like an angel sings,
> Still quiring to the young-eyed cherubins:
> Such harmony is in immortal souls;
> But, whilst this muddy vesture of decay
> Doth grossly close it in, we cannot hear it."

versal appeal of painting—will a library of poetry ever successfully compete with a picture gallery for popular interest? The Sistine Madonna can bring into visual unity the dignity of motherhood, the mystery of the Incarnation, and the emergence of the eternal into the temporal, as no poem could. The architectonic unity of a great cathedral can indeed be matched by Dante's *Divina Commedia*, and both require an elaborate technique for their full appreciation, but the great mediaeval poem also requires a sustained effort and a mass of learning which removes it from the majority of men. The accompanying music of rhythm in poetry may be as subtle as the themes and harmonies of the Eroica Symphony, yet is much less obvious than these. As compared with painting, architecture and music, poetry makes much more *primary* demand on the reader or hearer, and the printed page is far more removed from life than the outline and colour of the canvas, the carved stone and painted glass of the building, the directly sensuous excitation of the symphony. The very use of a medium that is the product of analysis,[1] as words are, creates a barrier that has to be climbed by an ardent imagination before emotion can be stirred. Yet, when all this is admitted, the far clearer articulation of poetic language, the unlimited range of its imaginative suggestion, and the greater scope of its descriptive power, make poetry supreme in the representation of spiritual reality. Take as an example, Shelley's "Ode to the West Wind". We have the successive pictures of the autumn wind sweeping the forest leaves before it, the storm wind carrying the rain and thunder-clouds, the sea wind lightly touching the Mediterranean or ploughing the Atlantic into great chasms. Then comes the appeal of man's helpless life—a leaf, a cloud, a wave—to that

---

[1] I do not, of course, forget the analytic work that precedes artistic creation; here we are thinking of the elemental form and primary appeal.

daemonic and dynamic energy of the universe which is symbolized by the West Wind, the prayer for inspiration that shall kindle the hope of a spring to follow the winter.

Suppose, then, that we wish to go beyond Shelley's poem, and to formulate a philosophy of the universe that shall justify its prayer. We shall be asking for the grounds of the faith that there is such a Spirit in the universe as that to which Shelley appealed, the faith of those ancient Semites who used the same word—*ruach*—to denote the wind of the desert and the supernatural energy which, they believed, sometimes possessed them. Their use of a single term for what we divide as "natural" and "supernatural" was intuitive, not rationalized. The same instinct which made Shelley apostrophize the West Wind as the energy of the Universe led those Semites to think of the wind of the desert as the simplest and most elemental force they knew, at once, in our parlance, both "natural" and "supernatural". They were not consciously symbolizing Spirit by wind; it is we who make the "natural" to be the symbol of the "supernatural". For us, who have passed beyond the naïve intuition, the question arises whether the word "Spirit", which in its own order symbolizes supernatural power, does stand for a reality which rational thought can justify. This illustrates and introduces the bearing of the symbolism of language upon theology, and in particular the adequacy of that linguistic symbolism in any statement or discussion of ultimate spiritual reality.

§ 3. *Adequacy of the Theological Vocabulary.* There can be few who have thought at all deeply about religion who have not sometimes pulled themselves up with "the previous question", i.e. have asked themselves whether the questions they are discussing should be put at all, in view of what seems the utter inadequacy of human thought and human language to handle such high themes. Nature herself passes out beyond our grasp; we can but describe, and sometimes explain, some of her phenomena. History, a mere fragment amid the immensities of time, is woven out of myriads of threads which we can never hope to trace. But how much less can man hope to pass beyond the very limits of space and time, nature and history, and venture to talk of God and eternity—especially in language necessarily drawn from the spatial and the temporal existence!

Once given, such a challenge must be met, and it can be met only by asserting the adequacy of the symbolism. We have emphasized the necessary symbolism of language in dealing with our experience in space and time, where it certainly meets our needs with reasonable adequacy. But our use of that language in regard to the eternal realm appears to be symbolic at two removes. In the first degree the word is a mere symbol of some experience. In the second, that experience is the symbol of something beyond itself. In many applications this is, of course, obvious. The vocal sound "rose" symbolizes a particular flower, which would *smell* as sweet had it been symbolized by the vocal sound "ipecacuanha". But, again, when Dante wishes to portray his vision of the saints in heaven, he writes:—

> "In fashion of a white rose glorified
> Shone out on me that saintly chivalry,
> Whom with His blood Christ won to be His bride."[1]

Here the word "rose" is universally recognized as a symbol extended beyond experience. The assembly of the saints beneath the throne of God is not identified, but compared, with the white petals of the familiar flower. But when we call God "Father", again using a symbolic vocal sound, which has a definite reference within our

---

[1] *Paradiso*, XXXI; in Plumptre's trans.

E

experience, do we mean that the nature of the unknown Being can be *compared* with that of a human father like Dante's rose, or that it is in some degree *identical* with it?

Some measure of identity of nature is certainly implied in the argument of our Lord: "If ye, then, being evil, know how to give good gifts unto your children, how much more shall your Father which is in heaven give good things to them that ask Him?"[1]  There is no force in the reasoning unless the symbolic sound "Father" possesses partial identity of meaning in both references.  Similarly, when the apostle Paul[2] argues not from below upwards, but from above downwards, and speaks of "the Father, from whom every fatherhood in heaven and on earth is named", he is not less implying a real identity of meaning, however imperfect the derived forms of fatherhood may be.

Our inevitable use of human language in regard to that which lies beyond experience raises and brings to a focus the great philosophical problems connected with our knowledge of reality.  The adequacy of all theological statement stands or falls with our attitude to this symbolism.  We may think, for example, of the views of the "Paris School", known as Symbolo-Fideism, and expressed by Auguste Sabatier and Eugène Ménégoz, not because of its intrinsic importance, but because it illustrates a widespread tendency in the modern attitude to religion, with both agnostic and pragmatic affinities.  Sabatier emphasizes the symbolic character of those confessions of faith which the Church calls "Symbols" in a different sense.[3]  All such theological propositions are, he argues, psychologically and historically conditioned, and have no absolute truth.  They need continual re-adjustment to contemporary culture, just as a man walking loses and

[1] Matt. vii. 11; cf. Luke xi. 13.      [2] Eph. iii. 14, 15 (R.V. mar.).
[3] *Esquisse d'une Philosophie de la Religion*, p. 407.

regains his balance at every step. Each believer will find that expression which his religious faith needs.[1] It follows that, as Ménégoz puts it, "the essential factor in salvation is the inward movement towards God, not intellectual adherence to some doctrinal tenet".[2]

The best recent reply to this general tendency (though without any specific reference to "Symbolo-Fideism") is that of Dr. Edwyn Bevan, in his important Gifford Lectures, *Symbolism and Belief*. His thesis is, while admitting the necessary symbolism of our theological language, to defend the adequacy of its reference to that which lies beyond experience. He considers in detail the symbol of "height", as when heaven is made the place of God, of time, as when we speak of the divine "purpose", of light—the "glory" of God, of spirit—the "wind" or "breath" of God, of divine "wrath", which so many would dismiss as mere anthropomorphism. He argues that the consciousness that such metaphors are symbolic may well go with the legitimate faith that nevertheless they express realities in the only way open to us. This, too, is the conclusion of Professor Urban, in a recent book on our subject, viz. *Language and Reality*. As he says (p. 706-7), "The concepts of space, time and number furnish the actual structural elements of objective experience as they build themselves up in language, but they fulfil their task only because, according to their total structure, they keep in an ideal medium, precisely because, while they constantly keep to the form of the sensuous experience, they progressively fill the sensuous with spiritual content." Any adequate discussion of the issues here involved would take us far beyond the necessary limits of this chapter. The whole question of Analogy, for example, as discussed

---

[1] *Op. cit.*, p. 410.
[2] In his article, "Symbolo-Fideism", in the *Encyclopaedia of Religion and Ethics*, XII, p. 151.

by mediæval[1] and later thinkers, would call for review, to say nothing of the problem of the relation of time and eternity which is fundamental to all philosophy. But if we are to claim adequacy for our symbolic language, certain principles are involved which must be at least indicated.

In the first place, as we have seen, some *correspondence* between the human and the supra-human realms must obtain, if our symbols are to have any real meaning outside our experience. The precise measure of correspondence claimed will vary from symbol to symbol, and indeed from the thought of one individual to that of another. There are still not a few believers who would take quite literally the descriptions of heaven in the Apocalypse. I have heard a simple-minded Christian, fond of simple music, state quite seriously that it seemed to him a wonderful dispensation of Providence that we should spend so much of our time in heaven in singing hymns, since music was one of the earthly experiences of which we never tire. I have read a typically American description of heaven, again offered as literal truth revealed in a vision, which ascribed to it a central lecture-hall, in which one of the "star" items was "Martin Luther on the Reformation". On the other hand, some of us who have looked up with awe to the starry sky have felt that no place within it all was worthy of Him who is Spirit. Yet we do not cease to believe that the spiritual realities to which we owe allegiance have their eternal home in Him, as we do not cease to use spatial metaphors to express spiritual reality, nor cease to ascribe to our metaphors a quasi-sacramental significance.

In the second place, it may be argued that such correspondence is unintelligible and indefensible unless there is some measure of spiritual *kinship* between God and man.

[1] Cf. S. Thomas, *Summa Theologica*, I, Q. xiii. 6.

The conception of man as made in the image of God is as vital to Christian theology as it is to the religion of the Old Testament. Originally, the phrase referred to outward form, but outward form, physical resemblance, was inseparable for the Hebrews from psychical likeness, since the physical organs had psychical attributes. In the course of history the conception has been sublimated, and the physical has been eliminated, with so much else that has served a temporary purpose. But unless there is such potentiality of real spiritual kinship as enables man to know God, and God to reveal Himself to man, so that enlightened human experience can faithfully reflect in its own limited way the activity of God, the symbolism of our language can have no meaning as applied to God.

In the third place, we are led to the view that the *actuality* of human history can enter into the eternal order because of this spiritual kinship. This means that though space belongs to those things which pass and perish in the using, time does not, and that time is itself part of the pattern of eternity. Only by this inclusion of time within eternity can we do justice to moral and religious experience, our consciousness of responsibility and our gradual achievement of creative fellowship with God. Here we should note the difference between the "truth" of poetry and the "truth" of history. In regard to poetry, it is no doubt true to say that "all experience, if it is to be available for poetry, must have reached a degree of intensity in which the question whether it is actual or not becomes irrelevant".[1] But the actuality of history is at once the fountain head from which Christian experience rises, and the sea into which it flows. The Christian religion is poetry, for it idealizes the prose of time and space, but it is more than poetry, since it is inseparably linked to the actuality of history. The problems here

[1] James Sutherland, *The Medium of Poetry*, p. 13.

are vast, but the issues are simple enough.  Let us put them in a practical way, suggested by the lines of our argument.

Religion is always some form of loyalty to the values created in the course of history and is always dependent on something beyond history.  It is shared by all sorts and conditions of men.  But the use of language brings its own difficulties.  The layman is often puzzled how to express his genuine experience without the technical discipline of the theologian, and the professional theologian is often painfully conscious that his theory far outruns his practice.  His technical facility enables him all too easily to juggle with words, and to deceive himself into thinking that he has the reality because he has the symbol for it.  He is tempted to think of the great themes he handles as the subjects of which he is master, instead of the masters to which he is subject.  He might then fruitfully recall the whimsical words of Apollonius of Tyana, as Philostratus depicts him.[1]  When he wished to cross the Euphrates, he was asked by the customs-officer what he had to declare, and replied, "I have with me Sophrosyne, Dikaiosyne, Arete, Encrateia, Askesis," to which the officer replied, "These maidservants must be registered." "That is impossible," said Apollonius, "these are no maidservants that I have with me, but my liege-ladies."

The measure of meaning in our symbolic language is given by the content which its terms have for us.  In the realm of moral and religious life that means ultimately the measure of our loyalty to the realities themselves. Few things are more strongly emphasized in Biblical religion, both explicitly and implicitly, than this—that knowledge depends on obedience.  To confess with the Collect that "all our doings without charity are nothing

[1] *Philostratus in Honour of Apollonius of Tyana*, Book I, Ch. 20; English trans. by J. S. Phillimore, I, p. 25.

worth" is only half the truth. The other half is that all our *words* about, but without, charity are worth no more, if only because they have no real content of meaning for those who utter them. In one of his sermons the late Professor H. R. Mackintosh reminded his hearers that the difficulty of the doctrine of the Atonement was largely made for us by the fact that we do not sufficiently know in real experience what sacrificial love means.[1]

But we must not forget the complementary truth of Christian faith—the doctrine of the Spirit of God, as creating the fruit of the Spirit within the believer. The Spirit can create His own language, even out of an unknown tongue, as when an Indian was so moved by the sincerity of John Woolman that he cried, "I love to feel where words come from." St. Paul passes from the thought of the criminal ignorance which crucified the Lord of glory to that of the saving knowledge given by the Spirit of God: "Unto us God revealed [things unseen and unheard] through the Spirit: for the Spirit searcheth all things, yea, the deep things of God."[2] The Pauline teaching of the *arrabōn*,[3] the "earnest" of the Spirit, the payment on account, out of that which will be fully paid at a later time, reminds us that what the Christian already has is a genuine part of knowledge concerning that which shall be. "Beloved, now are we children of God, and it is not yet made manifest what we shall be."[4] As Dr. Bevan says, "It is the combination of the 'now' and the 'not yet' which characterizes the Christian *Weltanschauung*."[5] The doctrine of the Holy Spirit is *the* doctrine of Christian experience, for it vitalizes all we venture to say about the unseen, by making our language sacramental, and so transforms "symbolic" into "real" knowledge. By the

---

[1] *Sermons*, pp. 176, 177.
[2] 1 Cor. ii. 10.
[3] 2 Cor. i. 22, v. 5; Eph. i. 14.
[4] 1 John iii. 2.
[5] *Symbolism and Belief*, p. 117.

truth of that doctrine, in the last resort, stands the validity of all we say about God and the Risen Lord and eternity. The symbols of time are taken up into the language of eternity, the language of divine activity, that language of God which is a revelation because it is first a redemption.

Possibly, some readers of this chapter may be inclined to make on it the comment of a distinguished psychologist, who had heard it read. The comment was, "Yes—but what then?" The comment is inevitable, and it ought always to arise in our minds when we are dealing with the more psychological side of theological and philosophical issues. It will be the aim of the next two chapters of this book to answer the question, so far as it concerns the relation of God and man within the sphere of redemption or revelation. It will be claimed that the inevitable symbolism of human language can sufficiently portray a genuinely creative activity of good or evil on man's part, and of redemptive grace on God's.

# CHAPTER IV

## THE ACTUALITY OF GOOD AND EVIL

§ 1. *THE Actuality of the Event.* In all our literature, there is no more familiar example of the difference between thinking and doing than Shakespeare's Hamlet. His first reaction to the ghost of his father, informing him that murder has been done, is to pledge himself whole-heartedly to the filial duty of vengeance. Yet only in the closing scene of the play, and then only upon the impulse of the moment, does he accomplish the deed. In the interval, he debates method, is swayed by circumstance, seeks confirmation, philosophizes upon the meaning or meaninglessness of human life, but does not act. Whatever be the cause of this inaction, whether or not, for example, it is to be traced with Bradley to his "melancholy" and disillusionment with life, first prompted by his mother's hasty re-marriage, there can be little doubt that the centre of the stage is occupied by the contrast between thinking and doing, in a world that demands action, rather than excessive thought about it:—

> "I do not know
> Why yet I live to say, *This thing's to do;*
> Sith I have cause, and will, and strength and means,
> To do't."[1]

Hamlet supplies the answer to his implicit question when he says:—

[1] Act IV, Scene iv.

"the native hue of resolution
Is sicklied o'er with the pale cast of thought,
And enterprises of great pith and moment,
With this regard, their currents turn awry,
And lose the name of action."[1]

The character of Hamlet, then, illustrates the distinction between any amount of thought about a deed, and that actual performance of it which requires definite volition. But we must also distinguish the volition, as the moral essence of the act, from its observed consequences. When we speak of the actuality of good and evil, we do not confine ourselves to the visible and external *consequences* of the volition. They belong to the act; indeed, in ordinary speech the doing of the thing willed *is* the act. In legal judgment attention is necessarily fixed on the visible and tangible result of the hidden volition. Yet, even so, that volition has to be taken into account. Killing is not necessarily murder; it may be "justifiable homicide". But, when we turn from purely legal to moral judgment, it is the volition that primarily concerns us. So far as the consequences of the volition entered, or might have entered, into the consciousness of the agent, they may affect our moral judgment of the volition. A trap-door left open, with consequent injury to someone, may be due either to mere carelessness, bitterly regretted, or to the deliberate desire to maim or kill. The consequences of an act may be judged quite apart from the volition of the agent. The removal of a tyrant may be a blessing to a people, even though the most enlightened of them may condemn the assassination which was its cause. An act once performed will have its own further consequences, quite beyond the volition of the agent, spreading out like the ripples on a pond when a stone has been flung at a water-rat.

[1] Act III, Scene i.

Clearly, then, we cannot escape from having to use the term "actuality" in a double reference. It may refer to the external event, which a spectator might have seen, the event which straightway passes out of the control of the chief actor in it, or it may refer to the inner volition, of which the accomplishment might have been hindered by circumstances, though the volition would yet be an event in the moral life of the man who willed it ineffectively. In the latter case, we cannot doubt that the divine judgment on its moral quality is unaffected by the presence or absence of external expression. In fact, an enlightened conscience will judge the unaccomplished evil volition as severely as if it had been accomplished, whilst thankful for the merciful restraint that hindered the act itself. Similarly, though "he meant well" is usually associated with some sort of weakness or failure, it at least conveys the absence of moral reproach. The good will, if it is really, not merely conventionally good, and really will, not half-hearted wish, is itself *essentially* the good act, whether or not the circumstances allowed it to become visible to any but God. The victory of Gethsemane does not draw its moral and religious quality from Calvary, though Calvary was needed to bring that victory into the other kind of actuality, as a focal point in human history.

This outer kind of actuality is less elusive than the inner. We have already[1] tried to characterize the actuality of history as being (a) irrevocable and irreversible, (b) serving to clarify thought or purpose, (c) providing a fuller expression of personality through an act of the will than the intellect alone could afford, and thus furnishing a new category for the manifestation of spiritual truth or reality. Words are often best defined by their sharpest contrasts. The immediate contrast with "actuality" is "potentiality". So long as an act has not been performed,

[1] Introduction, § 2.

an indefinable number of alternatives lie open, but with the performance of the act, all these are permanently excluded. Another feature of the "actual" is that it is always seen in retrospect, whereas the "potential" is always seen in prospect. This integral relation to the time-process must be constantly remembered, since it relates to that aspect of "actuality" which is our chief concern. The time-process can be said to exist for the sake of creating the actual, that which is brought into being once and for all and cannot, *qua* event, ever be altered.

From this standpoint, the historical event has acquired the character of "objectivity". This term is, itself, highly debatable in the realms of psychology and metaphysics, but it is here used simply to denote the quasi-independent existence of the actual, the fact, for example, that it henceforward limits the activity of any agent concerned with it, or with its consequences. It has entered into the moral and spiritual texture of the universe, and is woven into what becomes a new pattern in virtue of its presence. Because of its place in that pattern, it may acquire new meanings. The traditional act of "Jenny Geddes", in flinging her stool at the head of the dean reading from the Laudian Service-book in St. Giles', has been interwoven into the history of Scottish Presbyterianism. Not the least element in an acquired meaning is the fitness of the act, even if legendary, to become symbolic, and thus to express far more deep-rooted convictions or policies.[1]

§ 2. *The Good and Evil Volitions.*    The realm of human history usually means the whole of the events of which a record has been preserved, though, for our purpose, it may be extended to include all that might conceivably have been recorded, with such inferences to human

---

[1] Cf. Chapter III, "The Symbolism of Language".

volitions as the events justify. But, as we have seen from the example of Hamlet, there is another and inner world into which each of us can enter for himself, the world of

"Thoughts hardly to be packed
Into a narrow act,
Fancies that broke through language and escaped."[1]

This world extends from the first involuntary thought of a good or evil act up to the firm resolution to perform it, through all the bewildering and kaleidoscopic changes of consciousness and conscience. To this inner world also actuality belongs, in that extended sense of the term to which attention has been called. For it is a microcosm of spiritual activity, which is not less "actual" as a series of spiritual events than if each of them had found some external and visible expression. It is a world hidden from the direct observation of anyone else, often obscure and uncertain to the man himself. Yet, in a universe ultimately spiritual in texture, these unrecorded and elusive spiritual events are not less significant and important than those of the outer world. Indeed, we may and must go further than this, and say that to such a series of spiritual events the whole of a man's life is ultimately reducible. In any serious and intelligent retrospect of life, the outer events are all taken up into their spiritual meaning. We see them as bits of the pattern which we have made of life, and life has made for each of us. If that is so, imperfectly and incompletely, for man's view of himself, how much more must it be true of the significance of his life for God! We cannot think that the details of the time-process will remain *themselves* as part of any eternal order; otherwise eternity would seem to be no more than extension of time. We may think of the parallel afforded by the doctrine of "the

[1] R. Browning, *Rabbi ben Ezra*, XXV.

resurrection of the body". The thoughtful Christian will
hardly postulate the re-assembly of the scattered atoms
of which his physical body was composed, but is likely to
think rather of the preservation of the contribution made
by this body to spiritual personality through its intimate
partnership within the present order, and of a resurrection along the lines of St. Paul's thought of a body
sown in corruption and raised in incorruption, a resurrection to which flesh and blood, as such, cannot attain.
So we may think of the gathering up of the events of the
temporal order which concern us. They will continue to
concern us, but in their spiritual counterparts. They have
their place, as we have seen, in the actuality of history,
with all its problems and issues. But, in any evaluation
of the single human personality, it will be this central
spiritual actuality which counts, and stands over against
the judgment of God.

This deeper and more inclusive realm of spiritual
actuality, then, whatever the outer consequences, is the
peculiar sphere of moral responsibility. Only as outer
events issue from it, or are gathered up into it, will they
concern us in this aspect of our subject. It is not easy
for any of us to take this realm as seriously as we ought.
Almost inevitably, we tend to fall back into the thought
of the outer event as alone possessing actuality, and we
call John Bunyan morbid when he reckoned his greatest
sin to have lain in a wholly spiritual act—that he yielded
in thought and will to the haunting temptation "to sell
and part with Christ".[1] He had long resisted it. "But,
at last, after much striving, I felt this thought pass
through my heart, Let him go if he will; and I thought
also that I felt my heart freely consent thereto." Like
Esau, he found no place of repentance, though he sought
it carefully with tears. He felt his sin to be as actual as

[1] *Grace Abounding*, § 139.

that of Judas. Whatever elements of morbidity we may discern in his condition, we must at least confess that without the experiences of *Grace Abounding* the *Pilgrim's Progress* could never have been written. Bunyan felt the actuality of the inner world as few others have done, and out of his conviction came his power to make it real to us.

Many will be inclined to regard Bunyan's experience as an extreme example of "illusion". They regard the sense of sin as itself an artificial product of theology, and particularly of evangelical theology. That which was once felt keenly and intensely in the heyday of such experience is now, it is alleged, conventionally retained, though in much less vigorous form, only by those brought up in a suitable environment. Such a judgment is seen to be altogether superficial, even when we look at the facts of life merely as spectators. The actual presence of moral evil in human life is an undeniable factor in human history, and the recognition of it has inspired much of the serious literature in which that life is faithfully portrayed. Homer, Virgil, Dante, Shakespeare and Goethe can all be summoned to the witness-box. If moral responsibility for the existence of that evil belongs to men, their sense of sin is inevitable. This is confirmed, whenever we pass from detached observation of life as mere spectators to the inner experience of it which each possesses. The vocabulary will vary. The interpretation of the fact may be very inadequate. The personal attitude towards the various ways of dealing with the fact offered by various religions or types of religion may be one of indifference. But no man who is honest with himself and not shallow enough to be self-complacent, can avoid feeling a profound discontent with his own character, a discontent which seems to increase as that character develops into fuller appreciation of the spiritual values of life. It is this consciousness of moral failure that haunts all of us, and in the religious experience becomes the foundation of the sense of sin, as something deeper than regret, remorse, or even repentance for particular sins.

It crops up in the most unlikely quarters. As I turn over the pages of a book by one who describes himself as an "anarchic" journalist, without any religious faith, I come across a paragraph describing his chance entrance into a church in Paris during the celebration of Mass. He happens to catch the words, "Agnus Dei, qui tollis peccata mundi" . . . "Lamb of God, who takest away the sins of the world . . ." "Oh, God! what a dream. . . . If only He could!"[1]

But does not this practically universal sense of moral failure, by its negative character, hinder us from speaking of the actuality of evil as in any way comparable with the actuality of good? Is not the absence of the good that might have been at any one stage of man's development merely due to his finite nature and the necessary conditions of growth? In that case, the evil is left behind as man advances to something better, whereas the good is carried upwards to new levels. We should then have to speak of the actuality of good, but not of the actuality of evil, in the sense in which we are using the term. In one form or other, this is a widespread impression of to-day.

There is one inclusive and sufficient answer to all such objections. It is that the view they represent does not do justice to the moral consciousness of man. We are all aware, for example, of the inevitable conflict between our animal nature and our self-respect, or sense of duty. We know how appetite or the love of physical comfort may urge us to do what conscience forbids or to avoid doing what conscience prescribes. But so far as we blame ourselves at all for the commission or omission, it is because

[1] Michael Harrison, *Dawn Express*, p. 101.

we know that we were not willing to pay the price of abstinence or effort. We know that we could have done the better thing if we had wanted it enough, and we blame ourselves for that lack of will and its outcome. We do not blame ourselves for that in which there was no scope for our volition, or if we blame ourselves for carelessness or lack of thought, it is another kind of blame, and directed to another issue. We do not blame ourselves for an involuntary shrinking from danger, but only for the deliberate avoidance of it, when it was our duty to face it. We distinguish the desire to be approved by our fellows, which is one of the most potent factors in social life, from the "playing to the gallery", which leads us into conscious hypocrisy. However entangled with nature and circumstance our volition may be, we do practically recognize that, so far as it was our volition, we are morally responsible for it, and we condemn ourselves for failure to do what we knew was the right thing. We may venture to believe that inner self-condemnation plays a much greater part than self-approbation in the lives of most men and women around us. If that is true, it is highly significant, and has further consequences, to which we shall return.

It may be said here that any doctrine of the "fall" of man which makes sin logically inevitable destroys the essential principle of moral responsibility. The doctrines of the Fall and of Original Sin do not take any great place in modern theology, at any rate the doctrines in their classical forms. They are bound up with certain pre-suppositions of the historicity of Adam, of corporate personality, and (in the Augustinian form) of ascetic dualism, which few would accept.[1] But, in principle, the ideas go back to that sense of sin which we are discussing,

---

[1] See *The Christian Doctrine of Man*, by the present writer, pp. 163 ff., 187 ff. For a very full study, see *The Ideas of the Fall and of Original Sin*, by N. P. Williams.

F

and emphasize an important truth, though it is not to be
equated with "heredity" (as is often loosely done), nor to
be pressed to the point that all men are *necessarily* sinners.
So far as sin is made necessary, it ceases to be sin. The
same objection holds here as to the evolutionary doctrine
that sin is inevitable as a part of man's growth from an
animal origin. The truth is that we can never explain the
exercise of human freedom without explaining it away.
Freedom is a "first cause".

The evolution of man's nature from lower levels undoubtedly provides the *occasion* of much of man's sin, and
the same thing may be said of man's social environment.
The tradition of a society counts, of course, for evil as for
good. The influences of education, or the lack of it, the
quality of the home life, the kind of companionship which
surrounds adolescence, the intercourse of business life and
recreation, the groups called into being through political,
scientific, artistic interests—all these tend to develop
particular virtues and vices. The passengers on a "race
special" have as distinctive a look as the delegates to a
religious conference. Social environment is not less,
probably much more, a factor in personal conduct than
heredity. But it is only a factor, however important, and
still leaves unexplained that haunting sense of personal
responsibility from which man can never escape whilst he
is man.

We have, then, to assert the full actuality of moral
evil, whether existent only in inner purpose or displayed
also in outer consequences. It stands over against the
actuality of the good in both spheres, and gives rise to our
experience of a real conflict of opposing forces. The
conflict itself seems necessary for the establishment of
the good, *as we know it*. The law of tension between good
and evil, as the condition of man's effective knowledge
and possession of the good, is a law of our present life,

which we must simply accept. But this does not mean
that evil is forever the necessary foil of the good, and that
the good would become meaningless without the antagonism of the evil.[1] The good has its positive value, with
the capacity of unlimited extension. A community of
those who had learnt to be completely unselfish would
still have plenty to live for, in mutual service and in the
fuller co-operation of achievement. In the true artist,
the mastery of his art does not spell satiety, but preludes
his finest work. Why should this not be true of the art
of living?

§ 3. *The Social Origin and Divine Source of Morality.*
Our views on the *origins* of morality must not prejudice
our judgment as to its ultimate *source*. As to the former,
there is no reason why we should not accept the conclusion
of such an anthropologist as Westermarck, "that society
is the birthplace of the moral consciousness; that the first
moral judgments expressed, not the private emotions of
isolated individuals, but emotions which were felt by the
society at large; that tribal custom was the earliest rule
of duty."[2] The evidence for that statement can be seen
in his well-known volumes, as well as in a host of others.
It is probably true to say that for the average man of
to-day the pressure of public opinion is still the most
potent moral influence to which he is exposed. But such
an admission does not warrant us in the least in regarding
the moral consciousness as purely a social creation. All
it implies is that this is the historical form in which
morality has been evolved; its ultimate *source* is still to
seek. Here we are justified in maintaining that the values
of goodness, like those of truth and of beauty, demand an
explanation for which we must pass beyond human nature.

[1] Cf. A. E. Taylor, *The Faith of a Moralist,* I, p. 411.
[2] *The Origin and Development of the Moral Ideas,* I, pp. 117–18.

The sense of obligation which underlies morality points beyond itself to spiritual reality, which man does not invent, but slowly discovers. So construed, the moral consciousness becomes one of the most convincing grounds for theistic belief. The moral argument for that belief cannot here be reviewed. It is set forth competently and convincingly by such philosophers as W. R. Sorley[1] and Professor A. E. Taylor.[2] Those who accept it would claim that moral goodness possesses "actuality" in yet a third, though complementary sense, beyond that of historical actuality and the actuality of the inner life of man. They would assert that moral values have their home in God—"the concrete unity of all good in its one source,"[3]—and that we become conscious of them in proportion to our conscious or unconscious relation to Him. The Creator of man has endowed him with the capacity to discover and enter into possession of something which already exists. The history of the human race shows the gradual, and by no means always progressive, movement into the appropriation of this divine actuality; the development of the individual life is the miniature reflection of the process writ large in history.

Here we must distinguish sharply between good and evil, and not simply on *a priori* grounds. God's responsibility for the actuality of evil is confined to His creation of man, and His endowment of man with such a nature as is capable of initiating evil. In that initiation, social influences are usually involved, and, for anything we know to the contrary, there may be other spiritual influences from beyond the human sphere, such influences as were recognized crudely enough in the ancient belief in demons and in Satan. We cannot rule out the possibility of such extra-human influence, and the occasional

[1] *Moral Values and the Idea of God.*    [2] *The Faith of a Moralist.*
[3] A. E. Taylor, *op. cit.*, I, 101.

intensity of moral evil in particular forms may seem to call for such an explanation. But whatever we think on this speculative question, we must not make it more than a possible factor in the real initiative of man; that, the testimony of the moral consciousness forbids. The bargain by which a man sells himself to the devil is his own, and not made for him.

Man's initiation of good is not less actual than his initiation of evil, but there is an important difference to be observed. Whatever the evil forces which exist within human society or beyond it, moral goodness is always implicitly an assertion that the universe is on its side. "Serious living is no more compatible with the belief that the universe is indifferent to morality than serious and arduous pursuit of truth with the belief that truth is a human convention or superstition."[1] For "the universe", the theist says simply "God". The good act is related to God from the outset in a way different from the evil act. The good act has God on its side, and virtually proclaims "if God is for us, who is against us?" The co-operation of God thus recognized is not confined to the outer events of divine providence. In Christian theism, it is manifested in the inner operations of grace, from the first inspiration of the good thought to the resolute actualization of it in the good act. This sense of creative fellowship with God gives to moral good a quality quite different from that belonging to the creation of evil. Indeed, the very use of the term "co-operation" is apt to be misleading. It is not intimate enough to describe that subtle interweaving of the human purpose and the divine, that involution of the human and divine wills which is a characteristic of the good life become conscious of God. One of its greatest exponents has to say, not only "Work out your own salvation with fear and trembling, for it is God that

[1] A. E. Taylor, *op. cit.*, I, 61.

worketh in you", but even, "I live, yet not I; for Christ liveth in me". The greater the advance in the Christian life, the more conscious is the believer that it is God that worketh in him. The life of good is seen and felt to be more and more a surrender to superior forces—the doctrine of the Holy Spirit—whilst the life of evil is much more conscious of its own initiative and creative activity, except for the rare and abnormal cases of alleged spirit-possession, which need not here concern us. The evil man is ready to boast his achievements when his character is sufficiently depraved; the good man is more and more ready to give glory to God for whatever of good he has been enabled to accomplish, of which God is the ultimate initiator and supporter.

§ 4. *The Worth of History to God.* If we try to consider history *sub specie aeternitatis*, we can hardly doubt that it has a value for God in its entirety as well as in its individual agents. Behind it lies a vast and unimaginable pre-history, which seems out of all proportion to the product of the brief time-span of humanity. The slow and apparently devious movements of history do not obviously commend it as a moral lesson-book. The large masses of mankind still lying outside the influence of the world's highest moral and religious values assuredly suggest that God's ways are not as our ways, and His thoughts are not as our thoughts. In such aspects history offers a parallel to Nature. The universe seems too big to be wholly explained as the arena of human life, nor can we think of the stars as existing only for our aesthetic delight or for the exercise of our intellectual curiosity. Both Nature and history, it would seem, must have values for God which cannot be measured by our human standards, however true these may be in their proper application. Hebrew faith pictured God as delighting in the universe of His creation, quite apart from man,[1] though man occupied a unique place in His purpose. The scheme of human history, as presented in the Bible, suggests that, as a whole, it has a meaning and value for God, not to be resolved simply into the fortunes and destinies of individuals. God's honour is involved in the history of Israel as a people, and the history of mankind is represented as His concern from the very beginning. When we pass from the Old Testament to the New, we find the beginnings of a philosophy of history in the mind of St. Paul, for whom the great redemptive act of God has come "in the fulness of time", and human history is woven into a cosmic pattern. This includes the whole creation, groaning and travailing in pain until now, and destined to be delivered from its bondage of corruption. God is like a good farmer, interested in his fields as well as in his crops.

The upshot of such lines of thought is that we must think of the whole actuality of human history, apart from what has yet to be said about the individual agents in it, as deeply concerning God.[2] It is there before Him, on permanent and unchangeable record. It is part of His purpose, a great category of expression for that purpose, far richer than human intellect could ever supply, because of its inclusion of moral activity. So far as the actualities of history are evil, they defeat the purpose of God. So far as they are good, they carry out that purpose through the subtle yet simple "device" of human freedom within the appointed limits. God cannot ignore that record. "God's wrong is most of all."[3] If its past evil meant

---

[1] Prov. viii. 22 ff.; Gen. i.; Ps. civ.; Job xxxviii. ff., especially xxxviii. 4, 7:—

"Where wast thou when I laid the foundations of the earth? . . .
When the morning stars sang together,
And all the sons of God shouted for joy?"

[2] This is brought out supremely in Milton's *Paradise Lost.*

[3] Shakespeare's *Richard III*, Act IV, Sc. 4.

nothing to Him, neither would its past good. He must do something with the evil, and His honour is at stake. History, as well as individual men, calls for redemption. If time is, in some real sense, gathered up into eternity, then the actuality of time, transformed from mere succession into its eternal equivalent, will remain as part of reality, and will call for the transfiguring touch of God, unless His universe is to remain forever scarred and marred by the record of a divine failure.

# CHAPTER V

## THE DIVINE INITIATIVE

THE world is in sore need of God. He is needed as the ground of its interpretation, but that concerns the few. He is also needed as Redeemer from the power and guilt of sin, and that concerns us all:—

> "But where shall wisdom be found?
> And where is the place of understanding?
> Man knoweth not the price thereof;
> Neither is it found in the land of the living.
> The deep saith, It is not in me;
> And the sea saith, It is not with me."[1]

All that the spiritual life of man creates is imperfect, and continually points beyond itself to something more. In the realms of truth and of beauty, as well as in that of the good, man is conscious of responding to something beyond himself, something beyond all he can create, something which is authoritative over him because of its intrinsic quality, something which continually invites him to new adventures and discoveries in an as yet untravelled country. Because these values of which he is but partially aware are spiritual, the only ultimate home for them which he can conceive will also be spiritual. Since human personality is the only spiritual basis of such values within his direct knowledge, he is compelled to postulate personality, though of far higher scope and quality than his own, as the goal of his thought and faith.

[1] Job xxviii. 12–14.

73

§ 1. *The Purpose of God.* Neither philosophic thought
nor religious faith can find satisfaction in conceiving the
divine Person as the passive spectator of the universe.
On either count, He must be actively concerned in it. If
He is not the root and ground of its existence, as the
Christian doctrine of creation, for example, sets forth, we
leave the existence of the world with all its material and
spiritual values unexplained. But if He is ultimately
responsible for its existence, we cannot credit Him with
indifference to its present condition, without depriving
Him of that worth which is the condition of worship
(worthship), and the essence of religion. The only God
who can win our adoration and retain our faith is the
God who continues His initiative in creation by His
activity in redemption. In genuine religion, the emphasis
always falls on God, not on man. To neglect this is to
offer a substitute for religion, or to show grave misunder-
standing of its nature. Thus, in the interesting and instructive book called *The Discovery of Man*, by Mr. Stanley
Casson, which traces the progress and inter-relation of
anthropology and archaeology, there are frequent references to the "pride" of religion, which has led it to oppose
new knowledge, and it is said of man that "Religion is his
way of expressing his belief in his approach to the
Divine" (p. 322). But this is the exact opposite to a true
definition. It is God's approach to man, not man's
approach to God, on which the emphasis falls, and just
because of that emphasis, and all it implies, the fundamental religious quality in man is humility. So far as
there is pride, religion is absent. There is as much
humility in true religion as there is in true science. Both
are conscious, in different ways, of something more and
greater, something that exists apart from us, and is active
independently of us, whether that something more be
called Nature or God. The initiative is with God. We

live, because He first lived; we love, because He first loved.

Since God is personal, intelligent purpose must underlie this initiating activity, directing its operation from the beginning to the end. The will of God is the ultimate explanation of the world, and the purpose of God in creating, maintaining and redeeming it can be known to man only in the actualities of experience. We have no data for an *a priori* argument about God's ways. If we believe that the Christian experience affords the truest and fullest knowledge of God open to man, then we shall try to trace God's purpose both backwards and forwards, backwards into Nature, with its long line of man's ascent from lower planes of existence, forwards into man's future destiny, social and individual.

How far natural evolution itself reveals direction and purpose is still a matter of debate. Evolution is sometimes explained, for example, as due simply to "Natural Selection acting on random variation".[1] Bergson's *élan vital* (which alone could not carry us far) is dismissed as mere metaphor.[2] There is constant increase in fitness, but it is reached by the rough method of trial and error, regardless of costs.[3] The conclusion is that "we must give up any idea that evolution is purposeful. . . . It is the result of purposeless and random variation sifted by purposeless and automatic selection".[4] But, we may surely ask, even on the assumption of purposeless factors in the process, are we not still at liberty to recognize purpose in their combination, which admittedly produces "fitness" and human purpose itself? If the hope of the future depends on man's wise use of purpose, thus evolved,[5] are we not justified in claiming a purposive control of the earlier

[1] *The Science of Life*, by H. G. Wells, Julian Huxley, G. P. Wells, pp. 481, 489.
[2] *Op. cit.*, p. 488.   [3] *Op. cit.*, p. 490.
[4] *Op. cit.*, p. 491.   [5] *Op. cit.*, p. 493.

stages of the process? The truth is that as soon as a biologist admits the presence of any values at all—and how can he do otherwise?—he has debarred himself from ruling out of court the legitimacy of the teleological argument.

In regard to the future, those who believe that the Christian life at its best is the finest thing the world possesses will believe that it is God's will to carry this forward to full fruition, and to make it as universal as man's exercise of freedom allows. Whether there is any recalcitrance of Nature to the will of God, we do not know; we have no inside view of the sub-human. But we do know that in man there is a finite will which is permitted to conflict with the will of God, and that much of the evil of the world springs from this cause. The conflict throws into great prominence and clarity the divine purpose. This purpose, as interpreted through Jesus, is to guide and help man towards his true peace in doing the will of God, the true peace of fellowship with Him which is impossible without the harmony of the human and the divine wills. It must be a genuine *harmony*, and not a mere melody. The note of man's own creative power, a divine gift, must be brought into the full chord of the divine, to make the music which God desires. In attributing such desire to God, we recognize His self-limitation, but not any original limitation of His nature and being. He has willed to give man freedom, and to seek from man the freely given loyalty of an obedient will. In pursuit of that purpose, God will do everything that can be done, within the self-limitation of His purpose. Because of man's moral failure, there will lie on God the burden of redeeming both the individual man, so far as he is willing to be redeemed, and the long process of human history, which man's disobedience has marred. That redemptive work will provide a fuller revelation of the divine than creation and providence could afford. "In all the higher religions the promise of redemption from the world is more fundamental than the faith that the world is providentially ordered."[1]

§ 2. *The Contingency of History.* The divine initiative is fundamentally the activity of "grace", which we define for our present purpose as "the outgoing movement of God towards man".[2] This activity must sooner or later display itself in human history, whether we think of a divine initiative acting from without man's life inwards to his consciousness, or as acting from within his consciousness outwards—though we must never limit God's grace to the human consciousness of it. In either way, there must be some point of contact between the human and the divine, some "live point" at which there is the experience of an inflow of spiritual knowledge or energy. This contact may be made in innumerable ways, but, broadly speaking, it will be made from without through the mediation of the natural world or of other men (social tradition or individual testimony), or again from within, through the mediation of the thoughts and emotions which are stirred in the individual mind and heart by the activity of God.[3] In either way, whether primarily from without or from within, this divine activity will affect the course of human history, and constitute in its own ever-varying degree a revelation of God.

The events which condition these contacts, whether physical or psychical, will thus by their association with divine activity acquire a sacred character in the particular religious experience to which they belong. They are the threshold, door-posts and lintel of the divine entrance

[1] W. R. Matthews, *The Purpose of God*, p. 143.
[2] So A. E. Taylor, *op. cit.*, II, p. 3.
[3] On this, see *The Christian Experience of the Holy Spirit*, Ch. IX ("The Holy Spirit and the Individual Life"), by H. Wheeler Robinson.

into our life. But they cannot be separated from it, as easily as the metaphor might suggest. The form and content of revelation are blended organically, as body and soul. The relation of God to the world of things and men which He has created and sustains is far too intimate for us to separate the activity of Nature and man from that of God. It is the activity of God which constitutes the revelation, not the particular form which that activity assumes in our eyes, which depends on an analysis often wrong and always imperfect. The divine activity must clothe itself in actuality, in order to be either intelligible or operative. The actuality of the event, physical or psychical, thus brings in the feature of "contingency"— the contact with a whole network of other events. Here arises one of the major problems of revelation from the general or philosophical standpoint—the problem of contingency. The divine contact can never be wholly isolated and considered apart from the mass of physical and psychical contacts inter-related with, or mediating it.

(*a*) One difficulty arising from this intimate relation is that God acts, as it were, in disguise, and is not necessarily or automatically recognizable.[1] Because He can operate from within Nature and from within the mind and heart of man, He may be reduced to them in our interpretation of the revealing event. For many observers, God may become an unnecessary hypothesis, since the event seems explicable from physical or psychical causation. There may be an over-plus of alleged happening which defies such explanation, but this can be regarded as mythical or legendary accretion, or as due to the credulity of prejudiced observers.

This kind of difficulty exists only for those whose

[1] This concealment of God in His active administration should not be confused with the very different point that we can never wholly comprehend Him.

conception of God is more deistic than they realize. It is made by excluding God from the proper realms of His activity. If Nature is itself the constant outflow of divine activity, as any intelligible doctrine of creation requires, there should be no difficulty in His particular control of that activity in order to give some further revelation of Himself. When sounds are reproduced through the ether, the microphone modulates the carrier wave from the transmitting station so that we may hear an intelligible voice. Thus meaning is superadded to the output of mere energy. Similarly, may we not think of God superadding meaning to the continual outflow of His energy in what we call Nature? In saying this, we are not reducing the "supernatural" to the "natural"; rather, we are trying to lift up the conception of the "natural" to the level at which it may mediate personal communication. However anthropomorphic our language necessarily remains, it serves to describe a possibility (all that is needed to meet the immediate difficulty) which the theist should be able to grant. We are not suggesting that the activity of God is limited to the normal outflow of His activity. This He does use, to redeem and so to reveal. But the expectation of the theist should be that God has other modes of activity besides those with which He has familiarized us in Nature's "laws".

If our psychology were as advanced as are the natural sciences, we might find in it a similar regularity, though one more subtle and elusive, and one which is crossed by the new factor of man's own creative activity. Here, too, we might claim, as does the Christian doctrine of the Holy Spirit, that God works from within the ordinary processes of consciousness, as well as from without. We may come to recognize His activity within our own, even though it is quite impossible for us to analyse the complex product of the two factors. Just as the divine activity in Nature's normal ways veils the particular activity in some external deliverance, so the divine activity in the normal sustenance of man's conscious life veils the operation of His Spirit in guiding and helping man to live as he ought. Again, we must be careful not to limit the divine activity to the extent of our consciousness of it. As the embryo in the womb is nurtured by food of which it is entirely unconscious, so in the moral and spiritual growth of man there can be what the theologian calls "prevenient grace", preparing for the conscious response to God.

(*b*) In sharp contrast with the tendency to explain away revelation by natural causation stands the objection that physical or psychical events are strictly speaking *irrelevant* to moral and spiritual truth.[1] What connection can there be between the casting of lots and the divine oracle which was alleged to be given through it? Why should an ecstasy be made the condition of prophetic insight and utterance? Why (to take the supreme example in the Christian faith) should faith in the Messiahship of Jesus be historically linked with His resurrection from the dead? Is not moral and spiritual truth ultimately proved by its own intrinsic character, and therefore incapable of proof or disproof by any historical event, which belongs to an entirely different realm?

It may be supposed that the attractiveness of mysticism lies partly in the escape it seems to afford from the irrelevancy of mere events. The mystic claims immediacy of enlightenment from the unseen world, and often replaces the normal relation to history which characterizes the Christian faith by some form of symbolism. Thus Swedenborg claims to have been for some years "constantly and continuously in the company of spirits and angels, hearing them speak and speaking with them in turn", and regards his previous scientific studies as preparing him for

[1] On this point, see the further discussion in Chapters VI–VIII.

this revelation, since "spiritual truths have a correspondence with natural truths."[1] Jacob Boehme wrote towards
the end of his life, "If I had no other book except the
book which I myself am, I should have books enough.
The entire Bible lies in me if I have Christ's Spirit in me."[2]
Obviously, the Christian mystic is always indebted to the
Christian revelation. But, having reached a certain level
of experience, he may be ready to "kick away the ladder
by which he has climbed", or at any rate to regard
historical events as no longer integral to his relation to
God.

A somewhat similar tendency, in a quite different
application, may be seen whenever the moral teaching of
Christianity becomes its primary feature, and "the essence
of Christianity" is seen in what Jesus taught, rather than
what Jesus was and is.[3] The historical events are relevant
as the necessary vehicle and occasion of the moral teaching,
but once that is communicated, the historical events have
served their main purpose. Herrmann distinguished his
own position from that of Lessing ("historical facts are
valueless for religious faith") by admitting that necessary
truths of reason cannot be grounded on casual truths of
history, but by urging that historical events give the
courage to believe in the effective providence of God.[4]
True as this is, it falls far short of the Christian faith in
the Incarnation, which makes the historical event primary
and central, and the moral and spiritual life of the Christian
the secondary and peripheral result of this redemptive
work.

The principal answer to the charge or implication of
irrelevancy is suggested by the relation of body to soul or

[1] *The New Jerusalem and its Heavenly Doctrine*; Foreword by A. E.
Sutton, in 1938 edition, pp. ix, x.
[2] As quoted by Rufus M. Jones, *Spiritual Reformers*, p. 170.
[3] Cf. Harnack's *Das Wesen des Christentums*.
[4] *Warum bedarf unser Glaube geschichtlicher Thatsachen?* p. 29.

G

spirit. In our experience these are never separable. We know nothing, even in our purely human experience, of bodiless spirit. Our personality, so far as it is yet revealed in the present time-process, is always dependent on functions of a lower level than the purely spiritual. By this fact we are prepared to believe that the divine Spirit also will use means at a lower level of reality to disclose Himself and to enter into relation with man, and that we can no more expect to separate form and content here than in regard to ourselves, except by acknowledged abstraction. The same fact meets us when we think of the social organization of religion within the Church. If the Church is "the Body of Christ", we may expect it to offer the same intimate union of body and spirit. Its forms are a necessary limitation, but also a necessary function, of the expression and activities of its life. On the yet higher level of divine revelation, then, we may expect that in regard to spiritual as well as material "seed", "God giveth it a body even as it pleased Him, and to each seed a body of its own." That body, in the realm of revelation, is the historical event or events through which the divine activity operates in human history. We have here one important aspect of the great sacramental principle which runs through life, the use of lower levels by the higher, or as we may call it, the "kenosis" or self-emptying of Spirit.[1] The historical event may become on occasion the sacrament of God's approach to man, a sacrament in which the elements are transfigured by the use to which they are put, and the material and spiritual are blended into a new unity.

(c) But such a defence of the historical event as the necessary vehicle of revelation may still seem open to the criticism of its *externality* in relation to the truth revealed.

[1] Cf. *The Christian Experience of the Holy Spirit*, by H. Wheeler Robinson, pp. 81–85; also Chapter XIV, § 2 of the present book.

This is particularly felt by many as affecting the certainty of faith. The truth of the historical event—let us take again the Resurrection of Christ because of its centrality— will depend on the truthfulness of particular witnesses, whom we are not able to cross-examine. Their testimony does not wholly agree, and is moreover capable of more than one interpretation, e.g. as to the nature of the risen body. The conception of this held by the apostle Paul, who claimed to have seen the risen Lord no less than did the other witnesses, is certainly different from theirs.[1] How then can such an alleged event be made cardinal for Christian faith, without imperilling its certitude?

Such questions are not easy to answer by any formal argument. The evidence for this or that event will vary in quality, and there must be full historical criticism of it. In regard to some events, e.g. some of the miracles ascribed to Jesus, we are not necessarily bound to accept the interpretations of the witnesses or recorders.[2] Some of the events are not so bound up with revelation as to give them a vital place in the testimony, e.g. the story of the Gadarene swine. On the other hand, the Resurrection *is* vital to the subsequent faith of the disciples, and of most Christians. If Christ is the first-fruits of them that are asleep,[3] the relation of the event to the truth is much more intimate. The event is, in fact, the truth actualized in the particular case, and the charge of externality falls to the ground. Something of the same kind may be said for all the events that are really vital to the faith. The triumph of Jesus over the temptation to adopt "worldly" methods, following His consciousness of vocation at the baptism, the call of disciples, the ministry of healing, the acceptance of a Messiahship of suffering, manifested at Cæsarea Philippi, the agony of Gethsemane, the death on

---

[1] Cf. the whole argument of 1 Cor. xv. 35 ff. with Luke xxiv. 39, 43.
[2] Cf. chap. VII, § 2.          [3] 1 Cor. xv. 20.

the Cross—all these are not only integral elements in the biography of the "Jesus of history", but also closely involved in the revealing and redemptive mission of our Lord. In the sense indicated in (*b*) they are no longer external, but are fully taken up into the Personality of Jesus.

But the question of externality may be raised in a different way. So far as truth is alleged to reach us through the consciousness of a prophet, say of the Old Testament, or even of Jesus Himself, it may seem that we are still dependent on the testimony of another. Here, more than ever, we are deprived of any direct access to the ultimate source, the inner event, and our religious faith is necessarily second-hand. We believe—if we believe—because this or that authority has said this or that. Is it not better simply to say that we accept truth for its own sake, wherever it may be found?

The full question of authority in revelation must be deferred to a later stage of this book (Chaps. IX and X). Here it must suffice to indicate the line that will be taken, viz. that the response of the believer implies that there is something "objective", and so far external to himself, which springs from divine activity, whether that activity be recognized in the control of physical events, or in the heightening of the individual consciousness to the point at which it becomes "prophetic". In this sense, externality is essential. It is essential to faith (as James Denney once said to me) to seek a fulcrum outside itself. The subjective factor is not less essential to faith; it is in the blended unity of both that faith becomes living and active.

(*d*) One more difficulty, however, must be met in the present discussion. This is the *relativity* of the truth revealed to a particular generation and through particular

persons.[1] It is here, perhaps, that the limitations of a
historical revelation are most usually felt. Truth must
be permanent and universal; the historical revelation of
it will necessarily be in some degree transient and particular, if it is to be intelligible. The ethics of the Sermon
on the Mount are framed in view of a social group existing
within Judaism in the first century, whatever be their
wider implications. The Pauline interpretation of the
Cross is that of a Jewish rabbi, converted to the belief
that Jesus was the Messiah in spite of that Cross, and
preaching as a missionary in a world dominated by Hellen-
istic ways of thinking. What is their applicability to the
Western world in the twentieth century?

Let us frankly admit the relativity as inherent, necessarily inherent in the divine activity from the very
beginning. Only so could its human contemporaries be
awakened to a living faith. But it is a living and personal
faith which we believe God desires, not any formal
acceptance of a fixed body of truth. We must not confuse
the permanence and universality of truth as it exists for
God with man's fragmentary and often hesitating response
to it, as exhibited even in the prophets themselves. Truth
can never be absolute for man, as it is for God. It
is relative to the individual and the society from its first
reception, or it could never be received. The human
consciousness of Jesus Himself is a limiting condition of
the revelation that entered the world through Him—so
far as we regard it as a genuine human consciousness.
The particular circumstances which His recorded teaching
has in view were not those of the majority of the world's
inhabitants even at that time, and no mechanical application of them would have been possible everywhere in
the first century. It is a fallacy to think of the original
revelation as having qualities of absoluteness which it has

[1] Some aspects of this were discussed in Chapter II.

somehow lost in the course of time. Truth must always be born into the world through human travail, and it will always, even from the highest parentage, bear the marks of its lineage.

In practice, every religious community that looks back to an historical revelation admits this relativity by devising some method of re-interpretation, to meet new needs, through the living tradition of the faith. This process of re-interpretation may be naively unconscious, as in many evangelical appeals to "simple Biblical truth", or it may issue in a clear-cut formula such as that of the Council of Trent. In the latter case, the recognition of an institution authorized to declare the true interpretation (which means in practice the true interpretation for a particular age) will depend on certain presuppositions, which cannot here be discussed. The view here taken is that the Scriptural promise of guidance by the Spirit of God into the truth is no empty word, but is fulfilled in the experience of the individual believer and in the history of the Church, though it has not been vested in any external institution so as to guarantee human inerrancy of judgment.

Instead of complaining that this leaves man groping in the twilight rather than walking in the light of full day, we ought to ask what is the purpose of revelation. If we believe that it is intended to bring man into a fellowship with God which requires the activity of man's mind and will, then the very challenge of truth, as at first but dimly and partially discerned, is part of the educative process. Truth safeguards itself from being a mere "deposit" by requiring in the truth-seeker those very qualities which it is the purpose of truth to develop. Because of the variety of human response to it, truth flows as a river of God, changing its course to follow the changing valleys of the landscape of history, and not as a canal between the narrow banks of man's devising.

**§ 3.** *The Significance of Israel's History.* The fullest and clearest examples of the general principles outlined in this chapter may be found in the history of Israel, where we see historical revelation best illustrated. The length of the period covered (especially when we remember the post-canonical literature which bridges the apparent gulf between the two Testaments) and the variety of the types of religion which it offers, are matched by the relative fulness of the record. When we put aside later prepossessions, derived from the dogmatic positions taken by Judaism and Christianity, and study the literature critically in the light of its ancient environment, we shall see that the history of Israel is part of world history, not to be separated from it by any artificial theorization. Any claim that we make for the uniqueness of the history must be based on its intrinsic character. What we find is a religious experience arising in a Semitic setting, and conditioned throughout by that fact. No one can hope to understand the religion of Israel unless he begins with these Semitic origins, nomadic, Palestinian or imperial (Babylonia and Assyria). Throughout the centuries other influences, from Egypt, Persia, Greece and Rome, shaped and moulded the course of the history, and so, in varying ways and degrees, the religion. Finally that religion issued in two great related though contrasted types—Judaism and Christianity, so that we have a double check upon our interpretation, viz. that of origins and that of results. In studying the literature, we have always to remember that it has been selected and edited in the interests of post-exilic Judaism, notably as seen in the throwing back of the results of a long development to the beginning, so that the alleged "Mosaic revelation" largely anticipates a faith and practice which needed many centuries for their growth.

The first result of critical study is to bring out a remarkable diversity beneath the superficial unity of the Old Testament. Yet there is a real, though much deeper, unity to be discerned, as a reward of patient study and spiritual sympathy. This is the unity of the divine initiative, active throughout, ever working towards a fuller enlightenment and a larger measure of human response. The primary faith in Yahweh as the God of Israel, though only one amongst many gods, slowly moves forward to the conviction that He is the only God of the whole world—a conviction implicit in the great prophets of the eighth century and explicit in the "Isaiah" of Babylon. The crude justice and narrowly defined brotherhood observed within the nomadic clan, as the very condition of its maintenance in the desert, were gradually raised in quality and extended in scope until the ethics of Israel were universalized and became an essential part of the religion. The worship of God, similar in its sacrificial and ritual forms to that of other Semitic peoples, moved *pari passu* (except for the inevitable time-lag) with the higher conception of the Being worshipped, until the grosser elements were either eliminated or sublimated, and worship became, with whatever retention of outward ceremonies, primarily a worship in spirit and in truth. Such progress was not continuous and was not universal in Israel; the best is always represented by a minority in any nation. But the fact of the progress is unmistakable, and the most natural explanation of the fact is that of a historical revelation, ever proportioned to the response of individuals and generations.

The most characteristic quality of this revelation is that it is redemptive. This illustrates the repeated emphasis of our argument, that the revelation consists in a redemption, not the redemption in a revelation—which is what the ascription of a whole and complete legislation to Sinai is apt wrongly to suggest. The God of Sinai was known by His redemption of Israel from Egypt—that fact counted for more than any particular "words", few or many, which may have been linked with it. So, when the prophets speak to Israel, they do not appeal to an existent body of revealed truth, but to an active and living God, ready both to judge or to redeem His people. They interpret the contemporary history from the pages of memory, not from those of a Bible. They appeal to the Exodus as proof that the redemptive purpose and power displayed in it can be again manifested. For Deutero-Isaiah, the deliverance from Babylon was to be a new Exodus, faith in which was justified because there had been an old Exodus.[1] Naturally, when the actuality of redemption in history is religiously interpreted, redemption becomes a revelation, but the order and relation of the two are significant.

Another marked feature of Israel's history is its wealth of "mediation",[2] by which is meant the variety of the means by which God approaches or is approached. This ranges from the crudest physical event, such as the casting of lots in the use of Urim and Thummim, through the phenomena of Nature, such as the blowing of the wind in the trees or the burst of thunder in the heavens, up to the clearest utterances of the human conscience, that "lamp lighted by the Lord". Priestly oracle and prophetic "word" and the counsel of the wise man are all traced back to the inspiration of God. All along the line it remains open to us to accept the lower instead of the higher interpretation—to regard all these phenomena as due to the unpurposive operations of Nature or to purely human activities, without any divine purpose and control. Such alternatives of interpretation are always possible in historical revelation, from the nature of our experience.

---

[1] So also, e.g., in Jer. xxiii. 7, 8.
[2] Treated more fully in Part II.

The principle of mediation which underlies such revelation necessarily allows us to look downwards instead of upwards, and to be content with a lower instead of the higher meaning.

The most notable and the most important example of such mediation is afforded by the prophet. In him we see the meeting-place of the human and the divine more clearly than at any other point. The prophetic consciousness in Israel has its own psychological history.[1] It has the characteristic features of the general psychological ideas of Israel, together with certain abnormal possibilities, which appear to be linked with the dervish-like *nabi* and his "ecstasies". It also shows a high degree of moral development, and the faith concerning God that "nothing can be good in Him which evil is in me". But all this still leaves us with our feet standing on the earth. If we go on to say that in this and through this consciousness, by some leap of "sympathetic" faith on the prophet's part, God was enabled in fulfilment of His purpose to enter human history, then the statement constitutes a leap of faith akin to that made by the prophet himself. We can never eliminate that personal factor, in regard to either the outer or inner event. The interpretation, however warranted, can never be proved as something *wholly* independent of the interpreter.

This leads us to the part played by the prophet in relation to ourselves. We have compared our leap of faith, in sharing his conviction that God has veritably spoken through him, with that made by himself in the reception of the "word". But the comparison is only partial. In the realm of religious "discovery", the prophet is like the poetic genius, the scientific discoverer, the philosopher who inaugurates a new period. All of these appeal to data which it is believed that any man *of like*

[1] See more fully Chapter VIII, § 3.

*powers* could similarly interpret. But these pioneers hold the place they do just because they stand head and shoulders above the rest of us. We may be able to follow in their footsteps when once they have blazed the trail, but we could not lead the way ourselves. In proportion to our knowledge of them and of their work and character, we may be ready to follow them even where we cannot check their data—just because they are what they are. But in any case, their testimony adds something of no little importance to the intrinsic evidence of what they give us.

One significant feature of Israel's history should not be overlooked, because it helps to meet the difficulty already noticed, arising from the relativity of historical revelation. Faith in the election of Israel, expressed in the idea of a divine covenant, is a central element in Israel's religion, from the beginning to the end of the history. Israel was chosen to occupy a unique place and to discharge a unique mission in the history of the world. But does not the acceptance of such a belief, even in modified form, necessarily imply too narrow a view of history? Have not other nations been "chosen", in the sense that they also have made unique contributions to the world? We may freely recognize this, and yet maintain that Israel's service was unique and indispensable. Its particularity was the condition of its intensity. The true universality is not reached by thinning out our convictions so as to make them spread over as wide a surface as possible. It is reached by so intense a devotion to them that we penetrate nearer to the centre of things and so draw nearer to each other. That is the characteristic of Israel's religion at the best and in the best of her representatives. The moral and religious universalism of the Old Testament is found, where it is found, in the prophets and their most loyal disciples. It vindicates the particularity of historical revelation,[1] and all the more because it constitutes the historical preparation for a faith that claims to be universalistic in the widest possible sense.

[1] For a very thorough discussion of the problems attaching to this, see E. Troeltsch, *Die Absolutheit des Christentums und die Religionsgeschichte* (1902); see also the remarks of N. Söderblom, *The Nature of Revelation*, pp. 79 ff.

# PART II

# THE MEDIA OF REVELATION

VI. THE PRINCIPLE OF MEDIATION

VII. THE PHYSICAL MEDIA

VIII. THE PSYCHICAL MEDIA

IX. HISTORY AND REVELATION

X. THE CHRISTIAN REVELATION

# CHAPTER VI

## THE PRINCIPLE OF MEDIATION

OUR approach to revelation through the actuality of history takes for granted the closest interrelation of general history and experience with the special phases of both of them which enshrine the Christian revelation. This assumption is not an arbitrary one, derived from a reduction of Jesus Christ to one member of a pantheon, and of Christian theology to a mere branch of the comparative study of religions. It can appeal to the Bible itself, when this is historically and critically interpreted, for the Bible contains many ethnic elements and has drawn upon many cultures. The Semitic animism, the clan morality, the anthropomorphic conceptions of God, which often supply the content of the earliest portions of the Old Testament, and continue to condition the forms of its latest portions, are not easily separable from that prophetic consciousness through which we gain the highest revelation of the God of Israel. Nor can the Yahweh of Israel be ignored by those who serve and worship the God and Father of our Lord Jesus Christ. The arbitrariness lies with those who take the "absoluteness" of the Christian revelation to demand an unhistorical detachment from all this human life, in their laudable desire to magnify the uniqueness and majesty of that revelation.[1]

[1] For a fair statement and (to me) convincing criticism of the "Dialectical" theology as it bears on revelation, reference may be made to Professor John Baillie's *Our Knowledge of God*, especially pp. 17–35, where Brunner is allowed to criticize Barth, before his own (modified) position is criticized in turn. As is said by Söderblom (*The Nature of*

Whatever the difficulties raised by fidelity to history when a "special" revelation is brought into relation with a "general" revelation, such difficulties must be faced as the conditions under which God has chosen to reveal Himself. Some of them will be encountered in Part III of this book, where the Christian revelation is seen to be constituted by a divine redemption. Here we shall approach revelation as it is seen in general history, without fear that the Christian revelation will lose its uniqueness by such an approach. Since it is always through some form of mediation that God draws near to man in the actuality of history and experience, the principle of mediation supplies a convenient way of entrance to our subject. It has the great advantage of bringing us to the actual point of contact (in our experience) between God and man, instead of confronting us with *a priori* speculation.

The importance of mediation, and its conditioning influence on the particular type of religion of those whom it concerns, may be seen by contrasting three well-known figures of the Christian Church. St. Augustine begins his *Confessions* by bringing man's restless heart into direct relation with its Creator, in whom alone man's rest can be found. But the autobiographical prayer which forms the "Confessions" shows that between Augustine and God there are his doctrine of the Church, the sacramental means of grace which underlie Roman Catholicism, and Augustine's doctrine of predestination which underlies Calvinism. Calvin begins his *Institutes* with the words, "Almost the whole sum of our wisdom which ought to be considered true and solid wisdom consists of two parts, the knowledge of God and of ourselves". Between God and man, however, stands the whole system of ideas

*Revelation*, p. 171), "If you wish to have Christ, you must take history with him."

professedly drawn from Scripture which makes Calvinism the most impressive doctrinal statement of Protestantism. Newman begins his *Apologia* by describing his Calvinistic conversion at the age of fifteen, of which the permanent contribution to his development was, he says, that "of making me rest in the thought of two and two only absolute and luminously self-evident beings, myself and my Creator". Between them, however, there came to stand for him the authority of an infallible Church. All these representative men try to bring God and man face to face; the differences between them are seen in the different media which minister to that relation.

These illustrations are drawn from Christianity with its one personal Mediator[1] and its diverse media of idea, rite and institution, but they might equally be drawn from any of the great religions ascribing personality to God. They might come from the Persian religion, with Zarathushtra and the Gathas and the sacred fire, from Israel, with Moses, the Torah and the Temple, from Islam, with Muhammad and the Kur'an and the Ka'aba. Whether on the large scale of history or on the small scale of individual experience, religion brings God and man into relation by a great diversity of media, or by a great diversity of emphasis on similar media.

§ 1. *The Variety of Media.* Theoretically there is no limit to the possible media of religion, since the transforming power of the mind of man can give religious meaning to any object. Even in the more limited field of the intercourse of man and man, we see how wide is the scope of mediation—the gestures of the body, the sounds of primitive speech, the signs or marks that will develop into writing, the tribal rules that will develop into morality and the cult, the beginnings of art, the heirlooms

---

[1] 1 Tim. ii. 5; cf. Heb. viii. 6, ix. 15, xii. 24.

H

and ancestral objects that link the present with the past. For the intercourse of God and man the whole range of natural phenomena is open, and we know how rich and manifold has been its use. Besides this, there is the conception of man himself as in lower or higher degree a mediator between God and man, with all the varying levels of anthropomorphism which that mediation may entail. A review of the media of religion that was at all comprehensive would, in fact, become a history of religions. But our subject finds its reduction to the practicable if we think for the most part of the great theistic religions which develop a personal relation between God and man, and if we try to state the principles involved in such mediation, rather than to describe its many forms, except by way of illustration.

It will be a sufficient example of the variety of the media if we take a single religion, in which that variety is particularly remarkable—the religion of Israel. The religious wealth of the Bible, both in vocabulary and in idea, and the subsequent religious influence of the Bible on the faith and the worship of the three great theistic religions, are largely due to this variety. Six different types, at least, may be seen in the Old Testament. (1) There is first the way in which natural phenomena, physical events, are conceived to be under divine control, and therefore form a language of God. This may range from the sacred lot, Urim and Thummim, to the east wind that drove back the waters of the sea that Israel might cross into safety. (2) Again, there is that development of the moral consciousness which culminated in the prophets, with such epoch-making consequences for religion. This becomes an approach of man to God as well as an approach of God to man—a distinctive quality of true worship as well as the supreme means of revelation. If the use of physical events and functions yields the lowest

forms of worship, this medium can lead to the highest.
(3) Again, we find other "mediators", such as priests,
kings, and patriarchs, within the limited degree to which
the religion of Israel allows of personal mediation between
man and God (perhaps "representation" would be the
better word). The portrayal of the nation itself in its
vicarious suffering as the Servant of Yahweh marks the
highest point reached by this kind of mediation, higher
in its spiritual quality than that of any angel can be.
The absence of hypostases[1] from the strictly Hebrew
tradition is significant. (4) There is also the conception
of man's whole history as controlled by Yahweh according to a divine purpose. This conception the world owes
to Israel, who taught it to Christianity and Islam. It is
easy to see how the wide extent of this medium can
establish faith in the God of history and enlarge the scope
of divine revelation. Moreover, faith can so transform the
meaning of the events that there are unlimited spiritual
possibilities for their religious employment, of which
Israel made ample use. (5) Further, there is the cultus,
with all its connected or accompanying institutions, many
of them linked by faith to the history, since Israel saw
all things historically. Here the changing centuries shew
a bewildering variety of use, from Saul's stone of sacrifice
on the battle field down to the elaborate ritual of the
Temple and the first hints of the synagogue, a development full of colour and movement and noise, from which
issued the Book of Psalms as well as the Book of Leviticus,
besides a copious parallel development of private and non-
liturgical prayer. (6) Finally, there is the use of the
written Torah, already indicated in those psalms that call
to the study of the Law. The fixity and permanence
of the written Word clearly introduces a new kind of

---

[1] In Prov. viii, the Greek influence on the conception of Wisdom has
produced a quasi-hypostasis.

mediation, in the large sense of the term here employed, and a new type of nomistic religion was built on this foundation.

§ 2. *The Interrelation of Faith and Worship.* The most familiar example of mediation is in the regular worship of each man's particular faith. Faith can no more dispense with worship than sincere worship can dispense with faith. Whatever be the intellectual elements of faith, it implies a volition, and that volition finds definite expression in individual acts. That is simply stated in the words of the Apostle Paul, "If thou shalt confess with thy mouth Jesus as Lord, and shalt believe in thy heart that God raised him from the dead, thou shalt be saved."[1] But religious faith must be social as well as individual, and it is only in the common utterances and acts of worship that faith can find social expression. By that expression the individual faith verifies itself and educates itself. It needs that objective expression to correct its own subjectivity, even to maintain itself—for whose faith can dispense with the aid of regular inculcations and mutual encouragement? The necessary price paid for social worship is that spontaneity must accept the fetters of regularity, but that is itself a necessary part of religious education.

Ideally, the worship should correspond with the faith, and should be its natural contemporary expression. Yet it is inevitable that, in greater or less degree, religious worship should always carry with it survivals from the past. Within limits, that has its good side, even its indispensable side, since it reminds the worshipper that the community of worship is not to be measured by the visible persons of his immediate environment. On the other hand, probably all cults contain elements that have

[1] Rom. x. 9; the baptismal confession is doubtless in mind.

to be explained away, elements that have been retained from a stage of faith now superseded. The anthropologist would find in Elijah's crouching on Mt. Carmel, with his face between his knees, as he waited for the rain, the survival of an old cloud-making rite of sympathetic magic, as he would see in the water-libation of the Feast of Tabernacles another survival of the old rain-charm, whilst the words ascribed to Jesus at that same feast, "If any man thirst, let him come unto me and drink", are a further spiritualization of the survival.[1] The Vedic worshipper became conscious of immortality by the intoxication of the Soma-juice, and its use (as Haoma), though with no sanction from Zarathushtra, survives in Zoroastrianism. The survival of the Ka'aba and the well Zemzem into Islam from pre-Islamic religion is again a familiar example.[2]

Such things may serve to remind us that when a prophet arises, seeking to reform religion, the new idea which he brings is always related both positively and negatively to some existent cult. He has reached his idea through the discipline of that cult, as did Isaiah in his vision of the God of Israel. Yet the application of the idea may be a drastic reform of that cult, as was Isaiah's denunciation of those who trampled the courts of the temple to no purpose. No religion, no new idea of religion, can grow in a vacuum; it will always shew some continuity with its environment. Jeremiah could not have spoken of a new covenant of Yahweh with individuals, unless there had been an old covenant with the nation. The religion of Amos is not unfitly described as the Puritanism of the nomad in contrast with the agricultural culture of Baalism, whereas Zarathushtra exalts agriculture against the barbarism of the nomad. Muhammad's peculiar

[1] 1 Kings xviii. 42 ff.; Mishnah, *Sukkah* iv. 9; John vii. 37.

[2] Indeed this survival principle underlies the whole development of dogma. As Auguste Sabatier has said "Under the archaisms of words are hidden the neologisms of ideas" (*Philosophie de la Religion*, p. 403).

conception of revelation as a "reading" (Kur'an), something read to him from a heavenly book, is traced by Professor Andrae[1] to Muhammad's impression of the sacred books of Judaism and Christianity as essentially something employed in public worship, a public recitation, for which the Syriac name (*keryana*) is cognate with the Arabic (kur'an). There are thus definite limits set by existent worship within which the new ideas of the prophetic reformer can arise. In von Hügel's words[2] "the Prophets are full of conceptions and emotions derived from Symbolic and Sacramental Cultus". How much more will it be true of the ordinary man who grows up under the influence of the cult, that his ideas of religion will be dominated by it! Long before he can think for himself, if he ever does, these external impressions will be shaping his mind, giving both form and substance to his later religious development. The more elaborate the ritual, the more striking can the influence be; but the principle is true of the austere simplicities of Puritanism as well as of the colour and movement of Catholicism. This is part of the reason for propaganda by education which all religions employ in their missionary activities. It is also a reason why a change of religion in the developed man is so often of doubtful advantage; he must sacrifice so much of the outer form which is wedded to his spiritual convictions that very convincing reasons are needed to make the change spiritually profitable. In the Epistle to the Hebrews we have a valiant attempt to argue that the loss of the old forms of Judaism was well worth while because of the higher spirituality and permanent nature of Christianity; the argument illustrates the difficulty and danger of all change in religion involving an abandonment of the old forms of its worship.

---

[1] *Mohammed, sein Leben und Glaube*, p. 79.
[2] *Essays and Addresses*, 2nd series, p. 68.

On the other hand, there are definite limits to the elasticity of the media when interpreted afresh; only to a certain degree can we put the new wine into old bottles. Some parts of worship, like religious prostitution, must be ruthlessly amputated by a religion that claims to be moral. A cult that is fundamentally naturalistic, like Mithraism, cannot ultimately endure against the fundamentally spiritualistic conceptions of Christianity. In the long run, for better for worse, the institutions will tend to stamp their character on the ideas, in spite of all reformers, and in spite of the marvellous power of the mind of man to transform the meaning of things, a power which Wordsworth claimed as human nature's highest dower. Institutions and rites are prior in their influence on the developing mind; they are often more intense in their expression than the words that communicate thought; they endure from generation to generation, whereas the ideas alone will change with each individual in some degree. Worship is the body of religion, as faith is its soul, and it is the body that prescribes the limits within which the soul shall develop, and imparts to it some at least of its qualities. The reformer will often remind us that political thinking depends on political institutions, with the implication that some things which seem impossible with our present political institutions might well seem possible if these were changed. This is true, and it inspires the prophetic reformer in all religions; he attempts a seeming impossibility when he matches his idea against the momentum and vested interests of an institution; but he attempts it in the conviction that his impossible idea can be reinforced and made possible by some change of the institution.

§ 3. *Sacramental Mediation.* The use of the sacraments in religion is a special instance of the relation of faith and worship. It calls for some notice here, though obviously there can be no attempt to enter into the theological technicalities of the subject. But it may be suggestive to consider sacraments both from the lower approach of the anthropologist and from the higher interpretation of the philosopher, as instanced by the work of Dr. Marett and of Professor A. E. Taylor. Dr. Marett calls one of his books *Sacraments of Simple Folk.* He defends this use of the term by reference to the fact that *sacramentum* had a wide and elastic usage up to the twelfth century within Christianity itself. By a sacrament he understands a rite that is the technical organization of emotion in the interests of social welfare (as against magic), a rite which concentrates on some critical need by consecrating certain activities with reference to it. Religion, he argues, is dynamic, and "the sacrament . . . is the most dynamic of all ritual forms" (p. 9). It is a sort of spiritual health-exercise which brings *mana* into play. He proceeds to apply this definition to the ritual acts connected with the primary interests of savage life, viz. eating, fighting, mating, educating, ruling, judging, covenanting, healing, dying.

At the other end of the scale we have Professor Taylor's account of "Sacramentalism" in his Gifford Lectures.[1] The Christian sacrament is an instrumental cause of grace by divine appointment, according to what he regards as the characteristic faith of the Christian Church. He defends this faith on familiar lines, viz. that there are "natural" sacraments, as when physical food ministers to the mental life or when physical environment serves to awaken intellectual, artistic and moral activity. Why then, he argues, should we not believe, as theists, that God should use physical means also to minister to religious life, as "grace"? He pertinently remarks that "the

[1] *The Faith of a Moralist*, II, pp. 282–319.

ministry of the word" in the Protestant sense also depends on physical occasions. He concludes that the only proof that grace is mediated through the sacraments is the pragmatic one, viz. that the religious life nourished by sacraments is a higher kind of life than can be found elsewhere, though he admits the great difficulty of applying such a test.

The general principle of mediation would fairly cover both these statements, especially in view of the inter-relation of faith and event in all religious mediation. On the one hand, there is human activity in the ritual acts, and in the faith or "disposition" that is the minimum requirement for benefit; on the other, there is power available from beyond man's life, whether *mana* or the personal grace of God, which is believed to find occasion for its activity in the sacrament. The appeal to divine institution in the Christian sacrament is itself after all an appeal to faith, whether based on Biblical history or on the Council of Trent. In no way can we eliminate the fundamental interrelation of faith and event, already indicated; indeed, it is the one guarantee that the sacra-ment shall not be a purely mechanical form, which degenerates into magic. Nor can we ever hope to separate the activity of the Holy Spirit from the activity of man, by any demarcation of boundaries on deistic lines. In Protestant theology, the witness of the Spirit and the conviction of election and the final perseverance of the saints are all of them bound up with a human purpose, of which they might be called the higher aspect, and no subtlety of definition will ever separate them from it.

Here, as in so many other realms of life, such as the relation of subject and object in consciousness, our experi-ence is of a unity, which we have to analyse according to its presuppositions, whether they refer to *mana* or to

God. In either case, the faith that interprets and so far transforms the event must have an event on which to work, that is to say, some medium of its relation to the supernatural power.

This is not the place to enter upon any discussion of the sacramental question, and in particular as to whether Christianity is fundamentally and essentially an ethical or an ethico-sacramental religion. In the wider sense the issue is certainly a false one, since Christianity includes both morals and media; no religion can dispense with sacraments in the wider sense of the term, and no genuine Christianity could fail to be ethical in content. In the narrower sense which divides Protestantism and Catholicism, we may do well to remember that the categories of ancient thought do not readily fall into the sharpened antitheses of our modern thought, developed through centuries of controversy. An historical student of the New Testament may legitimately hold that it includes conceptions of baptism and of the Lord's Supper which are neither purely ethical nor purely sacramental in this narrower sense, but continue those symbolic acts of prophecy in the Old Testament which both represented and initiated the divine activity (according to the belief of the prophets themselves). We also do well to remember that the difference between the higher and the lower forms of our representation of divine activity and of our conception of its operation is a very little thing by comparison with the whole difference between the realms of the human and the divine. Belief in God and His active grace is so tremendous an act of faith that it has room within it for a whole host of smaller issues. These, like the earnings of the labourers in the Parable of the Vineyard, however much they mean to us, fall out of sight in comparison with the reality of divine grace.

§ 4. *The Relation of the Media to the Idea of God.* What is the relation to this belief in God of the particular media which a religion employs? Something of this we have noticed already in the general interrelation of faith and worship. But there is a Godward aspect of mediation which calls for special notice. The idea of God will always be conditioned by terms of thought drawn from the media of His worship. We should all agree so far with Auguste Sabatier that our thought as well as our language about God is "symbolic",[1] in the sense that it can never amount to a scientific definition; it cannot comprehend God though it can reveal Him, and God must use language intelligible to us if there is to be a revelation at all. It is possible to hold that all media, declarative or effective, are "symbolic", whilst we hold also to a certain spiritual kinship between God and man which enables these "means of grace" to mediate a true knowledge of Him, which always means *the truth of His relation to us.*

This symbolism is not, of course, arbitrary; it grows up unconsciously out of a living religious experience. But the quality of the media will always affect the quality of the conception of God. A good example of this is seen in the Jewish rejection of idolatry. The prophetic consciousness was a higher and better medium than any material representation of God could be. Therefore it not only survived but displaced idolatry; the lower media could not endure when once the higher had been experienced. The Christian[2] would claim that the person of Christ holds its unique position in his faith and worship because this highest category of his experience provides the highest conception of God which he can form. How could the cult of Cybele, with the Corybantic frenzy of its self-emasculated priests, permanently challenge "the pure

---

[1] See Chap, III.
[2] Cf. St. Paul in Acts xvii. 28 (man's kinship to God disproves idolatry).

religion and undefiled" of the God and Father of Jesus Christ?

In this connection the quantity as well as the quality of the mediating experience is of importance. The most striking example here is the contrast between the revelation of God in the religion of Israel and that in Islam. Both are a development of previous religion, and both have had a long subsequent history in which oral tradition has supplemented the written revelation. Yet when we look at the two sacred books, we see that Israel draws on the religious consciousness of some twelve centuries, whilst the Kur'an from the first to last bears the impress of a single man. Apart from any question of *quality*, there is a *quantity* of mediation here which not only yields an immeasurably greater religious experience, but also permits the use of a new type of mediation, that of the control of history through the centuries by divine providence and purpose. In another respect we may compare Judaism and Christianity. A Jewish writer has said, "Nor perhaps does a rigidly monotheistic religion lend itself to that variety of appeal and that richness of imagery which a Trinitarian belief enjoys."[1] We are not, of course, here comparing the truth of these respective ideas of God, but illustrating the fact that the range of the media does profoundly affect the range of the ultimate idea of God, whether that be justifiable or not. We might similarly ask what difference in response to the words and music of "The Dream of Gerontius" would be found in a Protestant and a Catholic respectively.

This is the proper place to notice that type of religious experience which is called "mystical", as claiming an immediate and direct relation of the soul to God. Mysticism is notoriously difficult to define, largely because of its many varieties. But its most characteristic features

[1] A. L. Emanuel, *Contemporary Review*, January 1918, pp. 88–92.

are its claim to immediacy in the relation to God, its inwardness in contrast with the use of sacramental media, and its emotional, rather than intellectual, emphasis. We may use the term to denote something which is found in many religions, and is more temperamental than ecclesiastical, without confusing it with the metaphysical mysticism which follows the negative way of absorption into the Absolute. The wider type ranges from the classical form seen in the experience of St. Teresa, who never ceased to be loyal to Catholic theology, and nurtured her soul on its sacramental system, down to the ordinary person who can remember some moment in which there was a deep and unifying consciousness of the Beyond which transcended the processes of conscious thought. So far as these experiences have a genuine content of knowledge they are always linked to the religious group and to the media it employs, whether or not the persons in question have themselves ceased to use those media. All our ideas are drawn from such media, and whatever stimulus we may gain from a contact with God beyond our powers of analysis, there comes a point at which that gain must be re-translated into terms of our conscious life. The healthiest mysticism has always recognized this. When St. Teresa has brought us to the very centre of her "Interior Castle", by a way which is like an inverted "Pilgrim's Progress", to the innermost chamber of "spiritual marriage", she tells us that its children are good works, and that if duty calls us from the presence chamber of the King, whenever we return, He will hold the door open for us. "Both Martha and Mary must entertain the Lord." The notable and historic concern of the Society of Friends with social service is due to the same healthy instinct, that even mysticism must find its own media of active expression, which will in turn react on the idea of God. Without such practical complement, mysticism may become an esoteric indulgence, as without clear thinking and sound tradition it may develop into wild extravagances and superstitious vagaries.

In largest horizon, mediation covers all history and all experience. Just as all the sensational stimuli and circumstances of a developing life contribute to its growth into independent consciousness and self-identity, so again they become the media of whatever vision it may gain of Reality beyond itself. It is interesting to notice how thinkers of very different schools agree (as they must) on this point. Thus at one extreme, Santayana says that spirit "must have, as the poet's mind has, its special memories and affinities, to load the dice, to follow a scent, to crave a particular issue. . . . Spirit is incarnate by nature, not by accident."[1] At the other extreme, von Hügel declares that Christianity is "irreducibly *incarnational*", and that "stimulations, vehicles and forms are (upon the whole and in the long run) as truly required fully to awaken the religious life as they are to express it and to transmit it, when already fully awakened"[2]. From the realm of poetry, as distinct from those of philosophy and theology, we have an apt illustration in the best-known of Keats' letters, in which he dismisses the phrase "a vale of tears" as a description of the world, in favour of "the vale of Soul-making".[3] He justifies this by the remark, "Do you not see how necessary a World of Pains and troubles is to school an Intelligence and make it a Soul?" When we combine this with his conception of beauty as the ultimate truth, the beauty which poetry is ever seeking to express by the concrete imagery begotten of this self-same experience, we see how fundamental is the principle of mediation for any approach to ultimate

[1] *The Realm of Spirit*, pp. 42, 43.
[2] *Essays*, First Series, pp. 230, 231.
[3] Letter to George and Georgiana Keats of April 1819; p. 326 of the edition of 1895, edited by H. B. Forman.

Truth. That which shapes us into personal consciousness itself becomes the medium of our knowledge of yet higher Being.

§ 5. *Basis for the Classification of Religions.* Finally, we may consider how far the principle of mediation helps us to classify religions. How difficult this task of classification is we see from the many different attempts at it, none of which has commanded general approval; it is as difficult as the related task, the definition of religion. Hegel classified religions into nature religion (including the religions of China, India, Persia, Syria, and Egypt), the religion of spiritual individualism (Jewish, Greek and Roman), and the absolute religion, which is a philosophical interpretation of Lutheranism; this scheme is not only based on insufficient knowledge of the religions, but is dictated by the determination to find his own system reflected in history. Siebeck did more justice to the intrinsic nature of the religions by dividing them into nature religion, morality religion, including Judaism and Islam, and redemptive religion, in the negative form of Buddhism and the positive form of Christianity. Galloway contented himself with the purely descriptive and external classification of tribal, national and universal. But, as he himself says, "The centre of a religion is the cultus."[1] The argument of this chapter has been that the principle of mediation expressed in the cultus will largely control both human faith and the idea of God. If this principle, therefore, is really applicable to the classification of religions, it should give us a division based on the essential character of the religions, and more objective in its application than are most of the schemes.

The first great class, on almost any principle, will be the nature religions, both those of primitive cultures and

[1] *Philosophy of Religion*, p. 47.

those more developed religions in which nature is still the principal substratum, such as the religion of Japan. The popular religions of Egypt and of Greece are also nature religions, in spite of their ethical accompaniments. Here, broadly speaking, we find natural phenomena, physical events, regarded as the chief media of contact with the spirits or gods revealed in nature. The quality of the religion cannot rise above a certain point because of the materiality of its media; higher needs may be met by an independent development of ethics, as in Egypt. On the other hand, amongst the Greeks we get a philosophic development which acts as a solvent at home and as an intellectual basis for other religions abroad.

The second class of religions will be those broadly characterized by their attempted rejection of the principle of mediation, whether natural or psychical, as in the religions of India. This is the direct consequence of that attitude to the world which seems to be the common ground of these religions—that life is not a blessing to be enjoyed, but a curse from which escape is to be sought, by Brahmanic absorption or by the Buddhistic and Jainistic Nirvana. Such an attitude leaves no room for mediation at all, in the sense we have been considering. Even so, such religions can be classified by their professed attitude towards mediation, and none of them, Hindu or Buddhistic, really escapes from it, as the popular development of these religions sufficiently shews.

The third class includes all the religions that have found their chief medium of contact with God in the prophetic consciousness. Here we have Zoroastrianism, Judaism, Christianity and Islam. It is significant that these, and these only, are the monotheistic religions. It would seem that the unity of the prophetic consciousness is needed to create the conception of monotheism. It is significant, also, that these are the supremely ethical religions, which

dwelling Bodhisattva by his recognition of the genuine things."[1]

In the method just illustrated a sort of rationality is apparent and this is often seen in the development of a pseudo-science of divination. The beginnings of astrology as well as its more systematic forms, passing into astronomy, often illustrate the application of scientific method. Very often divination links itself with higher beings by means of sacrifice or prayer or the use of some approved formula. Movements of birds are a particularly widespread method of divination, as is the inspection of entrails of sacrificed animals. In Babylon, for example, divination by the marks, etc., on the liver became a special science, from which country it seems to have passed to the Etruscans. Particular illustrations of the different kinds of divination are conveniently found in the long series of articles in Vol. IV of the *Encyclopaedia of Religion and Ethics*, and it is not necessary here to go into detail. But certain general characteristics of divination by physical media may be noted. However great and arbitrary the play of the interpretative minds, divination implies resort to an external happening beyond the control of the diviner. He needs, it would seem, the nucleus of an event, something sufficient to bear the claim that it brings knowledge from without. This event is the text of the sermon, which may wander very far from any meaning which can rationally be assigned to the text. Sometimes we can see a parallel to symbolic magic, as when like reveals like. Sometimes, no doubt, a whole body of precedent exists under which the new event is brought. But, in general, the essential feature is this reference to an external nucleus, credited with being the point of contact with abnormal sources of knowledge. There is clearly no intrinsic value in such reference, and divination by such means has

[1] H. Hackmann, *Buddhism* as *a Religion*, p. 185.

rightly been condemned by higher religions or the higher forms of religion.   Resort to an external event artificially linked to some power beyond itself is really an escape from moral responsibility.   The man who has to choose, and wishes to avoid decision, is drawn to believe that something or somebody can decide for him and that this decision will be for his good, or will yield true knowledge of the future.   On the other hand, we must admit that in the explicit recognition of a world beyond man's world, a world from which knowledge may possibly be derived, there is something which belongs to religion, something which is the grain of truth in the chaff of divination. When we think of the countless multitudes of men and women from east to west and from pole to pole who in their distress of mind and body have thus stretched out their "lame hands of faith" to the altar of an unknown god or to a god perhaps better unknown, we cannot but feel their kinship with those who by truer ways are seeking what they sought and finding a more adequate answer.

§ 2. *Nature and Miracle*.   Beyond the almost unbounded variety of resort to particular physical objects in divination (e.g. the casting of lots or the observation of animals and birds), there is the mass effect of the natural world as a whole, or in some of its more prominent features, such as the movement of the heavenly bodies.   Whereas in divination the initiative is often taken by men, eager to know the unknown, the physical world itself may seem to thrust itself on man's attention, whether by the cataclysms of earthquake, storm and flood, or by the more orderly movements of the stars or the alternations of the seasons, vitally affecting man's welfare.   Such phenomena inevitably become in course of time the media of revelation, since they are ascribed to powers beyond man's control, though intimately concerning his life.   The benevolent or malignant attitude of these powers is read through their supposed activities, and becomes the chief concern of magic and primitive religion.

Of course, we must avoid reading modern ideas of Nature into the primitive outlook. This was, generally speaking, particularistic and utilitarian, with the minimum of co-ordination or comprehension, and the maximum of pragmatic observation. Even to-day, it is difficult for the average townsman, so far removed from the direct production of the food on which his life depends, and so largely sheltered by artifice from exposure to the conditions of raw nature, to enter into the outlook of the farmer or the explorer. It is much more difficult to say what nature actually meant to primitive man, and to trace the slow progress of his thoughts about things through the recognition of *mana* in them, the ascription of souls or spirits to them, up to the conception of gods more or less detached from them, and able to control them, for man's good or his hurt. Even when the level of such polytheism was reached, the natural world must have seemed to consist of a number of compartments often overlapping, instead of a unity.

At the same time, we must not regard this primitive outlook as chaotic. Nature has always had her routine. From the earliest period of reflective observation, constantly stimulated by pressing needs, a certain order was apparent. Observation of the heavenly bodies, especially as developed in Babylonia, gave rise to the pseudo-science of astrology, the forerunner of astronomy. Across the background of the fixed stars, the sun, moon and the planets wove their ever-changing, yet orderly pattern. Some of these movements were quite obviously related to man's affairs, through the alternations of day and night, the succession of the seasons, the fertility of the soil. It was natural therefore to suppose that spiritual, as well as material, light was cast upon man's path through him who could interpret the changes of these heavenly bodies— natural also to link them with divine beings, whose will might be read through them. Upon the earth itself, the widespread fertility cults spring from a similar utilitarian motive. The Baalim, familiar to every reader of the Old Testament, represent local fertility gods, linked with some oasis and its springs, or some tree of luxuriant foliage, which the mysterious wind might stir to give an oracle or omen. Behind these local "lords", there was the widely practised cult of Ishtar (Ashtoreth) which spread so widely from Babylonia, in conjunction with the cult of Tammuz (Adonis), in celebration of the alternating seasons. This is often treated as the dominating "pattern" to which other religious interests have been subordinated.[1] On the other hand, we get a glimpse, through an Isaianic passage,[2] of the process by which agricultural lore was transferred to Yahweh, who, as a nomadic God in the first instance, had nothing to do with the fertility of the soil. To Him belonged rather the stormy phenomena of Sinai.

When the God of Sinai became the Lord of Canaan, and ultimately the Creator of the heavens and the earth, all Nature was seen as a revelation of His wisdom and power. Prophets and psalmists delight to hymn His praise in terms drawn from ancient mythology or contemporary ideas of Nature. "The heavens declare the glory of God and the firmament showeth His handiwork." Their ordinances, which are His commands, become the standard of reference for His equal fidelity to His spiritual promises.[3] When the promise of a future prosperity is given to a penitent and reconciled Israel, the terms are highly significant of the way in which nature is conceived to be dependent on, and so to reveal God: "I will answer the

---

[1] Cf. *Myth and Ritual*, ed. by S. H. Hooke.
[2] Isa. xxviii. 23–29.     [3] Jer. xxxi. 35–37.

heavens and they shall answer the earth; and the earth shall answer the corn and the wine and the oil; and they shall answer Jezreel."[1]  In modern terminology, we might say that there is here a recognition of "second causes"; the appeal of the people which God answers is mediated by the appeal of the growing crops to the earth on which they depend, as *it* depends on the rain from heaven, and as the blessing of the rain depends on Yahweh's control of the heavenly waters.

The passage is a salutary reminder that we must not think of the Hebrew outlook on nature as blind to its regular sequences; there was amongst them ample recognition of order in nature.  But neither must we set up this order as if it were in any sense an obstacle to Yahweh's more specialized activity in those "mighty acts" in which He is supremely manifest.  If we want to see Him overcoming obstacles, we must turn to the appropriations of Babylonian mythology in the prophets and psalmists which show Him as a new and nobler Marduk, defeating the dragon Tiamat, and substituting order for chaos.  But there is not anywhere the suggestion that "the laws of nature" are a restraint upon Him, for they are but the order which He has Himself instituted, and continues to maintain.[2]

For many people to-day, the difficulty felt about nature-miracles is partly due to the tyranny of this modern phrase "the laws of nature".  The metaphor of law (it is no more than metaphor) inevitably suggests a fixed and unalterable order, which cannot be changed without a violent interruption of an "illegal" kind, and is backed by independent sanctions.  But these "laws of Nature", as the physicist of to-day would be the first to admit, are

---

[1] Hos. ii. 21, 22; the terms are suggested by the name Jezreel—"Whom God soweth"—here given to Israel.
[2] Cf. especialiy Ps. civ. 27 ff.

nothing more than descriptions of sequences in phenomena. Enquiry into the ultimate causes of these belongs not to the physicist, but to the philosopher. That these descriptions, true of past experience, will also remain true for the future, is a well-founded expectation, on which our orderly life depends; it is in fact the school of our rationality, the necessary condition of any rational interpretation of the universe. It warrants the demand for full and satisfying evidence that any exceptional event, not to be explained normally, has in fact occurred. But again and again, it is the study of the exception that has led to the discovery of new forces operating,[1] and so to the advancement of knowledge. If there is, indeed, a spiritual and super-human world actively concerned with the material world, we may expect some evidence of its presence and activity, evidence that at first sight may seem to be a contravention of "the laws of nature", but which ultimately reveals higher "law", co-operating with these, whether from within or from without, whether through individual incidence or through comprehensive control.

This, of course, does not mean that every "miracle" alleged in the Bible or outside it, really occurred, or that, if it occurred, the explanation given by contemporaries is the true explanation. The "miracle" is simply an "object of wonder", inexplicable on ordinary lines by its observers and therefore ascribed by them to some higher power. It may cease to be an object of wonder to some later age of more extended normal knowledge. It may be more explicable in the realm of psychology than in that of physics, as a legendary expansion of some striking, though "natural", event. In particular, the true conception of miracle will be conditioned by the nature of the higher

---

[1] Cf. the stock example of the discovery of Neptune by the aberrations caused (in the motion of Uranus) through its unknown presence and the mathematical argument from these to the existence of a new planet.

power to which it is ascribed. It must be worthy of its source to be a miracle in the full religious sense.

On this high level, miracle is inseparable from Biblical religion and from the religion of all who rightly claim to stand in its succession. The supreme miracle of the Resurrection, thus conceived, is a mighty act of God, vindicating His Son. It was historically necessary, that His redemptive work might be known as divine, then and now. The direct evidence for it was confined to believers, as it must have been if spiritually conditioned and not a mere meaningless "event". That evidence is exposed to historical criticism, as in the case of any other event. But it must include all that flows from the event, as well as all that led to it. It must also look upward as well as forward, and include the estimation of its worthiness to reveal the God and Father of Jesus Christ, and to exhibit the new "law of life" in Him.[1] The precise *manner* of the Resurrection is of secondary account, and in truth the New Testament suggests more than one explanation of it.[2] But the *fact* is essential to the Christian revelation. Nature is here transcended by the transcendent God, whose immanent activity in the natural order is no limitation to His transcendent activity beyond it. It is rather the limitation of our descriptions of Nature which is here made manifest. It belongs to deism, not to Christian theism, to conceive nature as a closed system. Even human personality transcends the physical order; how much more will that be true of divine personality!

What has just been said shows the impossibility of making any absolute distinction between the psychical and the physical in the realm of revelation—just because the psychical (or spiritual) is always involved, even when

---

[1] Rom. viii. 2.
[2] Cf. St. Paul's argument in 1 Cor. xv. 35–50 that the resurrection "body" is "spiritual", and not of flesh and blood.

the physical is made the medium of their interrelation. This is especially apparent when we turn from particular events accepted as manifestations of deity to the more general impression made by nature upon man. It is not necessarily a surrender to subjectivism to say with Coleridge:—

> "—we receive but what we give,
> And in our life alone does Nature live."[1]

Here we must take account of two variables. On the one hand there is the multiplicity of Nature's aspects, ranging from the terrible majesty of the wind-swept ocean to

> "a hidden brook . . .
> That to the sleeping woods all night
> Singeth a quiet tune";

from the telescopic magnitude of starry skies to the atomic myriads revealed by the microscope, from the frozen solitude of Polar ice to the rank vegetation and crowded life of the African jungle. On the other hand, there are the not less infinitely varied moods of men, ever seeing in nature something to reflect the mood of the moment or of the age, so that Wordsworth on Calais beach finds that—

> "The gentleness of heaven broods o'er the Sea;"

whilst, across the Channel, Matthew Arnold on Dover beach hears only the

> "melancholy, long, withdrawing roar"

of the sea of faith.

---

[1] *Dejection* IV. The previous lines are also worth quoting as a warning against trying to make Nature's revelation wholly objective:—

> "Though I should gaze for ever
> On that green light that lingers in the west,
> I may not hope from outward forms to win
> The passion and the life whose fountains are within."

Even so, it is instructive to see how two such different men can draw together when they are trying to look more objectively into Nature's characteristics. For Arnold the supreme lesson that nature teaches him is

"Of toil unsever'd from tranquillity".

For Wordsworth's more developed vision of the meaning of Nature we must go to the famous "Lines composed above Tintern Abbey". He recalls the sub-conscious influence of his first visit, the unremembered pleasure which has influenced the unremembered acts of kindness and love. Then, penetrating deeper to its cause, he speaks of a vision that can lighten, because it interprets "the heavy and the weary weight of all this unintelligble world":—

"While with an eye made quiet by the power
Of harmony, and the deep power of joy,
We see into the life of things".[1]

That is not far from Arnold's "toil unsever'd from tranquillity". But Wordsworth's second visit records a deeper vision in those well-known lines which are the Magna Charta of the Wordsworthian lover of nature:—

"I have felt
"A presence that disturbs me with the joy
Of elevated thoughts; a sense sublime
Of something far more deeply interfused,
Whose dwelling is the light of setting suns,
And the round ocean and the living air,
And the blue sky, and in the mind of man:
A motion and a spirit, that impels
All thinking things, all objects of all thought,
And rolls through all things."

[1] We may compare Henry Vaughan's lines in *The Morning Watch*:—
"*Order*, The great *Chime*
and *Symphony* of nature",
(a reference which I owe to Professor Sencourt).

It is in that interplay of "thinking things" with the "objects of all thought" that the revelation through physical nature is to be made, if made at all. A new unity arises which has the quality of religious faith, even if it leaves the "presence" undefined. The experience is vital partly because it re-discovers the concreteness of life, which is obscured by our excessive habit of abstraction, just as John Stuart Mill had found, before he made this re-discovery through Wordsworth.[1]

Nature's beauty, order, serenity, majesty—all these acquire the force of an objective revelation, all the more objective because its media are physical, and always with us. For those to whom these qualities have been unveiled, the "miracle" of Nature as a whole will never cease to reveal God.

§ 3. *The Limitations of Nature-Worship.* Before we turn to those forms of revelation in which the psychical emphasis, rather than the physical, forms the starting-point, there is one historical aspect of divine revelation through nature which is important for the evaluation of religions. This is the rise of deities closely linked to the phenomena of nature, such as the Vedic storm god, Indra, or the Egyptian Nile-god, Osiris (in his original form). Nature-cults continue to bear the marks of their origin even when the conceptions of deity reach a relatively high level. But these higher conceptions are really due to a new psychical emphasis, and are not, properly speaking, products of nature-cults at all. Nor must we assume that *all* gods spring from ideas connected with nature. Of the Greek religion, a distinguished authority has

---

[1] *Autobiography*, Ch. 5. "What made Wordsworth's poems a medicine for my state of mind, was that they expressed, not mere outward beauty, but states of feeling, and of thought coloured by feeling, under the excitement of beauty . . . with culture of this sort, there was nothing to dread from the most confirmed habit of analysis."

remarked: "The higher beings are rarely recognizable as personifications of physical forces of nature, and it is only of a very few of them that a nature-origin can be posited or proved; and though many of them have special departments of nature for their peculiar concern, they are chiefly to be regarded as ethical and intellectual personalities . . . the dominant impulse was that which we call anthropomorphism."[1]

In our clearest examples of nature-religions, e.g. those of Egypt, India and Japan, the limitations are apparent. The deities of ancient Egypt are sometimes classified[2] into earlier derivations from aspects of Nature, such as the sun-god, Ra, and anthropomorphic abstractions, such as Maat, the goddess of truth (affiliated to Ra as his daughter). Both are incorporated[3] into the remarkable "monotheistic" revolution due to Ikhnaton in the fourteenth century B.C., which exalted Aton (the disk of the sun-god) to the supreme place. But the speedy break-down of this high form of religious faith is very suggestive of the difficulties encountered by such reforms in an environment of nature-worship.

As for the vast expanse of India's religions, any generalization is likely to be inadequate, if not erroneous. It is probably true to say that the worship of the Vedic Varuna offers "the closest approximation that we can find in all the ancient worships of India to a real ethical Theism".[4] But this does not represent the dominant trend of Indian development since "The place of Varuna is usurped by nature powers, unmoral and with undefined jurisdictions, melting from time to time into each other, and because unethical, more controllable to its ends by the rising power of the speculative intellect".[5] Along

[1] L. R. Farnell, *The Higher Aspects of Greek Religion*, p. 2.
[2] As by J. Baikie in the *Encyclopædia of Religion and Ethics*, IX, 217.
[3] Breasted, *Development of Religion and Thought in Ancient Egypt*, p. 338.
[4] Nicol Macnicol, *Indian Theism*, p. 13.     [5] Ibid., p. 18.

these lines was reached the Brahmanic pantheism of the Upanishads, whilst room was left for the jungle of nature-cults to maintain themselves within the all-embracing protection of a pantheistic philosophy of religion.

For Japan, it has been claimed that no people has possessed a keener appreciation of Nature,[1] and their national religion, Shinto, is fundamentally naturalistic, though crossed by elements derived from ancestor-worship (which belong to the group of psychical media). But Shinto is an official religion, and the old nature cults have not produced any spiritual equivalent to Christianity or Buddhism. In religion, as in so many other spheres, the Japanese have shewn themselves to be an assimilative, rather than a creative people, and their present-day attitude to religion appears to be syncretistic rather than distinctive. Such a tendency to syncretism is, in fact, one of the characteristics of nature-worship in general; it is the implicit confession of weakness or inadequacy, in contrast with the confident exclusiveness of a more virile faith, such as Judaism.

This quality of syncretism is well illustrated in Mithraism, the religion which is usually regarded as the chief rival of Christianity throughout the third Christian century. A glance at Cumont's impressive map[2] showing the wide-spread diffusion of Mithraic shrines through most of Europe will confirm this impression. That diffusion seems primarily due to the Roman legionaries, to whom Mithraism specially appealed. It is significant that only four years before the Toleration Edict of Galerius recognized Christianity as a *religio licita*, and six years before the Edict of Milan, decreed by Constantine and Licinius, placed it under full imperial protection, we find Diocletian, Galerius and Licinius at their meeting in Carnuntum

[1] M. Revon, in *Encyclopædia of Religion and Ethics*, IX, 233.
[2] In *Les Mystères de Mithra*, at end.

(A.D. 307) dedicating an altar to Mithra, which is still extant.[1] It is significant also that the "apostasy" of Julian took the form of an attempt to reinstate Mithraism of which he was a professed devotee.[2]

The central figure in Mithraism goes back to the god Mitra in the Rig-Veda, and especially to Mithra in Iran. He seems to have been ignored by Zoroaster in his concentration on Ahura Mazda,[3] but he reappears in the later Persian religion, adding to his original character of a god of light that of a vindicator of oaths and a warrior-god. In the form in which Mithraism spread through the Roman world, he becomes the great mediator between heaven and the realms beneath, perhaps in view of the light-bearing quality of the air,[4] and, in fact, a sort of Logos.[5] His typical representation on the well-known Mithraic altar-piece is that of a youthful figure in the act of slaying a bull. This sacrificial act liberates the life-giving fertility on which the earth depends. The scene depicted brings out clearly the naturalistic basis of the cult, and its astrological connections. This mystery cult had its sacraments and required a high standard of morality, but it remained a syncretistic solar cult with a myth at its centre. Not only did it assimilate Babylonian astrology, but it was also more or less linked with the Magna Mater cult and its *taurobolium*, the process of re-birth by baptism in a bull's blood. Mithra was also associated with Anahita, who is regarded as an Iranian Ishtar.

Cumont, our outstanding authority on this instructive type of religion, explains[6] its popularity as due chiefly to (1) its active morality, (2) its promise of immortality, (3) the interpretation of life which this mystery-cult could offer to the more speculative. He ascribes the weakness

---

[1] Cumont, *op. cit.*, pp. 49, 89 (ed. 3).
[2] Mithraism contributes later on to Manichaeism (light *versus* darkness).
[3] J. H. Moulton, *Early Zoroastrianism*, p. 140.
[4] Cumont, *op. cit.*, p. 129.   [5] *Op. cit.*, p. 141.   [6] *Op. cit.*, pp. 149 ff.

K

which ultimately led to its defeat by Christianity as due to the substitution of a myth for the actuality of history, its syncretistic compromises, and its ultimately materialistic basis.[1] Such an analysis amply illustrates the general theme of this section, viz. the limitations of natureworship. However high the morality associated with such a cult, the naturalistic basis for this morality is not enough. To be sufficiently well-founded and to provide a satisfying and enduring revelation of the divine, the morality must spring from the character of the divine personality, as will be argued in the following chapter.

It is a striking fact that the only successful and permanent forms of monotheism are those that spring from prophetic reactions against nature-cults and from the resultant interpretations of history. The three great monotheistic religions—those of Judaism, Christianity and Islam—all go back with greater or less clarity of emphasis to the prophetic religion of Israel. On the purely historical data we seem warranted in saying that no other foundation has so far supported a revelation adequate to man's intelligence as well as able to elicit an emotional response. The Yahweh of the Old Testament was not a nature-god, though He was ultimately seen to control the nature He had created. His great prophets would suffer no compromise with the nature-cults of Canaan. In their work we see clearly the crucial issue between nature and spirit,[2] which perhaps every generation—and none more obviously than our own (1940)—has to face.

[1] *Op. cit.*, pp. 206 ff.
[2] Cf. Söderblom, *The Nature of Revelation*, pp. 57–68.

# CHAPTER VIII

## THE PSYCHICAL MEDIA

A S we have already seen, psychical elements are involved in all use of the physical media of revelation, as, indeed, in the implicit symbolism of language (Chapter III) and in all sense-perception. Here, however, we are thinking of those media of revelation in which the emphasis is primarily psychical, even though it may involve some participation of physical elements. In the case of the physical emphasis, it is the apparent objectivity of the media which is most obvious, e.g. in the taking of omens, or the casting of lots. There may be nothing in the physical event which is intrinsic to revelation; the peculiar use made of it depends on something extraneous, such as the prayer or sacred formula, or the use of already consecrated media. But in the psychical media now to be considered, such as the phenomena of "possession" by a demon or spirit, there is fuller scope for mystery—the *mysterium tremendum* which, according to Otto, characterizes the numinous, whether in its physical or psychical manifestations.[1]

§ 1. *Dreams.* Dreaming is so frequent an accompaniment of sleep—except, perhaps, in its deepest form—that it might be regarded as normal. Its content is so closely linked to, indeed so constituted by, the content of the waking consciousness, that in some aspects it might be regarded as a mere variation of this. But there are some

[2] *Das Heilige,* Chap. IV *et passim.*

features of the dream that set it apart, and account for the remarkable place given to dreams in certain forms of (psychical) divination, as well as for the influence of dreams in confirming, perhaps in suggesting, the existence of disembodied spirits. Sleep is itself mysterious; the temporary withdrawal of a man from all his waking activities leaves room for many conjectures as to what the more dynamic part of him may still be doing. His "soul" seems absent from the body on adventures of its own. Thus from ancient Indian thought we have the warning: "Let no one wake a man brusquely; for that is a matter difficult to be cured for him, if the soul find not its way back to him."[1] As a modern example, we may take Doughty's report: "All the Arabs reverence a man's sleeping; he is as it were in trance with God."[2] The man's own memories of his dreaming will confirm, if they did not originally suggest, such conceptions. His "soul" has visited places far removed in space from his body, and has escaped from the limits of present time; he has seen the dead as though they still lived, and the living where their bodies could not have been. This discovery of a new and "spiritual" world, lying around the familiar visible scene, must have been of profound importance for early thought and religion. We can easily see how obvious a means of divination or revelation this experience offered, especially when it was brought under the aegis of a deity by "incubation", the practice of sleeping in a temple, e.g. that of Asklepios, the chief Greek god of healing.  In the dreams of the sleeper it was believed that his illness might be diagnosed, and its cure prescribed, by the deity.  Here we have a point of contact with the modern science of psycho-therapy,[3] in

[1] Bṛihadāranyaka Upanishad, IV. iii. 14; quoted by A. A. Macdonell, "The Ancient Indian Conception of the Soul and its Future State", in *The Journal of Theological Studies*, I, p. 502 (1900).

[2] *Arabia Deserta*, I, 249.

[3] Cf. W. Brown, *Psychological Methods of Healing*, pp. 29–32.

which psychology replaces the ancient faith, with the
same curative aim in view.

Every reader of the Bible will recall the great place given
in it to dreams as media of revelation. To the heathen
Abimelech, Pharaoh, Nebuchadnezzar, as well as to the
Israelite Jacob and Joseph, divine revelations are given
in dreams,[1] whilst another Joseph, in the New Testament,
is directly guided by the same means.[2] We may suppose
that dreams are often intended where "visions" are named.[3]
Certainly, the dream and the vision are coupled together
as means of revelation: "If there be a prophet among you,
in visions do I make Myself known to him, in dreams
do I speak with him."[4] Future outpourings of the Spirit
will be marked by the dreaming of dreams and the seeing
of visions.[5] Before Saul resorted to "the witch of Endor"
he tried divination by dreams and by Urim (the sacred
lot) and by prophets.[6]

The dreamer of dreams may divine correctly, and yet
his divination is not to be accepted as evidence against
the true tradition of Yahweh-worship.[7] Jeremiah gives
to the dream a quite subordinate value, though he does
not reject it altogether: "The prophet that hath a dream,
let him tell a dream; and he that hath my word, let him
speak my word faithfully. What is the straw to the wheat?
saith Yahweh."[8] Both Koheleth and Sirach speak con-
temptuously of dreams,[9] and the dream supplies an obvious
metaphor or simile for transiency and delusion.[10]

[1] Gen. xx. 3, 6; xli. 1–15; Dan. ii. 1, 3; Gen. xxviii. 12; xxxvii. 5–10.
[2] Matt. i. 20; ii. 12 ff.
[3] E.g. Gen. xv, cf. verse 5 (the stars are shining); Acts ix. 10. Some
visions may belong, however, to the "trance" state (Acts x. 10: "ecstasy")
and belong to the next section.
[4] Num. xii. 6, see Gray's note in the *International Critical Commentary*,
*ad. loc.*
[5] Joel ii. 28.      [6] 1 Sam. xxviii. 6, 15.
[7] Deut. xiii. 1–3.      [8] Jer. xxiii. 28; cf. xxix. 8, 9.
[9] Eccles. v. 3, 7; Ecclus. xxxi. 1 f. (R.V. xxxiv. 1 f).
[10] Isa. xxix. 7, 8; Job xx. 8.

Modern psychology has removed dreams from their ancient role; they are seen to afford entrance into the "subliminal consciousness". Knowledge of this is important for psycho-therapy, and helps to explain the remarkable phenomena of telepathy.[1]   There is no doubt that dreaming can afford an intensification of consciousness, as in the nightmare on the one hand, or in Coleridge's creation of "Kubla Khan" on the other. Not a few would claim that a dream-experience can clarify some situation of the relevant waking life, and we are probably influenced in our waking conduct by our dream activity in ways often unrecognized.[2]   Those who believe in the fact of divine revelation by psychical means can hardly exclude dreams from this recognition, as a potential medium of knowledge. But this recognition of them will not be based on their abnormality, but on their (psychological) normality, and it will be subordinated very definitely to that revelation which may be given through the moral consciousness and through the higher personality. The general chaos and disorder of the dream-world puts it far below the clear daylight of the waking consciousness. At the best, the "subliminal" revealed by dreams can be only a back-door by which intimations of a world beyond man may reach him. "The real affinities of the subconscious are rather with our primitive instincts and animal nature than with our higher faculties. . . . If man is to respond to the voice of God with any effect he must do so as a conscious, free, and intelligent being."[3]

§ 2. *Ecstasy and Possession*. The term "ecstasy" is used very widely and loosely to cover abnormal mental states of many kinds, but originally and strictly the

[1] Cf. F. W. H. Myers, *Human Personality and its Survival of Bodily Death*, Chap. IV.

[2] I could give illustrations of both from my own experience.

[3] W. B. Selbie, *The Psychology of Religion*, p. 85.

Greek term (*ekstasis*) denotes a removal or displacement, in particular that of the soul from the body (cf. our English phrase "out of his senses"). Thus the term properly applies only to a psychology which sharply distinguishes the soul from the body, as in the Greek dualism. It ought not to be used of the phenomena of Hebrew prophecy, which is based on a very different psychology, viz that the "soul" (*nephesh*) is the animating principle of the body (the real personality) without any independent existence.[1] In the Greek usage, "ecstasy" and the corresponding verb (*existasthai*) denote a transient madness, madness being a permanent ecstasy.[2] In connection with inspiration and revelation the madman or the mentally abnormal person has figured largely, since a natural explanation of pathological phenomena (as indeed of disease in general) is to ascribe them to invasive spirits. So the idea of "ecstasy" may become the basis of that of "possession" by spirits other than that of the man affected. Thus contact with an external spirit-world is established, through which the knowledge of "revelation" may be gained. On the other hand, it is often thought that the soul of the affected person may itself travel into the spirit-world and bring back the desired knowledge.[3] This is the theory which underlies so much apocalyptic literature, though here it seems often to have become a literary convention. For the clearest example of such "journeys of the soul" we may turn to the "shamanism" of primitive peoples in Northern Asia, though similar phenomena are found in many other places. Among the Altai tribes (north-west of Mongolia)[4] the shaman is the priest linked

[1] See my essay on "Hebrew Psychology" in *The People and the Book*, ed. by A. S. Peake.

[2] E. Rohde, *Psyche*, II, 19, cf. 60, 61 (ed. 2). Rohde collects the most important Greek references in his footnotes.

[3] For this distinction, see E. Bevan, *Sibyls and Seers*, pp. 134 ff.

[4] The following statement is drawn from W. Radloff's classical description in *Aus Sibirien*, II, Ch. VI.

with the spirit-world through his ancestors, and possessing the family lore which enables him to use the inscribed tambourine, offer the necessary sacrifices, and use the prescribed formulas. By nature or art he is capable of abnormal conditions, and in his "ecstasy" his soul can travel into the unseen by means of the soul of the sacrificed horse. He begins by sitting on the representation of a goose and by flapping his arms like wings, then captures the soul of the horse with a halter, and simulates the movements of a captured wild horse. After the elaborately detailed sacrifice of the actual horse, and the proper use of the tambourine and much other ritual, he signifies that he has reached heaven by his imitations of thunder or lightning, and the "ecstatic" state is intensified. Finally he returns to himself and informs the bystanders as to what he has seen or heard during this journey of his soul—"everything that is related to man's life and therefore is desirable to hear, e.g. about the coming weather, about sicknesses and pestilences which threaten, or whether he has here encountered another Shaman, what he has heard from him or said to him, or he speaks of misfortunes which threaten neighbours, of sacrifices which the people of the district are to offer, etc."[1]

We could not have a clearer example than this of "ecstasy" proper, accompanied by the journeyings of the displaced soul into the spirit-realm, to ascertain some of its secrets. The primitive character of the conception is here apparent from its accompaniments, but the conception endures to far higher levels, as in the ecstasies of the mystic, the most familiar being that of St. Paul, caught up even to the third heaven unto Paradise, where he heard "unspeakable words, which it is not lawful for a man to utter".[2]

[1] *Op. cit.*, II, p. 41.
[2] 2 Cor. xii. 2–4. St. Paul shews the Hebraic affinities of his psycho-

For the other type—that of "possession"—the best-known example is that of the Delphic Oracle. According to the usually received accounts the Pythia (the priestess of Pytho, another name for Delphi) drank water from a sacred spring and sat upon a tripod placed over a cleft from which vapour was supposed to arise and to pass into her body.[1] This *pneuma* was credited with being the source of the "inspiration" by which the Pythia gave the "probably quite unintelligible" utterances[2] subsequently interpreted by the officials (*prophetai*) and by them (in the earlier period) put into hexameter verse. Thus Apollo, the god of the shrine, gave his answers to those who duly sought his guidance. This is an example of "inspiration" as distinct from "ecstasy" proper and of revelation by psychical media, whether or not physical stimuli were used.[3] We may contrast the shrine of Zeus at Dodona[4] where the response was given by the rustling of the leaves of the sacred oak-tree, which illustrates the use of physical media (Chapter VII).

The place taken by the "ecstatic" or the "possessed" in primitive forms of revelation is doubtless due to the mystery of the abnormal which gives it a numinous quality. Such an idea has survived even into Christianity, whether in the early regard for the "gift of tongues" as a proof of the presence of the Holy Spirit, or in the renewal of such phenomena in the Montanistic movement of the second century,

logy by not being sure whether the journey was made by the whole personality (in the body) or by the inner part of it ("apart from the body"), which would be true "ecstasy".

[1] See Chrysostom's realistic account, quoted in Bevan, *Sibyls and Seers*, p. 157.

[2] H. J. Rose, in the *Encyclopædia of Religion and Ethics*, IV, 798.

[3] Professor H. W. Parkes, in his recent book, *The Delphic Oracle* (1940), argues against the resort to physical stimuli; the report of them is due to the agnosticism of later theory (see Ch. III, "The Procedure of the Oracle"). Cf. *The Cambridge Companion to Greek Studies* (p. 423). "The tale of the cleft and its intoxicating vapour lacks early authority." (E. A. Gardner.)

[4] *Iliad*, XVI, 234 ff.

or some forms of modern "revivalism". The genuineness
of such phenomena is beyond question, however explicable
by psychology (rather than by theology) for the modern
mind.  The fascination of the bizarre and unusual as
evidence of religious truth is still a feature of popular
"religion", and we need to remember the quite subordinate
place to which the Apostle Paul reduced them at Corinth.[1]
That such phenomena had their useful place in what we
have called the "ministry" of error (Chapter II) need not
be doubted.   But their wide-spread occurrence throughout
the world, at a certain stage of development, shows that
they do not verify any one religion beyond others. They
are "cradles" for temporary use, which the growing child
will leave behind him. The best illustration of this may be
seen in the Old Testament, with its development of the
"true" prophet, whose message was authoritative by its
intrinsic quality, from the earlier *Nabi*, whose authority
depended on the abnormality of the conditions under which
he spoke.   This is so important for our subject that it
requires separate and more extended treatment.

§ 3.  *The Prophetic Consciousness of Israel.*  In the
temple of Solomon the innermost sanctuary was a dark
chamber, and an early Hebrew poem contrasts this darkness
in which Yahweh has promised to dwell with the brightness
of the sun He has set in the heavens.   In that spiritual
temple of Israel of which the prophets are the essential
builders, there is also a dark chamber as the Most Holy
Place, over which are the words, "Thus saith Yahweh".
If we could penetrate its mystery, we should know the
last secret of personal religion,

---

[1] 1 Cor. xiv. 19.   These "tongues" were unintelligible utterances needing interpretation by one skilled to give this (cf. verse 13 ff.); they are
not to be confused with speech in foreign languages, as in the account of
Pentecost (Acts ii. 4, 8), though similar phenomena underlie that narrative.

> "the breath
> Of God in man that warranteth
> The inmost utmost things of faith."

But however eagerly, like the victorious Roman, we enter that windowless room, we shall find the ultimate secret as elusive as it was to him. Our study of the prophets can shew us the experiences of those who believed they stood in the council of God, what ideas they held of themselves and of Him, what apparent characteristics distinguished them from others. This is the proper province of psychology—the psychology of the Hebrews in general and of the Hebrew prophets in particular. But, fascinating as such studies are, they are only preparatory to the real thing. In the last resort, we shall know as much or as little of the prophetic consciousness as is the degree to which we share its essential and central experience. The value-judgments we make of a prophet's message pass beyond psychology, and imply a metaphysic.

In regard to the psychology of the prophetic consciousness, we may conveniently begin with the conclusions of Skinner, in his *Prophecy and Religion*. He describes three features as characteristic of Hebrew prophecy, viz. (1) the prophets are conscious of being intermediaries between Yahweh and the nation of Israel; (2) they possess remarkable insight into the providential significance of contemporary political events; (3) their experience contains a sub-conscious element (appearing chiefly in the form of the vision) which is not experienced in normal life. It is the last characteristic with which we are concerned, and it is better to approach it from the standpoint of Hebrew psychology, rather than through the modern terms which Skinner employs when he says that the revelation "wells up from the hidden depths of his [the prophet's] being, and clothes itself in symbols before his inner eye".[1] The

[1] *Op. cit.*, p. 13.

central question for us is, what was there in the form of the prophetic consciousness which authenticated it to the prophet himself and to those who heard him? The answer is to be drawn partly from the psychological ideas which the prophet shared with all his contemporaries, and partly from the special experience which marked him out as a prophet, which it is better to call "abnormal", rather than "ecstatic", since it included many elements besides that of ecstasy proper, whilst "ecstasy" corresponds with Greek rather than with Hebrew psychology.[1]

There are three main ideas in the psychological beliefs of the Hebrews which distinguish them from those current to-day. (1) They ascribed life and all the phenomena of consciousness to a principle which they identified with the breath (*nephesh*). (2) They ascribed psychical functions to the body—not only to the special organs, such as the heart, kidneys, and bowels, but also to the peripheral organs, such as the eye, ear, tongue, hand, and even to the flesh and bones. This "diffused consciousness" and localization of function was the almost inevitable result of their ignorance of the function of the brain and nervous system, and the absence, in their belief, of any central organ controlling the rest, and corresponding to the brain in the popular belief of to-day. There is no word for brain in the Old Testament, and we may conjecture that if a Hebrew wished to refer to it, he would have used a phrase like the Syriac, "the marrow of the head". (3) They believed in an invasive, wind-like spirit (*ruach*), which accounted for anything abnormal in human character and conduct. Whilst this word, *ruach*, is used before and after the exile, of human energies, it does not seem to be used in any pre-exilic passage with psychical predicates. This is an important and frequently ignored fact; the clear inference is that *ruach* was not conceived as a normal

[1] See § 2, *ad init.*

element of personality in the earlier period, and that all
assertions of Hebrew "trichotomy" are swept away.
But have we the right to speak even of a Hebrew "dichotomy"? Hebrew psychology has been approached too
often under the influence of Greek dualism. The famous
verse in Genesis (ii. 7) does not say, as is often supposed,
that man consists of body and soul; it says that Yahweh
shaped man, earth from the ground, and then proceeded
to animate the inert figure with living breath blown into
his nostrils, so that man became a living *being*, which is
all that *nephesh* here means. The verse is thus precisely
parallel to the main conception of Ezekiel's vision of the
valley of dry bones. The slain men are re-formed, according
to the Hebrew ideas of physiology, bone fitted to bone,
sinews put on them, flesh, i.e. muscular tissue, brought up
on top, and then the outer skin drawn over the flesh.
The *ruach*, which is at once wind-like spirit, and spirit-like
wind, here replaces the blowing of Yahweh into the potter's
figure, as the source of new energy; perhaps Ezekiel has
had more to do with the later use of *ruach* as a synonym of
*nephesh* than we have recognized. But the important
thing here is the conception of man as body, not as soul
or spirit. The Hebrew idea of human personality is an
animated body, not an incarnated soul. It is in full
harmony with this that the characteristic Hebrew view of
life after death is resurrection, not the immortality of the
soul. It cannot be proved that the *repha'im* of Sheol are
ever called souls or spirits in the Old Testament. The
*nephesh* is simply an animating principle, which ceases to
be anything when it ceases to function. Man, as essentially
flesh, stands over against God who is essentially spirit,
different in substance, though alike in form.

These general psychological beliefs make the phenomena
of the prophetic consciousness much more intelligible.
The Hebrew prophet, who naturally shared them, did

not think of his ego as either "spiritual" or unitary. His
body was a complex of localized functions, and his body
was himself. Hebrew has no proper word for, and no
organic idea of, "body". *Nephesh*, the animating principle
of the body, is really a quasi-material aspect of its life.
The Hebrew prophet, then, had not to conceive of the
direct and complete displacement of his ego by the spirit
of Yahweh; it was enough that there were many parts of
himself which might come under Yahweh's control. Belief
in an invasive spirit made easy the recognition of Yahweh's
power; the actual impulse to speak in His name would be
instinctively located in the mouth, imagined to be under
His temporary control. Thus Isaiah and Jeremiah both
experience in their inaugural visions a cleansing or consecration of the mouth, as the organ of which Yahweh will
specially need to take possession. It needs an effort for
most of us to comprehend the phenomena of dual personality, such as appear to be described in Isaiah xxi; modern
popular thought starts with the assumption of the unity
of personality. But the Hebrew prophet started from the
other end, the divisibility of personality. Just as Elisha
restores life to the separate organs of the dead child by
contact of mouth with mouth, eye with eye, hand with
hand, so the prophet could believe that Yahweh gave new
capacity of vision to his eye, or of audition to his ear,
without in any way interfering with the rest of his bodily
powers. Because we have lifted the phenomena of
consciousness into the psychical realm, we have to invent
a whole new vocabulary of "subliminals" and "complexes"
to explain them. But the Hebrew had the equivalent of
all this on his own psycho-physical level, through the
localization of function in the members of the body. If
we realize this feature of Hebrew psychology, it does not
illuminate the phenomena of the prophetic consciousness
alone; it also helps us to understand the reference to the

offending eye or hand or foot in the New Testament (Mark ix. 43 f.), the Pauline parable of the body and its members (1 Cor. xii. 12 ff.), the Pauline doctrine of sin, as the invader of the psychically conceived flesh. Such a belief is not, of course, confined to the Hebrews. It under-lies the whole of primitive psychology, from the ideas of the savage who eats the tiger's heart to gain the tiger's strength and ferocity, to the remarks of Galen, in the second century A.D., that the bodily organs possess a certain power of reasoning, knowing the functions they have to fulfil, or indeed cease to be organs and become animals gifted with reason.[1] We may in fact say that what popular thought holds about the brain to-day, speaking of it quite wrongly as if it had the human con-sciousness inside it, the Hebrews believed about many other parts of the body. Consequently they were much more pre-disposed for the detachment of any one element in consciousness from the rest, and for the recognition of divine "inspiration", through such detachment, by the Spirit of Yahweh.

All that has been said refers to the normal and everyday experience of the Hebrew, before we begin to think of the peculiar experience of the prophet as such. The point so far urged is just this—that much which comes to us under the declaration, "Thus saith Yahweh", is really normal experience of the reflective or intuitive kind, interpreted unconsciously through the current psychology, and assigned to Yahweh, when the call to be a prophet has once been heard. On the other hand there was an abnormal element in the experience of the Hebrew prophets which marked them out from their fellows. The evidence for this is well-known, and has been emphasized by Hölscher in particular, in his *Die Profeten*. It is not likely that a prophet of the classical period would have dared to

[1] *Use of the Parts of the Body*, XIV. 5.

prophesy without an inaugural vision such as Isaiah's in the temple, or an audition such as Jeremiah's, or such a characteristically peculiar experience as that of Ezekiel, when he ate the roll written within and without with lamentations and mourning and woe, and found it sweet as honey in his mouth. Some such experience was as essential to the equipment of a prophet as a "sudden" conversion used to be to evangelicalism, or as episcopal ordination to an Anglican clergyman. Moreover, we may expect such experiences to recur from time to time, and our expectation is fulfilled. The strength of Yahweh's hand must have rested on Isaiah many times in his long career, and the vision of the valley of dry bones was as "objective" to Ezekiel as that of the storm-chariot which opens his book. There is real psychological truth in the words of a New Testament writer that "no prophecy was ever brought by the will of man",[1] and we have a good example of this in the fact that when Jeremiah was consulted by the survivors of the tragedy of Jerusalem as to their future plans, it was not until ten days had elapsed that the word of Yahweh came to the prophet (xlii. 7). We are fully justified by familiar data in assuming that the phenomena of primitive prophecy were to some extent continued in the experience of the canonical prophets, just as the early phenomena of the gift of tongues in the New Testament were continued in the personal experience of the Apostle Paul, who thanked God that he could speak with tongues more than all his readers.[2] Yet such a prophet as Isaiah shows implicitly what the Apostle Paul says explicitly, that his emphasis is not on these external signs at all, but on the ethical realities and spiritual interpretations of the Spirit's work. In both instances we are warranted in saying that what is at the centre of the primitive form has been pushed to the circumference of the later.

[1] 2 Peter i. 21 (R.V. mar.).                    [2] 1 Cor. xiv. 18.

In regard to the extent of this "abnormal" element
in Hebrew prophecy, there is naturally room for wide
difference of judgment. We have to make a liberal sub-
traction from our records for the work of commentators
and editors, and for the repetition of prophetic common-
places without new prophetic experience. As already
suggested, the general psychology of the Hebrews would
provide *for the Hebrew mind* the idea of extraneous origin
for many experiences which we should call normal, such as
the deliberations of Jeremiah with himself. There are, in
fact, many varieties in the experiences of divine communication, which range from what is usually called ecstatic
prophecy, of which Ezekiel's trances form an extreme
example, down to the plain and homely recognition of
divine truth which we find in Jeremiah's purchase of the
field at Anathoth—"Then I knew that this was the word
of Yahweh."[1] Next to such abnormal experiences as those
of Ezekiel we may place the series of visions recorded by
Amos, probably representing his call to prophecy in its
original form. The night-visions of Zechariah are probably
not dreams so much as products of the borderland between
sleep and waking, if we may judge from his own remark,
"the angel that talked with me came again, and waked
me, as a man that is wakened out of his sleep".[2] The
intense visualizations of this particular state are well
known to modern psychology, under the name of "hypna-
gogic and hypnopompic illusions".[3] Then we have an
example of the strong conviction that may slowly emerge
through conscious or sub-conscious reflection, in the fact
that Jeremiah is at first unable to reject the prophecy of
Hananiah, though he doubts its undue optimism; but
subsequently he is given the warrant, "Thus saith Yahweh",

---

[1] xxxii. 8.                                         [2] iv. 1.
[3] Cf. F. W. H. Myers, *Human Personality and its Survival of Bodily
Death*, I, 124, 125.

L

to deny Hananiah's message and to foretell his death.[1]
The infidelity of Hosea's wife and his reaction to it afford
another example of the way in which Yahweh's message
may come through the experience of life, rather than
through any necessarily abnormal psychosis.   Finally, we
may take that sense of enduring fellowship with God which
Jeremiah supremely enjoys, as sufficiently constituting
him God's interpreter, and warranting him in his "Thus
saith Yahweh".   It is important that we should recognize
this wide variety of divine communication, before we
commit ourselves to the statement that every "Thus saith
Yahweh" represents an abnormal or ecstatic experience.
The prophets Amos and Zechariah, for example, clearly
distinguish their visions from other divine communications
they have received.   Jeremiah's own distinction of the
forms of prophecy is a suggestive parallel to Paul's valua-
tion of spiritual gifts—the lower is not denied, but it is
distinguished as lower: "The prophet that hath a dream,
let him tell a dream; and he that hath my word, let him
speak my word faithfully."[2]   There is a parallel between
Jeremiah's prophetic consciousness and that ascribed to
Moses in Num. xii. 6 f.:—

> "If there be a prophet among you,
> In the vision I make myself known to him,
> In the dream I speak with him.
> Not so My servant Moses:
> In all My house he is found trustworthy.
> Mouth to mouth I speak with him,
> Plainly and not in riddles;
> And the form of Yahweh he beholds."[3]

We can agree with Skinner's general conclusion, when he
speaks of the great prophets of Israel in contrast with
more primitive prophecy: "Visions and auditions, mysterious inward promptings to speech and action, are still

---

[1] xxviii.                                         [2] xxiii. 28.
[3] Skinner's translation, *op. cit.*, p. 196.

a part of the prophet's experience; but the field of revelation is no longer confined to them alone. The *meaning* of the vision passes into the prophet's thinking, and becomes the nucleus of a comprehensive view of God and the world, from which spring ever fresh intuitions of truth and calls to duty" (p. 220).

Whatever be the degree to which we recognize this element, the general truth must be urged that it in no way detracts from either the psychological significance of the prophetic consciousness or the sanity and practical efficiency of these prophets. The best argument here would be a detailed study of modern parallels. We may take the case of William Blake as an extreme example of the visionary type, with the Sadhu Sundar Singh as an Eastern example of one to whom the quasi-ecstatic condition has become habitual, whilst the plain and homely Quaker, John Woolman, would shew that occasional visions and revelations may accompany the work of a zealous and practical reformer. Blake by temperament, and his wife by sympathy, lived in a world of visions, which he translated by pen and pencil, from the time that he saw a tree on Peckham Rye "filled with angels, bright angelic wings bespangling every bough like stars". He saw once a fairy's funeral at which the body of the dead fairy was carried on a rose-leaf. At his brother's death, he saw the released spirit ascend through the ceiling, clapping its hands for joy. He believed that the great men of the past, Moses and others, came to him and allowed him to draw their portraits. He writes, "I am under the direction of messengers from heaven, daily and nightly", whilst in regard to one of his poems he says that his own part was simply that of secretary. All this, most sincerely believed, went with a character of genuine religion and generous kindliness which deeply impressed those who knew him. The Sadhu, again, who began his Christian experience with a vision like that of Paul on the way to Damascus, united his mystical raptures with a life of devoted Christian evangelism. His description of an ecstasy is of interest: "Whenever I am alone, always something new comes to me, and that in a language without words; I feel surrounded, as it were, with a wonderful atmosphere, then something speaks in my heart, then I am in a state of Ecstasy. No words are spoken, but I see all pictured; in a moment problems are solved, easily and with pleasure, and with no burden to my brain."[1] This, though at first rare, became an everyday experience to him, and may suggest the kind of continued fellowship with Yahweh which Jeremiah seems to have enjoyed. The Sadhu says further: "It is a waking, not a dream state; I can think on it steadily" (*ib.*). John Woolman, a leader in the Quaker movement of the eighteenth century against slavery, combined with his practical philanthropy the capacity to see an objectivation of the "Inner Light":—[2]

"Going to bed about the time usual with me, I awoke in the night, and my meditations, as I lay, were on the goodness and mercy of the Lord, in a sense whereof my heart was contrited. After this, I went to sleep again; in a short time I awoke; it was yet dark, and no appearance of day or moonshine, and as I opened mine eyes I saw a light in my chamber, at the apparent distance of five feet, about nine inches in diameter, of a clear, easy brightness, and near its centre the most radiant. As I lay still, looking upon it without any surprise, words were spoken to my inward ear, which filled my whole inward man. They were not the effect of thought, nor of any conclusion in relation to the appearance, but as the language of the Holy One spoken in my mind. The words were, CERTAIN EVIDENCE OF DIVINE TRUTH. They were again repeated in the same manner, and then the light disappeared."

[1] *The Sadhu*, by Streeter and Appasamy, p. 133.
[2] *Journal*, IV, *ad init.*

Such examples as these, which might of course be multiplied to any extent, are enough to shew us that "abnormal" experiences are always possible to particular temperaments, particular countries, or particular stages of education. The distinction between the normal and the abnormal in psychology is in fact just as artificial and as temporary as that between the natural and the supernatural. The normal life is itself a useful selection for certain purposes from the very varied possibilities of spirit. But when we pass to an evaluation of prophecy, the distinction of normal and abnormal ceases to have any meaning for us, as indeed does any question relating to the *form* of prophecy, in contrast with its *content*.

Before, however, we turn to this side of our subject, there is one other feature of Hebrew psychology (in the wider sense) which must certainly have entered into both the normal and the abnormal prophetic consciousness, viz. the idea of corporate personality. The prophet was one able to identify himself with both man and God, being the eye of Israel turned to God,[1] and the mouth of Yahweh opened to Israel.[2] It is the effective union with both which makes him the focus of revelation and discovery (the two being one). The man who cries, "For the hurt of the daughter of my people am I hurt",[3] stands in Israel's place as her representative; the man who chants the "Song of the Vineyard"[4] stands in God's, as His. The closeness of this double identification is explained only when we remember such things as the story of Achan and of the slain descendants of Saul, the doom of toil and suffering which came upon the race because of the sin of Adam, the Levirate marriage law, and the songs of the Servant of Yahweh—all of them examples of the group, instead of the individual, as the unit. It is difficult for us, with

[1] Isa. xxix. 10.
[3] Jer. viii. 21.
[2] Jer. xv. 19.
[4] Isa. v.

centuries of individualism behind us, to recall the sense of social solidarity in its ancient form, though the psychological doctrine of "race-consciousness" in our own times is a parallel to some aspects of it. Corporate personality is also the psychological root of the particular form taken by the prophetic teaching—the emphasis on social morality. But there is a Godward, as well as a manward, application of corporate personality.[1] Partly because of our strong sense of personality as necessarily individual (which may be, as Lotze argued, a real defect in our knowledge of what personality is), we find it very difficult to conceive how a Hebrew prophet could stand in the place of God, and speak for Him with absolute conviction. As students of Hebrew prophecy we sometimes almost desiderate the Greek doctrine of immanence to explain some of the phenomena. But does not the explanation partly lie in this doctrine of corporate personality? To those who could conceive the merging of the individual in the family and the clan and the nation it must have been much easier for man's personality to be conceived as temporarily merged in that of God. The Hebrew never lost grip of his own personality along the Pantheistic lines of Hinduism. But there are other ways of conceiving the experienced union of man and God, and I believe that, unconsciously and implicitly, though none the less really, the sense of corporate representation figures in Hebrew prophecy as largely as in Hebrew law.

What is the value of the prophetic consciousness for revelation? So far, we have seen that the Hebrew prophet

[1] Professor N. W. Porteous, in his essay on "Prophecy" in *Record and Revelation* (edited by H. Wheeler Robinson), p. 240, prefers to follow Heschel (*Die Prophetie*) in speaking of the prophet's sympathy with the divine *pathos*. But the two ways of approach seem to me complementary, rather than antagonistic. I should rather say that the prophet's sympathy with God was intellectually mediated to him by the thought-form of corporate personality, here meaning (temporary) membership in Yahweh's council. (Cf. Isaiah's audition of "Who will go for us?")

ascribed to the contents of his own moral and religious consciousness an objective origin and value, and that he did this because they were authenticated to him as divine communications, either through his inability to explain normal experience as we do, or through what we should still call "abnormal" experience. To what degree, and why, should we share his belief, whilst unable to accept his reasons for it? for that is what the theological part of our subject amounts to. The nearest approach to an answer that the Old Testament affords is found in its supreme prophet, Jeremiah, and particularly in his distinction between true and false prophecy. Here, too, as in the former part of the subject, Skinner's analysis will be found useful as a starting-point. The false prophets, he believes, were survivors of the old patriotism, from which Elijah divorced religion. Prophecy was in the first place dependent on conformity with the event for its verification; but Deuteronomy introduces the further test of conformity with the national religion.[1] Jeremiah denounces the false prophets as men of immoral life who prophesied smooth things for gain, who stole their messages from others, used their tongues whilst claiming that Yahweh was using them, substituted lying dreams for genuine visions. The true prophet, on the other hand, has stood in the council of Yahweh, has heard His word, and is sent by Him.[2] The net result of all this is that there is no psychological test as between true and false prophecy, though Jeremiah ranks the vision higher than the dream, and the audition perhaps higher than the vision. The immediate test is purely moral, being drawn from the substance of the message, though the prophet claims for himself an inner certainty, which springs from his confidential relation to Yahweh, and is naturally incommunicable. We must not, of course, forget that the ultimate

[1] xiii.     [2] xxiii, 9 ff., cf. xiv. 14.

test for the prophet as for ourselves must be that harmony with "the universe of discourse" which makes the ultimate *differentia* between sense perception and sense illusion. No man believes forever against the facts of experience.

We are building, therefore, on a historical foundation, laid by the man who reached the supreme heights of Hebrew prophecy, when we say that it must stand or fall by its intrinsic worth, and not by the accidents of its delivery. Coleridge has given classic expression to this truth in modern times; speaking of the Bible as a whole, he says, "I have found words for my inmost thoughts, songs for my joy, utterances for my hidden griefs, and pleadings for my shame and feebleness. In short, whatever *finds* me bears witness for itself that it has proceeded from a Holy Spirit."[1] It is worthy of notice that that is really the continuous argument which underlies more superficial reasons for belief in divine inspiration, through all the generations. Origen[2] says in the third century practically what we have just found Coleridge saying in the nineteenth: "from his own emotions he will feel that these books were the composition of no human skill, nor of any mortal eloquence".[3]

What are the philosophical implicates of such an attitude, so far as the contents of the prophetic consciousness are concerned? Chiefly, these three: the validity of the value-judgments of morality, the personality of God, and the "actuality" of human history. These are key-positions for those who would maintain, with the author of the Epistle to the Hebrews, that God spoke in the prophets. In regard to the first, the validity of ethical value-judgments, we may see such judgments already exercised in the consciousness of Jeremiah himself. He has hardly given

[1] *Confessions of an Enquiring Spirit*, Letter I.

[2] *De Principiis*, IV. I. 6; cf. Moffatt, *Approach to the New Testament*, p. 103.

[3] Eng. trans. by F. Crombie, in *Ante-Nicene Christian Library*.

us anything more illuminating than the words addressed to him by Yahweh:[1] "If thou wilt bring out the precious from the worthless, as my mouth shalt thou be". The prophetic consciousness is here virtually analysed as a spiritual value-judgment, just as an educated Quaker of to-day might analyse a message of the Spirit. The realm in which the prophetic consciousness operates is, as we have seen, supremely that of moral truth. The Hebrew genius has contributed little to the aesthetic wealth of the world, beyond its religious lyrics; and its service in the realm of intellectual values, pure and simple, is of small account. But its supreme contribution is admittedly in the religious conception of morality, an achievement in which the great prophets take the foremost place. The prophetic consciousness shews that morality *is* religion, when it is morality and not mere convention. The compulsion felt by the prophets, however mediated by psychological phenomena, was ultimately the compulsion of the moral consciousness, interpreted naturally as the will of Yahweh. But that compulsion is not peculiar to them; it is the universal characteristic of personality, when it reaches a certain stage of development, or indeed, when personality emerges at all. Our ethical systems may differ widely in their interpretation of this compulsion, but they have all of them to face the "I ought" (or as the idealist may prefer to put it, the "I must") as the central problem of ethics. For the man who believes in God, there can be no simpler, and it may be reasonably contended, no more satisfying, explanation than that this moral compulsion is ultimately due to the pressure of Divine Spirit upon human spirit, the transcendence of Him who is also immanent in the human consciousness. It may be freely admitted that there are other important ways of describing this ethical experience, as when we

[1] xv. 19.

use the Greek category of the ideal for the Hebrew category
of law.  But that does not affect the main issue—that the
appeal of the Hebrew prophets is to universal values,
which we cannot ignore without robbing ourselves of the
most essential attribute of human personality, as well as
abandoning the supreme contribution to revelation (apart
from the Incarnation) which history affords.

That which has been said leads directly to the second
implicate—the existence of divine personality.  The moral
values are personal values—that is, they cannot be conceived except as belonging to persons, experienced by
persons, and in relation, at least ultimately, to persons.
But if, by their own compulsions and attractions, they
prove their own objectivity, dominating our moral achievements, and are always able to vindicate their authority
as something greater than our own creations, they must
exist outside our own consciousness, and that can be in
personality only, since they are personal values.  The
Hebrew prophet, of course, does not follow out such an
argument, which would have been foreign to his way of
thinking.  He accepts an already existent, and but
partially moralized, Yahweh, and credits Him with the
largest morality known to himself.  Yet our modern
argument from moral values to the idea of God does no
injustice to the ancient intuition.  Indeed, there is a sense
in which modern theism itself owes much more to the
Hebrew prophet than it always confesses.  The three
great theistic religions go back to the Hebrew prophetic
consciousness, and it is from them that philosophy is
forever drawing both content and stimulus.  There must
be a God to explain before explanation, or the attempt at
it, is worth while, and we owe to the prophets the beginnings of the only vital and religious conception of divine
personality.  The obvious anthropomorphism of their
conception of Yahweh raises no real difficulty.  All our

conceptions of God are anthropomorphic, though there may be different levels in our use of anthropomorphism. If the spirit of man is in any real sense derived from, and akin to, the Spirit of God, then anthropomorphism is the only valuable line of thought concerning God; we shall know Him only as the prophets of Israel did, by the highest in ourselves. Ethical experience and theological construction act and react on each other: "moral standards", it has been said, "at first embodied in persons, slowly work free, so that persons are judged by them"[1], as when it is asked, "Shall not the Judge of all the earth do right?" Nor, again, need we fear the criticism that the personal theism into which the Hebrew prophets initiate us is after all limited to its foundation in the ethical values, whilst the beautiful and the true, not less than the good, have their home in God. As long as we can maintain that the *moral* values of personality are, in our present stage of development, the most essential to its growth and well-being, so long will the almost exclusive emphasis of the Hebrew prophets be justified. Through other peoples, and in other ways, the larger wealth of divine personality has been or will be made known to us by Him who is not the God of the Hebrews only; but the revelation through them remains central. It would take us too far from our subject to consider the realization of all values in an eternal consciousness of which we may be part, or to follow out the hint as to the ultimate nature of God given by the prophetic assumption of corporate personality.

The third important implicate of the prophetic consciousness we may call the assertion of the actuality of human history.[2] The divine revelation which the Hebrew prophets claim to bring is indissolubly bound up with the

---

[1] Dewey and Tufts, *Ethics*, p. 97.
[2] On this, see the fuller statement in the Introduction, § 2, and the Index of this book.

course of Israel's history; from that history spring alike its intensities and its limitations. These men claim to bring the Eternal into the time-order; in doing that, they raise the profoundest and most enduring problem of all philosophy. The real cause of many of our modern difficulties is to be seen here. It does not worry us that we are bound to conceive God on a larger scale than did the Hebrew prophet, or that prophetic morality should not be exhaustive; but is there not something alien to the modern mind in the thought of this larger God as really concerned in the affairs of a petty state of the ancient world? If, on the other hand, we so conceive God as able to contain both this, and a myriad other kingdoms, does not the intense reality of social and individual life, as the prophet lived it, seem to become a pale and meaningless shadow, a Sheol world even on earth? Certainly, the actuality of life is the postulate of all Hebrew religion, from the reward of the good man in length of days to the Messianic kingdom to be established on earth. The symbolic actions of the prophets, which Wellhausen has so suggestively called "religious drama amongst the ancient Hebrews", express our problem in miniature. Did all this count for anything? Do the acts of men still really count, the acts of time, in some real if transformed sense, amongst the immensities of eternity?

No formulas will help us here, though there are many. There is hardly a subtler or more comprehensive question than this, and perhaps the only answer to it is the venture of faith we all make by going on living. The Hebrew prophets made that venture as intensely as any group of men known to history, and that is part of the secret of their service to posterity. If, moreover, we feel how difficult it is to relate the time-series to a timeless God, we must remember that it is just as difficult to relate the empirical ego in each of us to the timeless ego; perhaps it is only in such communion with God as the prophetic consciousness exhibits that the relation is achieved. It is significant that Professor Hocking, in his study of *The Meaning of God in Human Experience* (p. 485 f.), should have turned from all other religious phenomena to those of prophetic consciousness, to find the typical assertion of this truth. "Of all fields of human creation," he writes, "that of the historic deed exhibits at its best this continuous descent of the idea into the particular. . . . By the prophetic consciousness I do not mean a knowledge that something is going to happen in the future, accomplished by forces beyond myself: I mean a knowledge that this act of mine which I now utter is to succeed and hold its place in history" (pp. 484, 503). I think that his challenging use of the phrase, "the prophetic consciousness", to describe the assertion of the actuality of human life, is amply justified by its best example. Hebrew prophecy is revelation, because it is actualization—true to God, because so true to man.

# CHAPTER IX

## HISTORY AND REVELATION

HISTORY, which gathers into its own unities both the physical and psychical media of revelation, forms the third realm in which the knowledge of God has been sought, and, as the Christian believes, found. In this chapter, we shall consider the general nature of historical revelation, reserving for the next chapter that particular form of it which belongs to the Christian faith.

The map and the dictionary are the chief tools of the historian. With these he works on the documents which are his material. The map represents the fundamental conditions in which begins every part of the history of mankind upon this earth. The map shows three great factors operating in succession—the hills, the rivers and the roads, the hills which decide where the rivers shall run, and the roads which are prescribed by the hills and the rivers. To read the map aright is to know the climatic conditions, the economic characteristics, and the whole material environment. On the other hand, the dictionary represents what may be called, in the largest sense of the phrase, the spiritual conditions of history. The dictionary is a book of words, and words mean both speech and the thought behind speech. The dictionary unlocks the historic documents in which the speech and the thought of other generations are enshrined. The essential test of the historian is that he can use with accuracy and with judgment the map and the dictionary, and so deal faithfully with the material and the spiritual conditions of human history.

Within the realm of history all the great religions have come into being, and their features always betray the place of their origin and the stage of spiritual culture at which they were born. The nature-worship and many gods of the Vedic hymns belong as essentially to the India of ten centuries before Christ as do the hatred of idols and the stern monotheism of Islam to the Arabia of the seventh century after Christ. The emphasis may fall on the material conditions, so that the gods represent heaven and earth and sky and sun and wind and storm and fire, as in the Vedic hymns; or it may fall on the moral consciousness of man, as in the higher Semitic religions. Ultimately the two can never be wholly separated, any more than a man's body and soul; material conceptions are spiritualized, and spiritual ideas may be materialized. All through the history of religions we may trace this constant interplay in the two factors. However varied be the material which is presented to the human consciousness, the mind of man is always striving to make a unity of it, which is the only condition of living with it and comprehending it. Man's mind is like a kaleidoscope. The jumbled fragments of coloured glass without pattern or meaning are given beauty and significance by the mirrors of the mind.

§ 1. *The Activity of God in History.* But can we go beyond man's mind to a greater, and believe that somehow and somewhere history can be the revelation of God? Is there any truth in the claim of the Time Spirit in Goethe's *Faust*:—

"Thus on the roaring loom of time I ply,
And weave for God the garment thou seest Him by?"

Certainly the product of the loom of time is not an ordered and complete pattern, but a very tangled web. There is much in history to exalt the conception of the human race. There are fine heroisms, noble sacrifices of self, patient and passionate loyalties, creations of beauty, achievements of thought, which seem not unworthy to be regarded as revealing God. But there are dark patches, ugly blemishes, in the story both of the individual and of the race, that seem to contradict any suggestion of God. Here history resembles Nature. What are we to make of *her* utter disregard of human desires, her relentless pursuit of ends beyond the individual, her heartrending catastrophes? If there be a God who has made and who upholds all this, is He handling an intractable material which He is not able to control? Has He established laws and forces with which He can no longer interfere? The theist would reply that God, in creating nature, has accepted certain conditions of His own devising, that He works by a multitude of secondary causes, and that nature may have ends and issues far beyond man's immediate comfort, though controlled to man's ultimate good. There is a parallel here with human history. There is much in both that seems to contradict any assertion of that divine activity which is implied in revelation. We cannot rationalize history. But if the human will counts for anything at all, and if God, who has created it, has chosen to accept its free activity within the limits He has appointed, then we shall have an explanation of many things in history that seem to deny God. We may still believe that the whole of history will be a full and adequate revelation of the divine purpose, but the end is not yet, and we may well find that some parts and stages of the history will reveal God more or less than others, just because another will than God's is being allowed to operate.

But "revelation" in religion means something much more definite than such general reflection of the divine in physical nature and in the course of human history. In the great religions which have maintained their dominion over man's heart and mind, revelation means that direct and purposive activity of God which discloses Him to man for man's good. Beyond man's search for God in physical nature or in the moral consciousness of man, there has arisen the great conception of God seeking man, and seeking him in more especial ways. Amongst the living religions, we find the doctrine of special revelation in Judaism and its historic successors, Christianity and Islam. We find it also in the religion of Zarathushtra, still alive amongst the Parsees, though much more obscurity rests on the beginnings of this religion. We find it also in the Bhakti development of Hinduism, with its thought of divine Avataras or incarnations, such as that of Krishna in the Bhagavadgita. The original Buddhism knew nothing of revelation, for the Buddha had no place for the gods in his teaching; but the subsequent development of Buddhism included many divine revealers and saviours. It is clear that no religion which is to retain the faith of men can dispense with the belief in divine revelation—the activity of the divine for man's good; that is one of the plain lessons of history. No god is worth worshipping who is unable or unwilling to help his worshippers, and that help, to be effective, implies a revelation of the divine nature and purpose. But not all of these religions of revelation can be called historical religions, in the sense of finding the revelation of God in human history. The Bhakti devotion of Hinduism or the ethical culture of Buddhism has little or no concern with history; the exact place and teaching of Zarathushtra are too little known to yield much for our purpose, which is the relation of revelation to history. We are left, then,

M

with Judaism, Christianity and Islam, as the religions
which can be called historical in the full sense, that is as
claiming to have received a divine revelation on the basis
of history.   The religions of the further East do not link
history and revelation; they are *in* history, but not *of* it.

§ 2.  *The Prophet in History*.   The first thing that must
strike us when we examine these religions of revelation,
Judaism, Christianity and Islam, is that they all go back
to the consciousness of a prophet, Moses, Jesus, Muhammad.   They are born within the experience of an individual
man, and they illustrate some well-known words of
Professor Whitehead: "Religion is what the individual
does with his own solitariness. . . . The great religious conceptions which haunt the imaginations of civilized mankind
are scenes of solitariness: Prometheus chained to his rock,
Mahomet brooding in the desert, the meditations of the
Buddha, the solitary Man on the Cross."[1]   The three great
founders of the three religions that concern us speak and
act under the sense of a divine compulsion.   They all
bear the marks of their historic environment; we cannot
interchange them; they belong to the human race in one
particular land and at one particular time.   Yet each of
them claims to speak and act, not for himself, but for God,
and history has so far confirmed their claim that what
they thought and did still remains central in the devotion
of many millions of the human race.   True, much which
has been ascribed to them by later generations is removed
to that later date by the touch of sane and sober historical
criticism.   Moses was a prophet who led Israel out of
Egypt, and interpreted that deliverance as the act of God;
his work was continued by many later prophets, and issued
at long last in a sacred book, which is an epitome of the
whole development, rather than a record of the teaching

[1] *Religion in the Making*, pp. 16, 19, 20.

of Moses.  Jesus, whatever else He was or is, was known
as the prophet of Nazareth, and the record of His life and
work in the Synoptic Gospels is much less elaborate than
the conception of Him which prevails in any of the Christian
Churches.  Muhammad, in the early years of the seventh
century after Christ, witnessed to his sincerity as the
prophet of Allah by the persecution he faced, before he
became a shrewd politician and a worldly-wise statesman,
whose sayings and doings themselves became an additional
revelation of Allah.  All these religions begin in a prophetic
consciousness.  What is the significance of this for revelation?

The significance is that man has found his highest and
most influential ideas of God through the highest category
of human experience, which is personality, and through
personality wrought to the highest intensity of conviction.
Just as, from ages immemorial, men have climbed the
mountain top to build the shrines for their offerings to the
gods of heaven, so in the spiritual realm, the highest point
of human nature has become the most effective contact
with God.  By no means every religion has done this.
Some religions all the time, and all religions some of the
time, have resorted to the lowest, rather than the highest.
They have tried to control God by the material means of
magical spells; they have sought exaltation by the intoxication of the Soma plant or by the sensual orgies of fertility
cults; they have claimed to fetter God to an institution or
to an organized society. But the theistic religions in their
origin, and at every recovery of the original breath of divine
inspiration, have turned to the highest experience of a
spiritual nature to hear what the Lord God would say
unto men. This is the mark of the prophets of Israel
denouncing idolatry and sensuality and social injustice, and
claiming that God speaks through the moral consciousness
of men rather than through the ritual of the living or the

mutterings of the dead.  How could an idol of even the costliest metal adequately represent God?  How could anything but the noblest testimony of the most enlightened conscience?  So Jesus in the Sermon on the Mount carried the great issues of morality and religion into the inner consciousness of the heart, and bade the man with hate against his brother leave his gift unoffered to God.  So did Jesus, when from the Cross He made forgiveness of the most cruel wrong the divinest thing in human history.  So also Muhammad, in spite of all his later compromises, when he denounced the idolatries of his contemporaries, and inspired men to deeds of the highest courage.

We are then faced by the fact that behind the sacred books of the three great types of monotheistic religion there is a prophetic consciousness, that is, a human will believing itself to be in such contact with God that its purposes are His, and that His will is revealed through it. This is the most important fact, and the *modus operandi* of the conviction is subsidiary to it.  The intermediary may be an angel, as for Muhammad and for some of the later prophets of Israel, such as Zechariah.  The condition may be an "ecstatic" state, as in the call of Isaiah or the abnormalities of the prophet Ezekiel.  At the highest there may be the direct consciousness of fellowship with God, as in the troubled dialogues of the prophet Jeremiah, or the untroubled consciousness of the prophet of Nazareth. These differences belong to the psychology of prophecy,[1] and though they are intensely interesting, they are secondary to the main conviction that human nature is capable of receiving the revelation of the divine.  This can be true only if there is a certain kinship between God and man, so that what is true for man at his highest is also true for God, with all the necessary limitations of historical

[1] See Chapter VIII, § 3.

conditions. This may be called the higher anthropomorphism, and all religion ultimately rests upon it. We have a simple example of it in the words of Jesus, "If ye then, being evil, know how to give good gifts unto your children, how much more shall your Father which is in heaven give good gifts to them that ask Him?" If, in our desire to exalt God, we make Him the "altogether Other", we leave it impossible for Him to communicate with man. However transcendent God is, the point at which He reveals Himself to us must be a point at which He becomes intelligible to us, that is, a point at which there is kinship between His nature and ours. This is a principle which some theologies have ignored or denied, notably the present-day Barthianism.[1]

But, if we grant this kinship, how are we to conceive the working of the divine inspiration within the prophetic consciousness? It is not enough to think of man's discovery, we have also to think of God's revelation, that is, of God's activity in bringing the prophet into truth, or truth into the prophet. Here, as in all genuine religious experience, we must refrain from putting asunder what God has joined together. When we try to analyse the convictions of a prophet, we must not forget that we are conducting a post-mortem, whereas the living experience is always a unity, in which the prophet forgets himself in God. We who come after may trace this or that line of the prophet's preparation, this or that endowment of his nature, this or that relation to his fellows, all of which are implied in the ultimate word of God which issues from his lips. But the essential thing for him and for religion is

---

[1] E.g. Barth (in opposition to Brunner), *The Doctrine of the Word of God* (Eng. trs.), p. 273: "the humanity and personality of sinful man simply cannot signify conformity with God, a point of contact with the Word of God. In this sense, as a possibility for God proper to man *qua* creature, the 'image of God' is not only, as we say, with the exception of some remnants ruined, but annihilated."

that all this is welded together into a hammer of God, as the prophet Jeremiah calls the word given to him. One of the most significant sayings about prophecy is that of Jeremiah himself when he is most depressed by the sense of abandonment and failure. God says to him, "If thou bring forth the precious from the common, thou shalt be as my mouth." This means that the highest he knows and feels is to be God's word to him and to his fellows. We find the same sense of unity everywhere when religion is most intense. Within Islam, we find a Sufi poem, quoted by Söderblom,[1] in which one who is tempted to doubt God like Jeremiah receives the message:—

> "O much-tried one,
> Did not I engage thee to my service?
> Did not I engage thee to call upon me?
> That calling 'Allah' of thine was my 'here am I',
> And that pain and longing and ardour of thine, my messenger;
> Thy struggles and strivings for assistance
> Were my attractions and originated thy prayer."

"Be comforted", is the divine word to Pascal, "thou wouldst not seek Me, if thou hadst not found Me."[2] But the highest expression of this unity of the human consciousness with the divine is that of Jesus: "All things have been delivered unto Me of My Father: and no one knoweth the Son, save the Father; neither doth any know the Father, save the Son, and he to whomsoever the Son willeth to reveal Him. Come unto Me, all ye that labour and are heavy laden, and I will give you rest." Thus at the "Land's End" of human experience we have the intuition that man's conviction *is* God's revelation.

§ 3. *The Actuality of History as Revelation.* Effective revelation includes teaching. The true teacher does not

---

[1] *The Living God*, p. 31.
[2] *Pensées*, II, 341 (Ed. Faugère, 1844).

simply or chiefly impart information to his pupils; he trains and inspires them in the art of discovery. He will direct their studies in the library or the laboratory, but certainly not by dictation. He will start them on some pursuit, and leave them free, within certain limits, to work out their own results. Somewhat in this way we may conceive God's activity to be exercised in all that leads up to revelation, though its consummation is always a disclosure of Himself. Within the little circle of our life we are free, but that circle is always part of a larger circle which overlays it, the circle of the divine purpose, directing, controlling, and so creating. There is no more room for mere dictation in God's revealing activity than in the work of a true teacher, who thinks more, far more, of the training of his pupil than of the communication of knowledge.

If revelation is not mechanical, neither is the true knowledge of history. This is not the mere accumulation of what we call facts; they are only its raw material. We cannot write or even comprehend history till we relate these data to one another, and trace their connections. There is something more in history than the study of cause and effect which underlies all the physical sciences. In such study we never get back to a real cause, but only to that which is an effect of some other cause. But in human history we are brought face to face with real causes, however limited their operation. The human will in great things or small is continually making history. We can never foresee its action in the same way as we can that of an acid upon a salt or of the sun upon a planet. The human will is continually making new beginnings. It creates something that was not there before. The spiritual world is not ruled by the laws of the physical world, though it has its own laws. Human activity is like the creative work of the artist. There is a whole world of difference

between his vision of beauty and the actual creation out
of it of some beautiful thing, whether it be a picture or
sculpture or symphony or poem.  Existence in thought is
one thing; existence in act and fact quite another.  Our
wills are constantly influenced by our thoughts, yet not
wholly determined by them.  So long as we are human
beings we have the power and the responsibility of choice.
No one doubts it in normal life, however difficult it may
be to explain it.  Indeed, it cannot be explained, except
by saying that personality has this power of taking up all
motives, desires, influences into itself and making them,
if it will, its own.  This is the experience of that inner
world, strange, mysterious, unique, which each of us makes
for himself.  But the great world of human history, with
all its social ramifications, is the same thing writ large.
We may isolate a single factor, such as the economic, and
usefully show its range and influence.  We may trace
back the French Revolution, for example, to the misrule
of generations, to the teaching of Rousseau, to the state of
Europe, but we must still leave room for the personal
activity of Marat and Danton and Robespierre and the
rest.  In the whole course of history something good or
bad is being created by personal agents, never to be
reduced to physical causes.  This is what we have called the
actuality of history, its quality of adding something new,
or of expressing in a new way that which before existed
only in idea.  The time-process, in which we are all agents,
and not mere puppets, is the partial and confused working
out of an eternal purpose, adding to it no new idea, but
giving to that purpose the quality of the actual.  Our
inner consciousness of being real agents is a true indication
of the reality of the whole.

It is surely significant that this quality of actuality has
been taken up into the three great monotheistic religions,
which are all based on a historical revelation, that is, a

revelation through real agents, who give actuality to the divine thought. The Old Testament is full of this; the God of Israel is known by what He does in history, as in the deliverance of Israel from Egypt. The New Testament is written round the life and death and resurrection of Jesus, which are interpreted as acts of God. Islam's creed is not simply, "There is no God but Allah", but also "Muhammad is the prophet of Allah", which brings the Moslem faith into the definite circumstances of history, and turns history into revelation. But history is active revelation only if time be more than the shadow of eternity, and an actual part of it, with a specific quality and a new value with which to enrich it.

It is significant also that the very conception of universal history, as we understand it, has been born of these great religions. It was Christianity that first taught the Western world the unity of the race, and the conception of a purpose working itself out in history. But Christianity learnt that truth from the Old Testament, from the apocalyptists such as Daniel, whose ideas go back to the prophets of Israel, who interpreted contemporary history in terms of a divine purpose. It is to Biblical religion that we owe both the modern conception of personality and the modern conception of the history in which that personality works out its destiny. We cannot reduce that history to the rational process which Hegel attempted to construe. But we can see how revelation interprets history and history becomes the actualization of revelation. We cannot successfully and completely join up and splice together the meeting of the human and the divine, either in the individual consciousness or in the history of the race. But we can see that history has meaning and spiritual value only as we do succeed in discovering within it both the human and the divine, and our discovery is made by what religion calls revelation, the high points of religious genius which

catch the light of dawn whilst the valleys are yet in the
twilight.

§ 4. *The Authority of Revelation in History.*   So far we
have been considering revelation purely on the basis of
history, without regard to the specific claims which it may
have upon us as being truth.   But we must now face this
difficult and thorny question of authority in regard to a
revelation through history.   The very fact that we have
gone behind the sacred books and the sacred societies to
the history from which they sprang, compels us to ask
what authority can attach to history when it is conceived
as the medium of revelation.   Lessing, it will be remembered, epitomized the movement of the German Aufklärung
by saying "contingent truths of history can never be made
the proof for necessary truths of reason".   Yet religion is
certainly never exhausted by the intellect, since it always
appeals to the whole of personality, with its emotional and
volitional capacities.   As a matter of fact, the thoughts
of religion have always been gained through some historic
personality in a given environment; the actuality of history
comes first, and reason comes in to interpret the rationality
of what history has given.

We must distinguish two different kinds of difficulty
which history occasions for revelation.   There is the
philosophical difficulty, which is indeed the great difficulty
of philosophy itself—how can the relative reveal the
absolute, and time become the vehicle of eternity?   Then
there is the historical difficulty in regard to historicity—
how can we ever be sufficiently sure of alleged historic
"facts" to make them the basis of religious conviction?

As to the first, all that can be said here is that if we
start with a dualism between time and eternity, we can
never hope to throw a bridge across the gulf.[1]   If the

[1] See Introduction, § 5.

eternal is the timeless, altogether different and alien from the time-process in which we live, then there can be as little relation between them as there is between God and man, if *they* are supposed to have no spiritual kinship with each other. But it is not necessary to start with such a dualism. The very view of history with which we have been working is that it is included in the eternal, that it is one form or aspect of the eternal. We need not think of eternity as unending time, or as simultaneity in which all time is gathered up into a single moment. We can think of eternity in the light of those moral and spiritual qualities which are our highest values in history, namely, in terms of purpose. We can believe that when we catch a glimpse of some true and worthy purpose being worked out here, still more when our own purpose is caught up into it, we are in touch with the eternal world. And this we must believe, if we are not to rob history of its spiritual values. The great claim of duty upon man, for example, is never explicable on the merely human level; it must come from something or someone above time, even whilst it is experienced within time.

From this standpoint, then, there is no reason to believe that what the prophets of Israel taught about their own land and people is not also eternal truth, and so qualified to belong to a divine revelation. Such truth will always be relative in form to its own age; we have no right to assume that the ethics of Amos or even of Jesus are directly applicable, as they stand, to every generation. But when they are seen as the temporal application of the eternal principle of the right relation of one human personality to others, when they are taken as the illustrations of an eternal truth in process of revelation, they can claim divine authority over us, as revealing eternal truth to us. If we deny this, we are simply denying that eternity can ever have intercourse with time.

The other difficulty as to the certainty of alleged facts of history is more difficult to meet, and perhaps it is impossible to meet it at all in any purely intellectual fashion. The thoughtful Christian of to-day often looks back with regret to his uninstructed days, when he perhaps felt no difficulty about the historicity of the Virgin Birth or the Resurrection or the other miracles associated with Jesus. We cannot hope ever to prove or disprove such things by the mere rules of historical evidence, and they never really were so proved or disproved. Our attitude towards them will be decided by more general considerations, such as the ways of thinking of a generation different from our own, which saw miracles where we should find other explanations, or the possibilities of a Personality admittedly unique amongst the sons of men, and of new powers emerging in him which are not seen in ordinary men. But what would be the value of a religious faith which was no more than intellectual assent to the conclusion of an argument? It might still leave the will of man unmoved, still be utterly fruitless in moral or religious result. All we can ask is that there be sufficient evidence to make belief reasonable, sufficient data for the eternal truths to gleam through the muddy vesture of our documents. The very lack of complete historical proof in certain cases may constitute a moral challenge; are we making the intellectual uncertainty an excuse for thrusting aside the related moral or religious appeal? The historian himself must often state a conviction which he cannot prove on the ground of precise evidence. The Christian also says, "I accept this death on the Cross and even this deliverance from death as essentially true, though I cannot understand its mode and manner; the influence of this faith on all subsequent history makes it impossible for me to think it historically untrue, and my own experience confirms history."

But this, it may be objected, is to remove revelation from the common ground of evidence and reason, and to make its appeal purely subjective, a matter of individual likes and dislikes. Certainly, part of the truth of revelation, part of its evidence, does consist in such an appeal to the individual. In the strict sense of revelation, it has not revealed God until it has made me see Him and won me to loyal obedience and trust. Dr. Edwyn Bevan concludes his skilful and eminently just sketch of the history of Christianity[1] with the words:—"the impulse to believe itself must come, if it comes at all, from the direct perception that a particular kind of life is the life most worth living. For those who have it the perception is a supernatural call—which, according as they will, they may follow or they may refuse". Our argument has been that this is of the very nature of religion at its highest, that it neither desires to, nor can, constrain men into an unwilling obedience, and that the training of the believer into a service which is perfect liberty is far other than a dictation of orders. If this be so, it is useless to compare the great religions as a mere spectator of them, and to expect to be able to prove that any one of them has absolute authority. When Festus wished to explain the faith of his prisoner Paul to King Agrippa, he could sum it up neatly in a sentence. He said that the Jews "had certain questions against him of their own religion, and of one Jesus, who was dead, whom Paul affirmed to be alive".[2] That is what it meant to the mere spectator—"one Jesus who was dead, whom Paul affirmed to be alive." But how much that affirmed fact meant to Paul himself, standing within the Christian faith! It is no longer a mere isolated event of history. Phrase after phrase of the apostle's burning speech leaps into mind as we try to

---

[1] *Christianity*, in "The Home University Library".
[2] Acts xxv. 19.

measure what *he* meant by affirming that Christ still lives —
"declared to be the Son of God with power, according to
the spirit of holiness, by the resurrection from the dead—
that I may know Him and the power of His resurrection,
and the fellowship of His sufferings, becoming conformed
unto His death—ye died and your life is hid with Christ
in God—I live, and yet no longer I, but Christ liveth in
me". That is how the bare formula of a faith glows and
quivers with iridescent light when we know it from within.

One thing we can claim for the Christian religion amongst
the faiths of history, even whilst we look on it from without.
At the centre of its alleged revelation there stands a man
unique in quality, standing in a unique relation to it, and
offering a unique Gospel. We cannot compare Jesus as a
mere figure of history with Zarathushtra or Buddha or
Socrates or Muhammad; none of them claims or holds the
same relation to God or man. The teaching of Jesus is
indeed largely parallel with that of the best of the Jewish
Rabbis; but Jesus, living and dying, is far more in Himself
than they. The Gospel, also, which springs from His
historic life on earth, is unlike any other offered to men.
Its peculiar quality has been admirably summarized by
Karl Holl: "Jesus inverts, as we may say, the customary
relations of religion and morality. Every other religion,
at least every other religion of high ideals, bases the
personal relation to God on the right conduct of man.
The more moral a man is—the term 'moral' being
understood in the widest sense, so as to include ritual
duties—the nearer he stands to God. But, for Jesus, God
begins the other way round. It is He who creates
something new with forgiveness. From this there springs
a real, close and warm relation to God, and with it, at
the same time, a morality which can venture to take God
Himself as its pattern."[1]

[1] *Urchristentum und Religionsgeschichte*, p. 22.

That is what is meant by the grace of God in Christ, and He actualized it in history by His whole attitude towards men. The revelation of this truth is pre-eminently the Christian revelation, and all else is subsidiary to this. The fact that this revelation came into history at a particular point of time, which for us lies in an ancient and remote world, casts no reflection on its eternal truth. In these days, we are not likely to claim, as did some of the Victorians, that history inevitably moves onward and upward by the constant evolution of something better, always leaving behind its own past. That is not true of civilization, or art or music or philosophy or any of the spiritual sides of man's nature, even if it were true of the material. In all spiritual achievements, and most of all in religion, we rise above the time-process, even whilst we work through it. History itself is the tribunal by which all such claims must at last be tried. In a wider sense than for Newman, "Securus judicat orbis terrarum", or for Hegel, "Die Weltgeschichte ist das Weltgericht".[1]

We may recall Lessing's moving parable of the three rings in *Nathan der Weise.* In a certain family a magic ring was handed down as an heirloom from father to son. It was to be given to the best beloved, and it had the power to make its wearer beloved of God and man. A father who had three sons could not decide which he loved best, so he had two other rings made exactly like the ring of power, and gave one to each of the three. After his death, they were inclined to quarrel as to which had the original ring, and they referred the matter to a wise judge, claiming that

[1] The actual words are Schiller's (*Resignation*) as Canon Peter Green points out in reviewing the first edition. That the history of the world is the judgment of the world is, of course, true only on a long view of history. Dr. Edwyn Bevan, in the composite volume called *The Kingdom of God and History* (ed. J. H. Oldham), pp. 59 ff., warns us of its untruth on short views. But he who believes in the God of history must surely hold that God will ultimately vindicate Himself in this sphere, as in every other.

each had received his ring from his father's hand. The
judge pointed out that the ring of power would itself
decide the issue in the course of time, for the most loving
and beloved would be its wearer.. Lessing has in mind
those three religions of revelation, Judaism, Christianity
and Islam, with which we have been chiefly concerned.
He does not mean that it is a matter of indifference which
men choose, and that conduct is all that matters. He does
mean, however, that the final proof of doctrine is in life,
which is exactly what we ought to expect from a revelation
made through life.

At the other extreme is the parable of Anatole France[1]
about the king who desired in his youth to possess a survey
of universal history, that he might learn its lessons. At the
end of twenty years his learned men brought him a dozen
camels, each bearing five hundred volumes, but the busy
king said, "Kindly abridge." After long periods they
brought smaller and smaller editions, till at last the
secretary brought a single fat volume—to find the aged
king on his deathbed. The old man sighed, "I shall
die without knowing the history of mankind." "Your
majesty," said the scholar, "I will summarize it for you
in three words: *They were born, they suffered, they died.*"

It is revelation, and the faith in revelation which makes
the difference between those two views of human history.
In countless ways, often unrecognized, the Christian
revelation has influenced man's outlook on life, and, not
least, his interpretation of history. To recognize history
as the medium of revelation at a particular point commits
us to a new view of history altogether.[2]

[1] *Les Opinions de M. Jérôme Coignard*, pp. 197–200.
[2] E.g. such as was outlined in the Introduction, which summed up the
axioms of a Christian interpretation of history.

# CHAPTER X

## THE CHRISTIAN REVELATION

PREVIOUS chapters have tried to show that all we know, or can know, of God is derived from what He has done in physical nature and in human history, and from that God-guided response to it in our consciousness which constitutes "Christian experience". There is an immanent presence and activity of the transcendent God within the whole natural order, which reveals Him as working through a multitude of secondary causes, veiling His direct activity from our eyes, and apparently often regardless of our individual lives and interests. There is a providential control of history, less easy to recognize, because it is crossed by the working of rebellious human wills, but able to subordinate them ultimately to the divine purpose. There is the constant activity of the Spirit of God, present in every human consciousness from its birth to its fullest surrender to God, yet again veiled by apparent identification with individual thought, feeling, desire, will, so that all seems our own, though it be God's. Along each of these lines, and the products or deposits which mark their course—-the order and beauty of the natural world, the traditions and institutions of history, the inner intensifications of ourselves which show us what we are or can be[1]—we may learn something of God from His initiative and activity. In fact, the revelation is always more or less blended through the convergence of

---

[1] Cf. W. James, *Letters*, I, p. 109. "At such moments there is a voice inside which speaks and says: '*This* is the real me!'"

these three lines into the unity of experience.    As Professor
A. E. Taylor remarks, "There are not really two water-
tight compartments of the historical process, a 'physical'
sphere and a 'mental' sphere; there is the one concrete
given process with its mental and physical elements
interrelated and interacting."[1]

For the Christian this revelation through history culminates in the historical Person and Work of Jesus Christ.
We are justified in using the word "culminates" of a
group of events embedded in history, and having a sequel
in other events, because we are speaking of spiritual
values, known through and in the temporal, but constituted
by their kinship with the eternal.    The culmination is
qualitative; the highest Alp is not necessarily on the far
horizon.    If Jesus Christ does indeed rise so high above
the rest of mankind as the Christian faith in Him implies,
the exact point of time at which He emerges is of secondary
importance.[2]    The fulness of the time for His coming
depends on the vital and intimate relation of His Person
and Work to all the factors of history, past, present and
future.    It is this relation, not the temporal occasion of it,
which is central to our theme.    His life, death and resurrection must not be viewed in isolation as a Barthian bolt
from the blue, any more than they can be explained as
purely human events.    They belong to two orders, the
human and the divine, the temporal and the eternal.
Yet they have the unity of a single life and work.    Our
approach to their interpretation is necessarily through the
human to the divine.    But it is of the essence of our
argument to remember that the human adds something to
the divine which is revealed through it—that actuality of
human life which is so much more than a category of

[1] *The Faith of a Moralist*, II, 169.
[2] On this point, see the excellent remarks of H. G. Wood, *Christianity
and the Nature of History*, pp. 154–56, already cited (p. xlvi).

thought,[1] or even than a mere symbol and shadow of the eternal.

In this chapter, then, we shall consider the revelation through history in its specifically Christian interest, and this, more especially, from the "evangelical" standpoint of Protestantism. Other approaches to the common faith of Christendom are, of course, possible and complementary, but, if they are to have much value, they should be made by those who live within the tradition they undertake to expound.

The theology of classical Protestantism has been sufficiently characterized by its historian, Otto Ritschl, as controlled by four chief factors, or "courts of appeal", viz. the supremacy of Scripture, on which all the Reformers were agreed, the centrality of "saving faith", especially amongst the Lutherans, whilst the Reformed Church more or less subordinated this to the doctrine of election, the reference to the œcumenical creeds of the early Church, and the validity of human reason in general. It is instructive to notice the modifications of these theological positions which are represented in modern evangelicalism. The doctrine of the supremacy of Scripture, as the only rule of faith and life, has been profoundly affected by literary and historical criticism, and by the comparative study of religions. It is still maintained, but virtually on the ground that the Bible is the source-book rather than the text-book of Christian doctrine, the sufficiently accurate record of a religious experience which is normative and authoritative. Similarly, the emphasis on saving faith is continued in the demand for an individual and intelligent reception of the Gospel as constitutive of full fellowship in the Church; but the psychological study of Christian experience has thrown into prominence the subjective factors of a personal response to Christ, and has seemed to

[1] Cf. Taylor, *op. cit.*, II, p. 166.

offer an alternative explanation of conversion. In regard to the œcumenical creeds, these would still be accepted in substance by most evangelicals, but there would be found amongst the Free Churches a general disavowal of any formal authority belonging to them. Finally, the appeal to the validity of human reason, which is implied in such a theological structure as Calvinism (of course in strict subordination to the supremacy of Scripture), has been both weakened and broadened. There is much less confidence in human ability to construct a systematic theology, but there is a much wider recognition of other human values, e.g. the sociological, as belonging to the Kingdom of God.

All these changes conspire to make it difficult for the educated evangelical to formulate a clear and convincing doctrine of revelation. He cannot take refuge in an impossible theory of verbal inspiration, though he may be as convinced as ever that God is revealed in and through the Scriptures. He cannot appeal simply to the evidential value of Christian experience, for that appeal itself implies an interpretation of psychologically conditioned phenomena. The Christian consensus of faith is likely to be much less convincing in the light of historical and comparative study, whilst the authority of the Church is moral rather than intellectual, and is for him in any case subordinate. He believes that God is revealed in many ways of useful activity beyond the Church, but it is not easy to correlate these different realms whilst preserving the central significance of the revelation through Jesus Christ, who has no direct relation to these other values. There seems no way out of these difficulties, except by a more searching analysis of what is implied in assuming a revelation through history, for it is in that assumption that these difficulties are brought to a point.

Evangelical faith claims to be a direct personal response to a historical revelation of God in Jesus Christ. Directly we try to state that in philosophical terms, we see that we are faced by what may be called the cardinal problem of all philosophy, the relation of time and eternity. A historical revelation means a revelation temporarily conditioned, which means, at least *prima facie*, that its eternal values are no longer present as such, but only as represented through temporal equivalents. How, in particular, can the transcendence of God be represented in forms of immanence? The moral beauty of Jesus Christ may sufficiently represent the character of God, but how can any human life, least of all a life that ends with a Cross, establish the triumphant transcendence of God? Yet that is precisely what Christian faith affirms, and is essentially concerned to affirm, on the ground of the historical revelation. In some sense, the immanent must be also the transcendent. This is the philosophical theme of which the Christian doctrines may be called theological variations. The doctrine of the Incarnation is applied philosophy, working on the data of the Christian experience of Christ. The unending endeavour to correlate the divine and the human in Jesus Christ is the concrete handling, in a particular instance, of the problem of time and eternity, and is worthy of at least as much respect. The problem becomes central in the doctrine of revelation, and any doctrine of revelation will be at least an implicit claim to offer a solution of it. Is it irrational to suggest that such a doctrine, if we could state it adequately, would itself be the real solution of the philosophical problem? We cannot hope to bring the eternal into the temporal by any intellectual scheme that could presume to comprehend both in a larger unity; but Christian faith projects the temporal into the eternal and ultimately rests on an epistemology of its own.

§ 1. *The Actuality of the Historical Data.*   The starting-point for any enquiry into the validity of such a claim is obviously in the actual historical happenings.   By the actuality of the history is here meant, in the first place, the assumption that certain events more or less faithfully recorded in the Old and New Testaments did occur, and that we may gain a sufficiently accurate knowledge of them by a critical use of the relevant documents.   Modern criticism of the Bible has done this immeasurable service to a doctrine of revelation—that it has driven us back behind the literature to the life, and within the life to those psychical factors which are of the essence of true history. In the Old Testament such criticism has thrown into prominence the consciousness of the prophets of Israel as central in formative influence on the history.   That influence was modified in many ways, as by the compromise with the cult which issued in Jewish legalism, by the use of devotional forms which created our present Book of Psalms, by ethical applications seen in the Wisdom literature, by adaptation to new needs seen in apocalyptic. But the prophetic consciousness is essentially the interpretation of contemporary history by the light of faith in the God of Israel as morally active.   We cannot understand the contribution of the prophets if we divorce them from the happenings of their own times.   They bring their own intuition of moral values to bear on the careers of conquerors, the ambition of statesmen, the rise and fall of empires.   They find in the migration of Bedouin tribes from Egypt the evidence of the redeeming activity of God, and they find in the deportation of Israelites to Babylon the not less clear evidence of the punitive activity of God, vindicating His moral order.   The events themselves are, of course, capable of other explanations, but this was theirs, and their interpretation became itself a new event of far-reaching consequence for the subsequent history.

Through the actuality of their interpretation of other actualities, God was revealed to their contemporaries and successors. It is not otherwise when we pass to the New Testament, with its central experience of a filial consciousness which continues on a higher level the prophetic consciousness of the Old Testament. In the central figure of Jesus, that filial consciousness is directly shaped and conditioned by external events. Within the limited range of His public life we see Him accepting a ministry of a particular kind, addressing Himself directly to the needs of His contemporaries, accepting as the will of God His Father the destiny which His own moral passion thrust upon Him, and apparently interpreting His own death as a new event of deep significance for God and man. The principle is precisely the same—the transformation of the event into a new fact by a new interpretation of it. All this is continued in the reproduced and secondary filial consciousness of His disciples. The whole theology of Paul may be regarded as an elaborate re-interpretation of the Cross of Christ, in order to mediate Christ's filial consciousness in the form of "adoption" into sonship. That theology, in turn, becomes a new constitutive event in the Bible history, and a new starting-point of alleged "revelation". It is, indeed impossible to speak of bare events at all; even the Synoptic Gospels are an interpretation of Him who lived to die, and died to live.

We may trace the same interrelation of faith and event down to any present experience of the Christian revelation, and indeed, we must so trace it, in order to grasp the meaning of revelation for evangelical faith. The reaction of such faith is in principle the same whether it be directed towards the naively conceived figure of Jesus in the untutored mind or the critically sifted reconstruction of the scholar. There is an event, or rather a series of events, and there is an interpretative reaction to the events.

The events themselves, no more now than in the first century, carry on their face their inevitable interpretation. Even though, as read in the Bible or presented by a Christian preacher, they are accompanied by such an interpretation, they enforce no inevitable conviction of their truth *as revelation*.   It is of vital importance for the understanding of our subject that we try to see the precise point at which a man's relation to Jesus Christ becomes evangelical faith, and so gives the renewed actuality of revelation.   Face to face with the Jesus of history, he may be moved to compassion at the sight of such suffering, physical and spiritual; to indignation, because it was unmerited; to admiration, because it was so bravely borne; to wonder, that human nature could issue in so fine and beautiful a thing as this self-forgetful, self-surrendering love for man and God.   He may even go so far as to try to build his own life on this pattern, and to take its principles for his own.   All that is deeply significant, and of very real value; but it is not yet evangelical faith.   It does not meet those needs of the human heart in all generations which are its deepest needs—the sense of moral impotence, when in the grip of evil habit, hated even while continued, the sense of guilt before God, vaguely or clearly felt, the sense of alienation from other men, whom it is a duty to serve, the sense of insecurity and helplessness before poverty, sickness, death.   All these are expressions of one fundamental need—to discover some sufficient Power at the heart of things, able and willing to deliver from the inner captivity, the outer alienation, the constant dependence on happenings over which there can be no human control.   In other words, man's deepest need is for God, such a God as the God and Father of Jesus Christ, and such a personality as that of Jesus Himself, linking the human to the divine, with the immanent become the transcendent.   This is the cardinal point in the intuition of evangelical faith—the recognition in loving trust that this Jesus is the same yesterday, to-day and forever, and that He is God manifest in the flesh, that His love is the love of God at the very heart of the universe, no longer overthrown by the world, but triumphing over it. This act of trust and grateful love, which interprets the actuality of the events as the sufficient evidence of God entering human history, is the essential moment in the intuition of evangelical faith. It is reached by no merely historical evidence and by no merely rational inference. The Christian explanation of such an intuition is that it comes by the Spirit of God, which is the theological way of saying that God is present, and therefore active, to the believer through his experience of Christ. Such an explanation, which frankly resorts to the divine as the direct ground of the human experience, may seem to some the Achilles-heel of the argument. But it is an essential part of the argument, and is consciously such to Christian faith. No explanation can indeed be given why in presence of the historical facts some respond with this act of faith and some do not, except the previous moral development. But there is a partial parallel in the different realm of æsthetic value-judgments, though the moral element is there much less prominent. In both cases, we may refer to the influences of training and environment which undoubtedly condition the ultimate attitude. But in neither case do they lead to something inevitable; if we could guarantee the result of Christian education, it would be the denial of that very freedom and moral responsibility which is one of the chief prerogatives of human personality. Christian faith is the free response of the human personality in its full unity to the disclosure of divine personality in Christ.

§ 2. *The Godward Significance of the History (Redemption).*

We cannot, therefore, wholly rationalize the act of faith, or be content to define it as "an act of the intellect under the command or direction of the will".[1] But we may recognize within it the conviction that there is a Godward significance in the history, and see that this is essential to the very nature of evangelical faith. This comprehensive conviction underlies the whole view of history taken in the Bible, and makes it, in a very special sense, historical revelation. God is known by His activities, and the history ideally written would be the convincing declaration of those activities. In this conviction the Jew and the Christian are one; the difference between them is that the Christian finds special values in certain parts and aspects of the continuous history which the Bible records. What does this mean, when we try to give it a philosophical statement? We must not diminish the actuality of the history on its human side, any more than did the prophets of the Old and the apostles of the New Testament. Cyrus pursues the course of his ambitions undisturbed by any thought of Yahweh's "I gird thee, and thou dost not know me".[2] Peter says to the Jews of Jerusalem, "Ye killed the Prince of life . . . in ignorance ye did it, as did also your rulers, but the things which God foreshewed by the mouth of all the prophets, that His Christ should suffer, He thus fulfilled."[3] The Biblical interpretation of the human acts claims for them a superadded significance for God. The human volition is taken up into the divine, without thereby losing its human actuality. However difficult it may be for us to deal with the time-honoured problem of responsible human activity within the will of God, we must not evade it by shifting our point of view,

---

[1] St. Thomas, *Summa Theologica*, II, ii. q. i ff., as summarized by M. C. D'Arcy in *The Nature of Belief*, p. 302, though it should also be remembered that for St. Thomas grace takes possession of the root-unity of the soul below the distinction into intellect and will (q. vi).

[2] Isa. xlv. 5.                    [3] Acts iii. 15–18.

and treating the human simply as the working out of a
foregone conclusion. That would be to rob human life of
all real significance, whereas we want to find out its
significance for God, whilst admitting its significance for
man. The working solution of Christian theism is, of
course, to conceive that by an act of self-limitation God
has given a real though limited freedom to men, always
within the sphere of His own activity. If this view be
taken, then we must ascribe to the actuality of human
history a real significance for God, at least not less than it
has for the human agents of it. If it adds nothing to the
range of His purpose, creates no thought that is not
already His, introduces no risk for His universe, whatever
risk it may involve for the individual finite will, yet it
must add something of vital significance to Him, in order
to be part of His purpose. We seem to be in presence of
a category of actuality,[1] not reducible to thought, not
identical with the idea, though its scheme is contained
within the idea. A new *depth* of being seems to be added
to the thoughts of God when they are actualized through
human wills. Perhaps we may get a useful suggestion of
what this means from the analogy of the artist. Between
his vision of beauty and his creation of the beautiful there
is the difference of actuality. By his acceptance of the
limitations of his medium, he is enabled to add a quality
to his vision that was not there before, though he may
have added nothing to the vision itself which was not his
from the beginning. Thus Quintilian says of the statue
of the Olympian Zeus by Phidias that "its beauty seems
to have added something even to the traditional religion".[2]
Of course, the analogy breaks down in one respect when
applied to God, whose thoughts as willed must be identical

---

[1] See Introduction, § 2.

[2] XII. x. 9 "cuius pulchritudo adiecisse aliquid etiam receptae religioni
videtur". I owe the reference to *Jew and Greek: Tutors unto Christ*, by
G. H. C. Macgregor and A. C. Purdy (1936), p. 207.

with His activities.   But may we not conceive the significance of history to God as comprehensively consisting in
this quality of actuality which He calls into being through
the limiting medium of human wills freely exercised?   If
we look at history in that way, we may escape one of the
great perils of theology—the substitution of fictions for
facts in regard to God.   We rule out theories of "docetism"
and "acceptilation".   We say that the events which have
a real meaning for us have a not less real meaning for
God, though we have to express that meaning in anthropomorphic terms which we know to be inadequate.

It is then the assertion by faith of this significance for
God which gives to the facts of the Gospel history their
significance for man as revelation, and conditions the
content of that revelation.   There is first of all the vision
of God's purpose in human history, the glimpse of God at
work in the making of human souls, the disclosure of the
kind of soul He is making, the goal of the society of human
souls which He is constituting, whether this be seen in His
handling of His prophets or of His Son.   There is the
emergence of God as manifest in the flesh through that
Son, the divine initiative and all that it implies for human
hopes.   There are the achieved values of the process as
well as of the goal, the achieved values seen supremely in
the Son Himself.   There is the transformation of the moral
evil of the world into the occasions of divine grace, of
which the Cross of Christ becomes the supreme example,
and the prophecy of a like transformation of all moral
evil, which must lie at the heart of the doctrine of the
Atonement.   Central and comprehensive of all this activity
is the actuality of the love of God, the sacrificial love
which accepts suffering due to sin and by its acceptance
transforms it into a medium for revealing grace.   That
suffering is the joy of God, since it is the spontaneous
outflow of His own nature as sacrificial love into the

actuality of human history. Here is the pivotal fact for evangelical faith, which awakens its ideal response of grateful and loyal obedience. There may be a hundred ways of describing the quality and function of God's suffering love, but its fundamental category is *actuality*.

§ 3. *The Manward Significance of the History* (*Revelation*). The actualization of God's redemptive love in Christ itself constitutes the revelation of that love, and it is proclaimed to men in the Christian Gospel. In the Pauline interpretation of that Gospel, it is the good news of an accomplished deed, which has changed the relation of men to God before they hear of it. This emphasis may be clearly seen in Paul's consciousness of himself as an "ambassador" on behalf of Christ.[1] He says that he is in the grasp of Christ's love for man, that through the actualization of this love God was reconciling the world unto Himself and that the declaration of this to man is "the word of reconciliation", primarily because of what God has done. Such reconciliation on the human side is simply and solely in the act of faith, whatever moral consequences may flow from it; on the divine side, it is through what God has done in Christ. So, in the first paragraph of Luther's *Commentary on Galatians* we read: "In my heart this one article reigneth, even the faith of Christ."

This living and active presence of God in Christ to Christian faith is essential to the conception of revelation. The Word of God as recorded in Scripture or preached by the evangelist is not conceived simply as a word about God; it is a sacramental means by which God the Holy Spirit makes Himself present to faith. Human words are always a body animated by the more or less of vital truth they derive from the speaker and the hearer. The marvellous power they can exert is not in themselves, but in the

[1] 2 Cor. v. 20.

contact they make between mind and mind.   In the early
days of wireless, a lady said to Marconi, "How wonderful
this wireless is!"   "Not half so wonderful", he rightly
replied, "as the fact that you and I are talking now."   An
intelligible word spoken to me brings my mind and personality into contact with another, and is sacramental through
his informing spirit.   If the other be God, then the Word
of God is sacramental to His Spirit; it becomes one of His
acts, however many human links there may be in the
chain.   This is another way of stating the doctrine of the
*testimonium spiritus sancti internum.*   As Calvin puts it,
"The Word itself is not fully certain to us unless confirmed
by the witness of the Spirit. . . . God sent the same Spirit,
by whose virtue He had administered the Word, to complete His own work by the effective confirmation of the
Word".[1]   It is only as we recognize this Real Presence of
God in the Word, the immediacy of His contact with us in
it, that justice can be done to the place given to the Word
of God, that is the Gospel, in the evangelical tradition.
It controls the theory of worship, which is the recognition
of the worth of God as known by His Word.   The sacraments proper are themselves forms of the Word, acts
which preach Christ.   The Church is constituted by the
reception of the Word and exists to proclaim it.   No
doubt the differences of ecclesiastical type here suggested
are those of emphasis rather than principle, and all
Christian Churches share more or less in these as in other
conceptions already noticed.   But the only justification
for the large place given by the evangelical to the sermon
in public worship is his theory that the Word of God, the
ideal subject of the sermon, is the most effective means of
arousing the spirit into recognition of the worth of God.

It is this sacramental conception of the Word of God
which also justifies us in speaking of the universality, the

[1] *Institutio*, I, ix. 3.

finality and the authority of revelation. Here we can speak in less general terms than those of the previous chapter. If the declaration of God's acts in the past can be infused with spiritual power so as to make present contact between God and man, it becomes a new act of God, with limitless powers of continuity and adaptation to new needs. Surely, no small part of the difficulty often felt as to the fitness of historical happenings to be the medium of divine revelation springs from the neglect of this essential principle. Think of Jesus Christ simply as a figure of the past, with all the inevitable limitations of the conditions in which he lived, and it is difficult or impossible to conceive a permanent and universal relation between that isolated figure of history and the soul of mankind. But if God be present in the Word which re-presents Christ, if the Holy Spirit can make use of that Word, there is a virtual escape from the temporal limitations, which indeed become themselves sacramental. It has been said of Christ that "At every step of His life He let loose another secret of God's love." (Robert Barbour). That is not the unbridled rhetoric of the preacher, if we allow the eternal to have anything at all to do with the temporal. It seems to be one of the qualities of Spirit that it must always be embodied in that which is lower than itself in the scale of reality; we know nothing of disembodied spirit. Yet in the communion of spirits, even of finite spirits, we transcend the bodily conditions which made that communion possible. The historical circumstances of the revelation are similarly transcended in man's fellowship with God, without any loss of their original actuality. Jesus Christ is the same yesterday, to-day and for ever because the God we know in Him is the same. But the constant necessity to re-interpret the primary events of revelation, to relate them to new needs, is the very condition of the active *presence*

of God.  The inevitable element of subjectivity, which
seems at first sight a weakness in the evangelical doctrine
of revelation, is the way by which the warmth of actuality
and the ever-renewed adaptation of God's revelation is
made ours.

But how far may it be claimed that such a revelation
as we have in Jesus Christ can be exhaustive of human
values, or sufficiently comprehensive of them to be final?
It is obvious that no historical appreciation of the Gospel
can read into it the values of all the ancient world, to say
nothing of the modern; nor are we prepared to-day to take
a negative attitude towards those values.  Yet it does not
seem necessary to trace the whole of the divine revelation
to Jesus Christ; all that the evangelical Christian is
concerned to maintain is the supremacy of the values for
which He stands.  Those are admittedly the ethical, and
in the broadest sense of the term, the ethical values are
the universal and dominating values of life.  To say that
the Christian faith should be concerned with them in the
first place, and only secondarily with the intellectual and
æsthetic aspects of life, is not simply an act of piety to its
historical origins in both the Old and New Testaments; it
is also the implicit recognition that the social relation of
person with person, which issues in morality, is the most
vital and comprehensive factor in human life, and therefore
stands in closest relation to the comprehensive universality
of the Christian faith.

The ultimate authority of revelation, on such a presentation as this, must clearly be intrinsic.[1]  Whatever place
be given to the formative and classical experience of the
Bible, or to the pedagogic and disciplinary guidance of
the Church, their authority is that of the light of the moon,
a reflection of the sun's.  The intrinsic authority of the

[1] Cf. what was said on this point in the latter part of the previous
chapter, as well as in the Introduction.

Word, however, does not lie in its intellectual or æsthetic qualities, or simply in its moral appeal; these it has or may have, but they are all the conditions of something else— the presence of the God whose nature and purpose are revealed in the Word. It is the nature of God which is the only final authority in all truth, and the Word of God is authoritative because it testifies to that nature and convinces of the truth of Christ through the power of His present Spirit, who is Himself.

In this attempt to expound the concept of revelation for evangelical experience, the key-word has been "actuality"—the actuality of what God has wrought through the freedom of human personality, and supremely through the personality of Jesus Christ. But it is impossible to separate "revelation" in the Christian sense from "redemption", for which the key-word is, as we shall see in Part III, "transformation". It is the abuse of that freedom that has prevented the whole course of human history from being a perfect revelation of God in its own order. But the abuse which the theologian calls "sin" has itself the quality of actuality,[1] and as such its consequences have been wrought into the working out of God's purpose by that transformation which is the prerogative of spiritual beings, divine or human.[2] Sin has been made the supreme occasion of grace, by God's attitude towards it. Human penitence is the transforming attitude on the human side, bringing man to God's side, with something of God's vision of moral evil. The transformation of one actuality into another belongs to the essence of redemption and of the Gospel which declares it.

In one of England's southern counties there is a height commanding a noble landscape, which bears the sinister name of "Gibbet Hill". The site of the

[1] See Chapter IV.
[2] This is more fully explained in Chapter XIII, § 4.

O

ancient gallows is marked by a cross bearing on the four sides of its supporting column these four happily chosen phrases: *In obitu pax, post obitum salus, post tenebras lux, in luce spes.*  As I read them one day in the bright sunshine, I felt anew the transforming power of the Gospel, and I sat down to read the penitential psalms with a renewed consciousness of the meaning of divine redemption.  The transformation of that grim spot by its new monument was the actualized echo of the transformation wrought on Calvary, and the prophecy of that final transformation of meanings which is the supreme form of actuality for spiritual beings.  For them the ultimate fact will always be the *meaning* of the event, and that truth is the basis of an illimitable hope.

# PART III

# THE FACT OF REDEMPTION

XI. THE REDEEMER

XII. THE MEANING OF REDEMPTION

XIII. THE REDEMPTIVE SUFFERING

XIV. THE REDEEMED

# CHAPTER XI

## THE REDEEMER[1]

§ 1. *THE Suffering Messiah*. The title, "Messiah" (Christ), is the first distinctive category in order of time to be applied to Jesus. Its significance for our purpose is twofold. On the one hand, it linked His Person and Work with the actuality of history, and enabled Him to take a definite place, however erroneously conceived, in the conceptions of Jews and of Jewish Christians. On the other hand, it was capable of such transformation in His own consciousness, and in the Gospel of the early Church, as to bring out the idea of a suffering Redeemer.

"We preach a Messiah who has been crucified", said the apostle Paul,[2] and the context shows his full awareness that this is a paradox, a stumbling-block (*scandalon*)[3] to the Jew and folly to the Greek. The "folly" can be illustrated from what the apologists say of their opponents: "Herein they declare our madness, that we give a second place next to the unchangeable and ever-existent God, the Creator of all things, to a man who was crucified."[4] The "scandal" lay in declaring a condemned criminal to

---

[1] The scale of this book does not allow of a longer discussion of Christology than this chapter contains, but perhaps enough has been said to indicate the outline of one, in relation to the general theme. The method adopted has been to take successively the six titles or descriptions of Christ most important for our subject.

[2] 1 Cor. i. 22; this seems to be the force of the perfect participle following the noun.

[3] Cf. Gal. v. 11.

[4] Justin, *Apol.* I, 13; cf. Lietzmann (*Handbuch zum Neuen Testament*) on 1 Cor. i. 22, where other parallels are given.

be the anointed of God, who should redeem Israel, so replacing Moses and the Torah by Jesus and the Cross. It had been a "scandal" for St. Paul himself, until his vision of the risen Jesus convinced him that this was indeed the Messiah of God.[1] So he had come to accept the preaching of the apostles before him, and to recognize with them the Old Testament basis for a crucified Messiah—"the things which God foreshewed by the mouth of all the prophets, that His Messiah should suffer."[2]

But the paradox had already been accepted by Jesus Himself. It would now be generally admitted by New Testament scholars that the Messianic consciousness is a necessary element in His own interpretation of His life. True, He seems to have had little use for the "Davidic" form, a typical example of which may be seen in the Messianic expectation of the Psalms of Solomon (xvii. 23 ff.). From His temptation onwards, He turns aside from a kingship of this earth. In reply to the challenge of the high priest, "Art thou the Messiah, the Son of the Blessed?", His affirmative answer shews affinity with the other, transcendent form of Messianic expectation, found in the apocryphal and pseudepigraphical literature, and notably in the Similitudes of Enoch.[3] But, accepting the form, He transformed the content of Messianic belief, by interpreting His Messiahship in the light of the Suffering Servant of Isaiah liii.[4] This interpretation may begin with His baptism; it becomes explicit only after Cæsarea Philippi, when Peter's confession acknowledges Him as Messiah. From that point onwards He seeks to lead His disciples

[1] Cf. Rom. i. 3, 4, 1 Cor. xv. 8, Gal. i. 15, 16, and the narratives of his conversion in Acts.

[2] Acts iii. 18.

[3] Mark xiv. 61, 62: cf. Enoch xlvi. 1 ff., 4 Esdras xiii. 1 ff.

[4] For details, see *The Cross of the Servant*, by H. Wheeler Robinson, pp. 66 ff.

into the idea of a *suffering* Messiah, the mission to which He had dedicated Himself, and which He fulfilled in His Passion.

It is no exaggeration to say that this is the most original and daring of all the characteristic features of the teaching of Jesus, and it led to the most important element in His work. There has been no success in all the endeavours made to find previous or contemporary identification of the Messiah with the suffering servant of Yahweh.[1] The Targum of Jonathan for Isaiah liii. does give a Messianic application to some parts of the chapter, but, by a most artificial ingenuity, ascribes all the suffering to the people, not to its Messiah. This is very significant for the main line of tradition. There is no evidence of a suffering Messiah in previous or contemporary Judaism to explain the conception in the consciousness of Jesus.[2]

The title, "Messiah", was in itself of transitional rather than of permanent importance, except that in its Greek equivalent it supplied the abiding name "Christ" to the great unnumbered multitude of believers in Him. The first creed, "Jesus is Messiah", belonged to the circles of Jewish Christians, or of those Gentiles who had come under Jewish influence. In the Gentile world generally, it was soon replaced by the creed, "Jesus is Lord", more appropriate in claiming the central place for Jesus within the whole horizon. But the older title had served its purpose well. It linked the old and the new Israel, and effectively brought out, by the very contrast of name and content, the place of the Cross in the redemption of the world.

---

[1] See the copious passages collected by Strack-Billerbeck, *Kommentar zum Neuen Testament*, II, pp. 273 ff., and by Driver and Neubauer, *The Jewish Interpreters of Isaiah LIII.*

[2] Cf. J. Klausner, *Jesus of Nazareth*, p. 201. He connects such ideas as did arise in Judaism later with the troubles of the Bar Kokhbah revolt, 132–5 A.D.

§ 2. *The Risen Lord.*   According to the New Testament
narrative of the Ascension, the disciples of Christ were
left looking steadfastly into heaven, where a cloud had
received Him out of their sight.[1]   They have been looking
up ever since, though the significance of their attitude may
now need a more spiritual reference.   In New Testament
times it was inevitable that the reference should be spatial
in the literal sense.   The heaven of the Bible is necessarily
conceived in spatial terms, even though its implications
altogether   transcend   spatial   reference.   Thoughtful
Christians to-day have realized the impossibility of conceiving a solid firmament with a heavenly palace and
throne set upon it.   As we look up to the starry universe
and try to travel through space, we are like Noah's dove
which found no rest for the sole of her foot.   In greater
or less degree we realize that the natural home of the
spiritual is in spiritual personality which altogether
transcends space.   We come back from the stars above
us to the consciousness of a divine presence within, *though
not only within.*   If we can no longer believe, in the literal
sense, that God dwells in the high and holy place, we
may be all the more certain that He dwells with those of
a humble and contrite spirit.   But we can express His
transcendence only by the use of spatial terms,[2] so that
in this sense it is still necessary that the heaven must
receive the risen Lord.[3]

It is easier, however, to see that terms drawn from space
are necessarily metaphorical when applied to the eternal
world, than to make the same admission in regard to
terms drawn from the duration of time.   How are we to
conceive the continued existence of the risen Lord after
His Ascension?   The temporal enters into our spiritual

[1] Acts i. 9, 10.
[2] See Edwyn Bevan, *Symbolism and Belief*, pp. 28 ff.
[3] Acts iii. 21.

experience to a far deeper degree than does the spatial. In fact we cannot conceive of personality, as we know it, except in terms of successive phases. The fact that Jesus dwelt for a time on earth and the faith that His personality *continues* to exist in the realm of things spiritual cannot be eliminated or ignored.

We may regard this post-existence of Jesus Christ as the supreme example or limiting case of the problem which arises in regard to men in general. The Redeemer is unique, but if the redeemed continue to exist in some sense in or with God, then He is in this sense, as in others, the first-born among many brethren. His unique place in the temporal order necessitates a unique place in the order of post-existence, but to some extent at least there is a similar problem in regard to all human existence after death. How do redeemed men continue to exist in or with God? Our natural answer to such a question must, of course, be in terms of redeemed personality itself.[1] "Without holiness no man can see God"; this is one way of saying that it is the quality of the personality which marks its nearness to God and its whole relation to God. If, then, we try to conceive the relation of the unique personality of the risen Lord to the Godhead, we have to think of Him as being still the supreme revelation or expression of God. We can understand better the naive vision of the Sadhu Sundar Singh, who, when admitted to heaven, asked to see God, whereupon he was told that no one could ever see God other than in Christ, who alone was visible.[2] Admittedly this line of thought does not help us much metaphysically, but it is important as indicating our line of approach. It suggests that Christ, whether here on earth or in His continued existence beyond earth, is the redemptive personality of God Himself. The

---

[1] See, further, Chapter XIV, § 3.
[2] *The Sadhu*, by Streeter and Appasamy, pp. 54, 55.

belief that the human personality of the Redeemer has
been appropriated, assimilated or in some way taken up
into this divine personality indicates the importance of
that actuality of history on which so much emphasis has
been laid.    It suggests that God is speaking to man by a
redemptive activity which needs the category of historic
actuality as its only adequate language, and that this
language is adequate because its product can be taken up
from the temporal into the eternal.[1]

§ 3. *The Pre-existent Christ.*   What then is to be said
about the pre-existence of Christ?   This, it will be noticed,
is a problem of a different kind, and the approach to it is
different both historically and logically.   The Christian
faith and experience demand the belief in the continued
post-existence of the risen Lord, but belief in His pre-
existence before the earthly manifestation is not so much
a demand of faith and experience as of inevitable speculation.   It is just because we find it impossible to regard
Jesus simply as a man amongst men, just because we give
Him a unique place on earth and a unique place after the
days of His flesh, that we are compelled to ask whether a
similar uniqueness attaches to Him prior to the earthly
manifestation.   Here again we must admit the possibility
that a similar question can be raised and has been raised
in regard to all human personality.   We do not know
whether our spiritual self is created along with the body
it inhabits or uses, or whether it has had some previous
existence.   On this question different opinions have been
held in the Church.[2]   But even if we were to believe that
in some real sense pre-existence belonged to all human
personality, this would not supply the element of unique-

[1] See, further, § 6.
[2] See *The Christian Doctrine of Man*, by H. Wheeler Robinson,
pp. 161 ff.

ness which must attach to Jesus. Nor can we dismiss the problem by speaking of a pre-existence simply in the thought and purpose of God. The prophet Jeremiah was, as Duhm puts it, a divine *thought* before he was born, and there are parallels to this kind of pre-existence in the Jewish conception of the Messiah and elsewhere in Judaism. But this kind of conception is not adequate for our purpose. The speculation of the Apostle Paul in Philippians ii. and the general concept of the "Heavenly Man"[1] have their value as attempts to supply a pre-existence background, such as the history seems to require. They are parallel with the Logos conception to be noticed a little later. All such attempts to penetrate into a realm beyond our knowledge are expressions of what is felt to be a necessary implication of Christian faith and experience. Jesus Christ, as He is known amongst the sons of men, is so related to the whole purpose of God that He cannot be an accident of history or even a man accomplishing a divine purpose. In some sense He belongs to the eternal being of God and that which He became on earth and continues to be in heaven belongs to the divine order from all eternity.

§ 4. *The Son of God*. Amongst the terms which have been employed to express this relation, that which lies nearest is the term "Son of God". It is consecrated by the use which Jesus Himself made of it. It has a rich connotation directly suggested by the filial consciousness of Jesus. Both at the baptism and at the transfiguration, the divine voice describes Him as "My beloved Son".[2] The title sets the father-son relation in the forefront of our Christologies and its dogmatic use through many

[1] Cf. Bousset, *Die Religion des Judentums im Neutestamentlichen Zeitalter*, ed. 2, pp. 404 ff
[2] Mark i. 11, ix. 7.

centuries has given it a commanding position.[1]　Origen
delivered it from some of its obvious limitations as a
metaphor by postulating an "eternal" generation of the
son.[2]　This paradoxical qualification, of course, lifts the
relation of the son to the father out of time.　The very
necessity of it should warn us against a too facile
application of the metaphor of sonship to the doctrine
of the Trinity, especially the too prevalent "social"
doctrine which thinks of a Father and a Son and of the
Spirit as a more or less vaguely conceived *relation*
between them.　Much professed Trinitarianism is really
Binitarian.

But even apart from the perils we incur in trying to
base the doctrine of the Trinity upon a single metaphor.
however consecrated, we are not justified in using advanced
Trinitarian doctrine as the premise of our Christology.
For this would involve an argument in a circle.　The
eternal sonship is itself an assumption based on the
historical and cannot, therefore, be made our starting-
point in explaining the historical.　Both for the New
Testament experience and for our own to-day, man's relation
to God is always ultimately to divine *unity*.　We need to
hold fast to the Pauline explanation of this experience
(Eph. ii. 18) that "*through* Christ we have our access *in* one
Spirit *unto* the Father".　This intensive approach alone does
justice to the unity of the Christian experience. The proper
place of Trinitarian doctrine is as a sequel to the Christology
and involves a further converging approach through an
adequate doctrine of the Holy Spirit.[3]　If, as has so often
happened, we try to start with a Trinitarian doctrine built
on an isolated metaphor, we shall never reach a satisfactory

---

[1] It is suggestive to contrast the rival cult of the Magna Mater and its
very different content.　Cf., also, Chap XI of *The Śāktas, by* E. A. Payne.

[2] *De Principiis,* I. ii. 4.

[3] Cf. *The Christian Experience of the Holy Spirit,* by H. Wheeler
Robinson, Chapters X, XI and XII.

result. But if we start with our experience of God in Christ as of the actuality of God's redemptive personality manifested in the space-time order, to which we belong, we are more likely to do justice to the great and permanent Christian values in the first place and to secure the right foundation for any subsequent theology to be constructed upon them.

§ 5. *The Logos.* The most important speculative attempt made by the early Church to interpret the Person of Christ was through the use of the Logos conception. This term was an inheritance from Greek thought, prominent in Heraclitus as the immanent reason in the world, and made fundamental by the Stoics as the divine law of the world, the principle underlying all the phenomena of nature and the life of man. In Philo's attempt to reconcile Jewish faith with Greek thought, the Logos becomes the central and comprehensive mediating principle between God and the world. The function of the Logos is likened to that of Aaron who stood with his censer between the dead and the living (Num. xvi. 47). The Logos is a suppliant of the mortal to the immortal, an ambassador of the ruler to the subject, "neither unbegotten like God, nor begotten like you, but in the middle between the extremes, as hostage to both."[1]

The convenience of such a mediating conception, expressing at once the inner will, thought, purpose on the one hand, and its outer expression in act on the other, is obvious. It gave to the interpretation of the Person of Christ a duality of reference, Godward and manward, which explains the continued popularity of Logos theology, from the Prologue to the Fourth Gospel, through the Apologists

[1] Ritter and Preller, *Historia Philosophiae Graecae*, 610, quoting from *Quis rerum divinarum haeres sit*, 42; cf. C. Bigg, *The Christian Platonists of Alexandria*, ed. 2, p. 45.

and the Platonist theologians of Alexandria, down to Apollinarius. It enabled the creative Word of God to be effectively linked in thought with the redemptive Word. Indeed, the Logos has in the former respect close affinity to the Hebrew conception of Wisdom, as the creative agent of God.[1] Those passages in the New Testament[2] which give to Christ a cosmic place are apt to puzzle the thoughtful but untutored reader, who cannot see how "Jesus of Nazareth" can have all created things ascribed to Him, and who does not realize that the historical figure has in such passages been interpreted in a new speculative setting supplied by contemporary thought. That such speculation has its peril—that of losing grip of religious values—is amply illustrated by the doctrinal conflicts of the early Church. The Logos conception did not save Arius from creating a sub-divine mediator, nor Apollinarius from creating an unhuman Saviour. The omission of the term Logos from the Creed of Nicaea (though it stood in the basal Creed of Caesarea), and the substitution of the term "Son of God", may mark both the sense of danger from intellectualism, and the recognition of a greater value for religion in the filial relation of Jesus to the Father. It is claimed by Dr. W. R. Inge[3] that the Logos-doctrine "belongs to a permanent and very important type of religious thought, and can never lose its value". This may be true of the use of the term to indicate some necessities of a sound and adequate Christology. But we must beware of the tendency to take refuge in it, as though it solved, rather than stated, the problem. The useful ambiguity, the double reference, of an ancient term is no justification for its uncritized use to-day by those who no longer share its presuppositions.

[1] Prov. viii., Ecclus. xxiv., Wisdom of Solomon, vii.
[2] E.g. Col. i. 16 ff.
[3] *Encyclopædia of Religion and Ethics*, VIII, p. 138.

§ 6. *The God-Man.*[1] The modern approach must be made through our conception of personality, which offers a great difference from the thought of the ancient world. It can fairly be said that "Greek philosophy began, as it ended, with the search for what was abiding in the flux of things".[2] This primary interest in ultimate "nature" (φύσις) rather than in "activity" may be seen both in the cosmologies of early Greek speculators and in the more systematic schemes from the Stoics onwards.[3] It is reflected also in the theology of the ancient Church, necessarily dominated as it was, in the Græco-Roman world, by Greek philosophy. Thus the Christian interest in personality and indeed the very conception of personality (which is so largely due to the Christian doctrine of man) had little opportunity to exert their influence on Christology. The problem of the Person of Christ presented itself chiefly as that of reconciling two different "natures", the human and the divine, both assumed to be somehow present in the one Person. The Chalcedonian statement (ἐν δύο φύσεσιν) is unsatisfactory to us because, as has just been said, it was trying to answer a question different from that which we put. We conceive of reality in terms not of abstract "nature" but of concrete personal activity and personal relation, whilst "Greek thought conceived of personality, however spiritual, as a restrictive characteristic of the finite—a transitory product of a life which as a whole is impersonal".[4]

(*a*) What is the significance of this cardinal term, "personality" (for which there is no real equivalent in the ancient

---

[1] This term (Θεάνθρωπος), first used by Origen (according to Bethune-Baker's *Early History of Christian Doctrine*, p. 150), is here used without reference to his Christology, or to any other historically connected with it. For Origen's view of the Incarnation, see *De Principiis*, II. 6; the term occurs in II. 3.

[2] Burnet, *Early Greek Philosophy*, p. 15.

[3] Windelband, *Geschichte der Philosophie*, p. 210.

[4] Pringle-Pattison, *The Idea of God*, p. 291.

conceptions and terminology)?  It includes self-conscious-
ness, sufficiently continuous to have the character of
permanence or identity, individuality as affording a
unique outlook on the universe, and activity, in the sense
of creative initiative.  With the last-named is closely
linked the character of the person.  His "will" is not a
segment of his personality; it is the man himself in whole
purposive activity.  If this view of "will" is taken, it is
difficult to see how two wills can ever co-exist as such in
any personal activity.  Of course, there are in man the
familiar phenomena of moral conflict and of the divided
heart, prior to the act, but in the act there is the unity
of a single or predominant purpose, and that unity so far
reveals the character of the person.  We also properly
speak of the will of man as acting in obedience to, or in
harmony with, or under the guidance of the will of God.
But here it is still the unity of a single human will that
issues in the act, whatever lies behind or within it.

In actual fact, the unity of personality is always in
process of becoming, and is never perfectly achieved,
however near saint or sinner may approach to it in completeness of surrender to good or to evil purpose.  Here
especially we see the sharp contrast between our modern
conception of personality, as essentially dynamic, and the
ancient conception of human "nature", as static.  That
which makes personality the supreme and most fascinating
reality in this world of ours is just the ever-moving, ever-
varied interplay of thought and feeling which constitutes
the inner life of each of us.  Here, at any rate, we escape
from the intellectual world of abstractions, lifeless because
frozen into rigidity.  Here, too, we escape from what seems
to us a world of mechanical law and external causation.
Each of us stands at the centre of a little world which he
has made his own, a world of light and warmth and colour,
controlled by his own power of selective attention.  All

these characteristics of personality, including the very
sense of individuality, have been acquired through its
development in a social setting. In the technical language
of psychology, the self implies a not-self, whether of
things or other persons. The infant learns slowly to
distinguish his own toes from its mother's fingers, and
the child his body from his inner self. The discipline of
the will is learnt only by fellowship with others whose
constraint imposes necessary limits, beyond those already
imposed by natural objects. The ideal values of life, in
which alone spiritual life consists, are first recognized in
other persons. The sense of social solidarity, which can
raise all the individual values to a new level and give
them a new horizon, is not based on some intellectual
inference from the abstraction we call "human nature",
but is acquired in the intercourse of life, through actually
living with others, and sharing their life.

But beyond all this, which is matter of experience and
observation, the most important aspect of personality has
yet to be indicated, viz. its potential relation to higher
forms of its own reality. It has already been urged that
the values cherished by human personality point beyond
themselves to their previous existence, in independence of
the human response to them. Our sense of obligation to
them finds no other adequate explanation. But the only
home for such values which we can conceive must be
personal; their very meaning is bound up with this
assumption. They link spirit in time with Spirit in
eternity, and they prophesy, however dimly and obscurely,
their own fulfilment in ampler and richer forms.

Many questions spring to our mind as to both the
origin and destiny of human personality.[1] But our
immediate concern is with the bearing of what has been
said upon Christology. If we knew more about ourselves

---

[1] Soo, further, Chapter XIV, § 3 ("Personality and the Life Beyond").

P

we should be in a much better position to formulate a doctrine of the Person of Christ. If we approach that doctrine along the lines of our human personality, i.e. if we assume that His manhood is truly ours, however much more than ours, we shall ascribe to it a genuine individuality of outlook, the unity of a single will, and the social solidarity with all men of One who recognized to the full the ties that bound Him to His fellows. All this, at least, is amply corroborated by the Synoptic Gospels, through which we come nearest to the "Jesus of history". But if, having said this, we feel the need to say more, the need to claim for Him a unique manhood that makes Him also God manifest in the flesh, it will not be by trying to add the divine to the human, or by dovetailing the divine into the human, or by sacrificing the human to the divine.[1] It will be by some deeper view of what human personality already is, a view that will at least enable us to conceive it as the fitting vehicle of the divine, and capable of becoming the "temple" of the divine itself under the limiting conditions of a particular historical environment and in the texture of a particular national history.

(*b*) This intensive approach to the manhood of the Redeemer obviously implies, as its *sine qua non*, the kinship of the human and the divine. This does not mean, as in some forms of humanism, the deification of man, or that every man is regarded as potentially divine. Nor does it mean the pantheistic reduction of the transcendent God to an identity with His creatures. It means that there is no such permanent gulf between man's "nature" and God's as would make impossible the indwelling of the human by the divine. We are indeed already committed to think

[1] Here the pre-Chalcedonian Christological controversies and the Chalcedonian statement are of great value. They eliminate some of the wrong roads by a process of experiment, even if they cannot tell us the right road.

of God as "the Beyond which is akin"[1] by other considerations.

Unless there is kinship, God's spiritual activities must forever remain unintelligible to man, and there can be no revelation and no redemption involving man's responsive activity. Unless there is kinship, we renounce the New Testament doctrine of the Holy Spirit as the indwelling Christ, continuing His work from within the human spirit. Unless there is kinship, the goal of life as fellowship with God becomes inconceivable. "Now are we the sons of God and it doth not yet appear what we shall be." As Dr. Edwyn Bevan says, "It is the combination of the 'now' and the 'not yet' which characterizes the Christian *Weltanschauung*."[2] If it be said that the adoption into that sonship is already an act of grace, and implies no "natural" kinship, the sufficient answer is that such adoption can make actual only that which was potential, and potential kinship is already kinship, even if a kinship far below the level of the conscious relation of the Christian to God,[3] and a kinship temporarily denied by man's sin.

When once we have put aside the tendencies of Greek dualism, which have so often obscured the interpretation of Scripture, this kinship of men and God is seen to be thoroughly Biblical. It is implied in the primitive story of the creation of man; into the nostrils of this unique creature God uniquely breathed the breath of life. True, a prophet can contrast man, who is "flesh", with God, who is "Spirit";[4] but this contrast is by no means to be identified with the Greek distinction of material and spiritual natures. We should think rather of the contrast between the corruptible and the incorruptible which emerges in 1 Corin-

---

[1] W. R. Matthews, *God*, p. 10.
[2] *Symbolism and Belief*, p. 117 n.
[3] It is this fundamental principle which, if accepted, bars acceptance of any form of Barthianism.
[4] Isa. xxxi. 3.

thians xv.,[1] or, as we might say, between the finite and
the infinite.  For St. Paul, spirit, not flesh and blood,
inherits eternal life, and spirit is the innermost life of man.[2]

Because of this kinship, human personality is potentially
capable of being brought into perfect harmony with the
divine, to a degree we cannot define.  From the standpoint
of the divine, the result would always involve limitations—
those necessarily springing from a particular historical
environment.[3]  But from the human standpoint, the result
would be expressed wholly in terms of achievement, i.e.
positively and not negatively.  The point to be emphasized
here is that, on the purely historical plane, no distinction
could be drawn in the result, between human personality
perfectly achieving the potentialities of its kinship with
the divine, *in a given environment*, and divine personality
manifesting itself *in the same environment*.[4]  There is, of
course, a difference, and one of the highest importance, in
respect of which of these interpretations we emphasize.
But the difference is one of interpretation, not of historical
actuality.  Even if we think of supernatural powers
exercised by such a personality, we cannot say that they
are not due to the raising of human personality to a level
beyond that reached by any other man.

This line of approach to the unique personality of
Jesus, unique in the sense defined in § 2, is not meant
to suggest in the least that it affords a complete
explanation of the emergence of that personality.  On the
contrary, the more we recognize His uniqueness, the more
are we driven to seek some unique explanation of it,

[1] Cf. B. Duhm, *Das Buch Jesaia, ad loc.*
[2] Rom. viii. 16, 2 Cor. vii. 1, etc.; cf. *The Christian Doctrine of Man*,
by H. Wheeler Robinson, p. 110.
[3] Note what is said later on "Kenosis" (especially XIV. § 2.)
[4] Cf. Archbishop Temple, *Christus Veritas*, p. 125: "God in terms of
our own experience. . . . Man as he is in his truest nature, which is
only made actual when man becomes the means to the self-expression
of God."

whether by special "miracle" (e.g. the Virgin birth) or by the divine control of history and environment (which would not be less supernatural) or by such a general conception of "the Word made flesh" as is expressed in the prologue to the Fourth Gospel. Such lines of interpretation may be regarded for the moment as alternatives. The significant fact is that Christian thought has been compelled to resort to such explanations because it was faced by a unique historical actuality.

Just what that actuality would contain, in the way of achieved values, could not be determined *a priori*. The Christian faith in a divine Redeemer, living and dying as a man amongst men, does not form the conclusion of a philosophic argument, though it supplies the datum for the beginning of one. The place actually taken by Jesus in history and experience shows that He does satisfy the highest moral and spiritual needs of men, so that they have been continually urged to apply to Him the highest categories their thought provided.[1] The precise form of these, however important and illuminative in itself, is always secondary to the actuality of the redemption which He is believed to have wrought.[2] It is through that actuality as an integral part of His life on earth that we must always approach any doctrine of His Person. We make unnecessary difficulties for ourselves when we assume that any one type of doctrine is sacrosanct, e.g. the Chalcedonian doctrine of two natures. What is really vital is that we should strive to do justice to the highest truth expressed by such doctrines, the truth that God was in Christ, reconciling the world unto Himself.

Our approach to the Person of the Redeemer through

[1] Cf. H. T. Andrews, *The Christ of Apostolic Faith*, p. 163.
[2] Cf. Grensted, *A Short History of the Doctrine of the Atonement*, p. 33: "It was indeed by the fact of Redemption that rival doctrines of the Trinity or of the Incarnation were tested. This is the key to the history of the great heresies of the fourth and fifth centuries."

human personality will always need for its complement the study of His redemptive work, what He has wrought *for* us (Chapter XIII) and *in* us (Chapter XIV).   As Man, Jesus Christ is known to us in a definite context of history, that context which justifies the apostle in placing His coming in the fulness of the time.[1]   When we approach Him along the lines of this context (as did the author of the Epistle to the Hebrews, in his opening verses) we may use the spatial figure of an *ascent*.   But Christian experience of the redemptive activity of God through Christ has always found it necessary to ascribe this to a divine *descent*.   The great and permanent redemptive values cannot be adequately assigned to one who is, after all, merely man, however exalted his manhood.   Christian thought has rightly argued that the redemption of man must be wrought by God, and not merely by God's deputy.   The tremendous impact of divine grace on the human heart must derive its momentum from the divine initiative.   Only God's shoulders are strong enough to carry the burden of man's sin.

Where and how do this ascent and descent meet?   That is the peculiar problem of every type of Christology which tries to do justice to both features.   There is a tunnel constructed in the eighth century B.C. which links the Virgin's Spring outside Jerusalem with the Pool of Siloam. An inscription tells of its excavation simultaneously from above and from below, and there was natural anxiety as to whether the two excavations would meet.   That anxiety was relieved when a rift in the rock enabled each party of miners to hear the others, though three cubits remained to be hewn through.   So also the Christian theologian must ask himself whether his lines of ascent and descent will happily meet, whether his theory succeeds in bringing together the divinity and the humanity of the

[1] Gal. iv. 4.

God-man, so that the waters of life may flow through without interruption.

Already it has been argued that unless there is some kind of spiritual kinship between God and man intercourse and revelation are impossible. Equally inconceivable without the reality of kinship would be any real Incarnation, for this implies that human personality is no alien sphere of God's presence and activity. Does this kinship warrant us in tracing a continuous line of ascent to God, at some point of which Jesus is conceived to stand? Such a conception is plausible by its apparent simplicity, but it conceals rather than solves the problem. Are we not unduly exalting our human nature if we think that the finite can so pass imperceptibly into the infinite, the temporal become the eternal, man become God? Will not the inevitable tendency of such an ascent through Christ still leave Him on the manward side of a gulf as yet unbridged?

We get nearer to the right conception by reference to the inclusiveness of spirit.[1] Mental phenomena are characterized by their inclusion of that which is external, whereas physical objects remain external to each other. Our contact with the outer world is maintained by the transformation of sensational stimuli into particular perceptions, which again are taken up into the new unity of general conceptions. We may see a similar principle of inclusion in the successive stages of our analysis of material phenomena by which the separate sciences are constituted. There are different levels of abstraction, and therefore of assimilation, in the successive data of physics, chemistry, biology and psychology which the single object may yield. In the movement of an animal, for example, we can distinguish the physical strains and stresses of muscular activity, themselves inseparable in existence

[1] See further, on this point, Chapter XIV, § 3.

from the chemical constituents of the blood, and these
again from the biological assimilation of food. Yet the
resultant movement is a unity, however dependent on the
successive levels which our mental analysis discerns. Still
more complex is the unity of consciousness in the man
who observes the animal. When we think of his moral
relations to his fellows, we see how one life may become
dominant in another, whether by way of sympathy and
compassion, or by way of admiration and hero-worship.
Such inclusion of one life within another is, naturally,
distinct from the spatial inclusion of the embryo within its
mother's womb. But it is an inclusion which may be
none the less "real" in the full ontological sense.

When we try to apply this line of thought to Jesus
Christ, we have always to remember that we are looking
up, not down, and that we cannot therefore expect to
comprehend, to grasp together as one, that which is
admittedly beyond our experience, viz. the relation of
transcendence to immanence. We cannot even claim to
enter into the consciousness of Jesus, and even if we could,
that earthly consciousness would not necessarily be the
measure of the ultimate reality. But glimpses are given
us of a unique relation to the Father, in particular the
notable declaration, "no one knoweth the Son save the
Father, neither doth any know the Father save the Son."[1]
Perhaps we should better describe this relation as His
dwelling in God, rather than as God's dwelling in Him—a
conscious life in God, through which was actualized the
"Real Presence" of God on earth. We may indeed find
suggestive if remote parallels to this *parousia* in the partial
and intermittent surrender of the saint to God, through
which God by His Holy Spirit continues His dwelling upon
the earth. Here the unity is manifested in the identification of the divine and human wills, but we cannot reduce

[1] Matt. xi. 25 ff., Luke x. 21 ff.

to a formula this miracle of grace in the saint, and far less in the God-man. We need not, however, doubt the result— that in approaching Christ we approach God Himself, so far as man may yet know Him. One way of describing this result is to speak of a divine "Kenosis", though this "self-emptying" of God in the Incarnation does not necessarily mean the acceptance of any of the theories historically associated with the term. We might also describe the Incarnation as the supreme example of that sacramental principle which runs through the universe, by which the higher is necessarily actualized and so revealed through the lower, the deity by the humanity. Such a view, again, might honestly use the Johannine statement, "the Word became flesh and dwelt among us."

The problem of the relation of the human to the divine in the "Jesus of history" has its analogue at a higher level still, when we attempt to think of the relation of the God-man to the Godhead. Let it be fully admitted that here, as in regard also to the Incarnation, our human experience offers no example of such an inclusion of full personality within a higher form of Being. The psychological analogies offered by Augustine,[1] such as the inclusion of memory, understanding and will within the unity of personality, obviously fail us as constructive data. Even the concept of personality cannot be applied to extra-human Being without the elimination of certain characteristics of personality in its finite forms. Such are its continued "becoming", without finality, its constant suggestion of something higher than itself, its exclusive individuality of consciousness, notwithstanding that this is built up by a multitude of inclusions. When we speak of divine Personality,[2] we have to conceive Being which

[1] *De Trinitate*, viii. 14, ix. 3 ff., x. 13, xii. 4 ff., xiv. 3.
[2] See, further, Chapter XII of *The Christian Experience of the Holy Spirit* in this series.

includes all that belongs to the highest forms of personality, including that of the God-man, yet without the limitations that necessarily attach to personality *within the time-order*. This is a hard demand, but the alternative would be to forfeit our highest and most spiritual category in relation to God.   He cannot be less than the best we know, however far beyond He goes.   The greater must include the less— that seems to be one of the great laws of the spiritual life, whether we think of the inclusive mystery of our own human consciousness, or that higher mystery by which the human characteristics of Jesus are taken up into the real personality of the God-man, or finally that ultimate mystery of His inclusion in the Being and activity of the Godhead.

At each of these stages of the problem of spiritual inclusion, the easiest way out of the difficulties would be to minimize the actuality of the included element, and so to be enabled to fix our attention on that which includes it. Thus in regard to ourselves, we may pass lightly over the physiological basis of psychology, and treat the "soul" almost as if it were a disembodied entity.   In regard to Christ, men have been attracted to some form of Docetism, or at least to the Apollinarianism which mutilates human personality in order to facilitate its union with the divine. In regard to the Godhead, the simplest solution has often appeared to be some form of modalistic Monarchianism, such as the Sabellian, which would make the God-man a transient manifestation of the One God.   But such temptations must be sternly resisted.   The unity of the Godhead must be maintained at all costs—better Sabellianism than Tritheism—but God will be robbed of His highest glory if the redemptive activity of the Redeemer be not actually and permanently divine.   That is why such repeated emphasis is here laid on the actuality of history, as the only firm foundation for our faith in Redemption and Revelation,

# CHAPTER XII

## THE MEANING OF REDEMPTION

§ 1. *THE Metaphor.* Like most of the great terms of our religious vocabulary,[1] the word "redemption" conceals a metaphor, that of "buying back" by the payment of a price. In fact it is from the same root as the word "ransom".[2] It emphasizes, therefore, the objective character of the work of Christ. Perhaps for this reason, as well as because of the cruder developments of the "ransom" theory of the Atonement (see § 4), the word "redemption" has become somewhat old-fashioned, and more general terms, such as "atonement", "salvation", "reconciliation" are preferred as expressions of what Christ has done for man. All these admit of greater emphasis on the more subjective side of man's deliverance from sin than does the term "redemption". But for that very reason the more objective term is here preferred. Whatever the crudities of the metaphor of paying a ransom may be, when it is made the basis of a doctrine of the Atonement, there is little danger from them provided we remember that the term is metaphorical, and do justice to the truth involved in other metaphors, such as those drawn from sacrifice or from penalty.[3] Neither of these should be interpreted as the payment of a price, and thus confused with the idea which underlies "redemption". The ransom paid for a slave or prisoner by which he

[1] See Chapter III.
[2] "Ransom" is from the Old French, *rançon, raençon*:— Latin *redemptionem;* see *The Shorter English Dictionary*, s.v.
[3] See §§ 2, 4.

obtains his freedom, is not a sacrifice or a penalty, except in a very loose and metaphorical use of these terms. But ransoming does imply a definite activity, independent of any action or response of the person affected. Throughout the history of our faith, the Christian conception of salvation has been based on what Christ has done for man, and generally in this "objective" sense. In Him, God's initiative has been seen, doing something for man which he could not do for himself, something which had to be done for him as well as something to be done in him through his response to this act of grace. The word "redemption" is, in fact, a challenge to those who would argue that the activity of grace and its objective character consist primarily in the creation within history of a local point of "influence" upon men.

§ 2. *Redemption in the Old Testament.* The terms "redemption", "redeem", "redeemer" occur altogether one hundred and thirty-two times in the English Old Testament (A.V.) and almost always[1] render terms derived from two Hebrew roots, *padhah* and *ga'al*. The related English term, "ransom", occurs as a verb twice as rendering *padhah*,[2] and twice as rendering *ga'al*,[3] and nine times as a noun, eight of which render a word from a different root, *kopher*.[4] This noun denotes the price paid in compensation for a forfeited life,[5] or less directly for each Israelite enumerated in a census.[6] It is not to be accepted for the life of a manslayer[7] and judges are condemned for acceptance of a "ransom".[8] Though a man's wealth may provide a "ransom", the wronged husband will not accept it, and it

---

[1] The exceptions are Ps. cxxxvi. 24 (*paraq*) and Neh. v. 8 (*qanah*).
[2] Isa. xxxv. 10, Hos. xiii. 14.         [3] Isa. li. 10, Jer. xxxi. 11.
[4] The ninth is in Exod. xxi. 30, from the root *padhah*.
[5] Exod. xxi. 30, that of the owner of a goring ox.
[6] Exod. xxx. 12.                   [7] Num. xxxv. 31, 32.
[8] 1 Sam. xii. 3, Amos v. 12, Job xxxvi. 18 (on which see Dhorme).

cannot be given to God so as to secure escape from death.[1]
More general and figurative uses are illustrated by the
statement that God has given to Cyrus, Egypt, Ethiopia
and Seba as a ransom for Israel.[2]

The fundamental idea of the verb *padhah* also is
to "ransom", as by payment of an equivalent for
what is released. Thus, if a Hebrew bondwoman, who
has become her master's concubine, cease to please
him, he must not sell her, but must allow her to be "redeemed", i.e. ransomed.[3] When Jonathan had broken the
taboo laid by Saul on the eating of any food, and the
oracle indicated him as the offender, his father was ready
to have him killed, but his popularity as a victorious
leader in the fighting led the people to demand that he be
ransomed, and this was done in some unstated way,
probably by the substitution of another in his place.[4]
Ancient Israel regarded the first-born of man and beast as
belonging to Yahweh.[5] This may have meant originally
the actual sacrifice of the first-born son, and the story of
Abraham's intended sacrifice of Isaac might then be a
record of the transition from such human sacrifice to the
sacrifice of an animal substitute.[6] The actual stage
reached in the early literature is, however, that expressed
by the words: "thou shalt set apart unto Yahweh all that
openeth the womb, and every firstling which thou hast
that cometh of a beast; the males shall be Yahweh's.
And every firstling of an ass thou shalt ransom with a
lamb; and if thou wilt not ransom it, then thou shalt
break its neck: and all the firstborn of man among thy
sons shalt thou ransom."[7] On the other hand, no man's
wealth can be his ransom when the appointed hour of

---

[1] Prov. xiii. 8: vi. 35: Ps. xlix. 8.
[2] Isa. xliii. 3: cf. Job xxxiii. 24: Prov. xxi. 18.
[3] Exod. xxi. 8 (E).
[4] 1 Sam. xiv. 24 ff.
[5] Exod. xxii. 29.
[6] Gen. xxii.
[7] Exod. xiii. 12, 13, cf. xxxiv. 20.

death has come: "None can by any means redeem (*padhah*) his brother, nor give to God a ransom (*kopher*) for him".[1] We see clearly, then, the point of departure of the term *padhah*; it denoted originally an equivalent in real or assumed value given to release from some bond or taboo. In more figurative use, which is our concern in theology, it will naturally denote the activity of God in delivering man from any disability or constraint, whilst the actual payment will usually drop out of sight, attention being fixed on the *result*, the deliverance or escape from the constraint. So, a man saved from imminent death will be able to say "He hath ransomed me from going into the pit, and my life shall behold the light."[2]   To Israel it is said, "Yahweh brought you out with a mighty hand, and ransomed you out of the house of bondage, from the hand of Pharaoh, King of Egypt."[3]   A late passage relating to the dispersed Israel says: "He that scattered Israel will gather him, and keep him as a shepherd doth his flock. For Yahweh ransoms (*padhah*) Jacob and redeems (*ga'al*) him from the hand of him that is stronger than he."[4] Here the metaphor of a money payment underlies the term "ransom" as applied to deliverance from exile; yet we can no more insist on actual payment as essential to ransom or redemption in such metaphorical use than we could insist on the literalness of the accompanying metaphor of God as a shepherd, and ask what the shepherd's staff did in this rescue. The point is that Israel is to be restored from exile; the precise manner or means of the restoration is not in view.[5]   If, however, the figure demands reference to the price paid, rather than to the deliverance

---

[1] Ps. xlix. 7.                              [2] Job xxxiii. 28.
[3] Deut. vii. 8.                             [4] Jer. xxxi. 10, 11.
[5] Cf. R. H. Kennett, *Ancient Hebrew Social Life and Custom as indicated in Law, Narrative and Metaphor*, p. 3: "attention is almost invariably directed towards the *effect* of what is used as an illustration rather than to its progress or to its external characteristics."

wrought, a different term (*kopher*) can be used, as was the case in the passage cited above (Isa. xliii. 3), where the meaning is that Cyrus will actually receive compensation for his service in delivering Israel from exile, by becoming a world-conqueror and by absorbing Africa into his dominions. But ordinarily we must emphasize the general result and not press the metaphor of redemption in all its possible bearings.

The figurative use of *padhah* reaches its furthest Old Testament development in such words as those of the psalmist: "*He* shall ransom Israel from all his iniquities."[1] Here we must not unduly spiritualize. The cry for help *de profundis* is partly, at least, a cry for deliverance from the calamities brought by sin. The ransoming means the escape from them. The outward sign of "forgiveness" is restoration to prosperity, though forgiveness undoubtedly meant more than this to the devout Israelite. Nowhere, in fact, is this word *padhah* used of redemption from sin alone; it always means deliverance from some tangible and visible menace, which may or may not be regarded as a consequence of the suppliant's sin.

The parallel term, *ga'al*, is similar in idea, but has characteristic developments. Like *padhah*, it denotes the buying back of something to which the right has been lost. A man who has sold a house has the right of redemption (*ge'ullah*) for a year.[2] If a man has sold himself into slavery as payment of debt to a "stranger or settler", "one of his brethren may redeem him; or his uncle, or his uncle's son may redeem him, or any that is nigh of kin unto him of his family may redeem him; or if he be waxen rich, he may redeem himself."[3] Here we note the peculiar quality of this term, *ga'al*; it is appropriated to the right and duty of the kinsman to be a redeemer. Two incidents will illustrate this. Hanamel, the cousin of the prophet

[1] Ps. cxxx. 8.    [2] Lev. xxv. 29.    [3] Lev. xxv. 48, 49.

Jeremiah, came to him, saying "Buy my field, I pray thee,
that is in Anathoth, which is in the land of Benjamin:
for the right of inheritance is thine, and the redemption
is thine; buy it for thyself", and the prophet does this in
full legal form.[1] We should express this by saying that
Jeremiah's relationship to Hanamel imposed the obligation
of purchase, not simply morally, but also legally. In
the Book of Ruth, the kinsman's duty to redeem the land
of Naomi apparently included the obligation to marry
Ruth, by a quasi-Levirate marriage. The kinsman is
ready for the purchase of the land, but not for the marriage.
He therefore formally renounces his duty by drawing
off his sandal and handing it to Boaz "in the gate", in
presence of the elders. This enables Boaz to take his
place as "redeemer".[2]

Another aspect of the kinsman's right and duty expressed
by the term *ga'al* is that of blood revenge, the primitive
justice which demanded blood for blood, the blood of some
member of a group, for blood shedding by this or some
other member of it. In the Hebrew form of this wide-
spread practice, the "avenger of blood" is a near kinsman
of the slain man, who claims an equivalent life from the
slayer or his group. The avenger or "redeemer" is the
*go'el*. In the famous words of Job, "I know that my
redeemer liveth",[3] the meaning of the term is very different
from that given by Christian associations. He means
"my blood avenger" who will vindicate my shameful death,
and rehabilitate me after death in the eyes of men. When
Yahweh becomes a *go'el* or "redeemer" He acts towards
man as would a worthy kinsman, vindicating the position
and honour of his kin. Deutero-Isaiah thus uses the
term in regard to the redemption of Israel from exile,
promised through Cyrus: "Fear not, for I have redeemed

[1] Jer. xxxii. 7 f.                      [2] Ruth iv. 1–11.
[3] Job xix. 25, cf. Deut. xix. 6, etc.

thee: I have called thee by thy name, thou art mine".[1] Again, God says: "I have blotted out, as a thick cloud, thy transgressions, and as a cloud, thy sins: return unto Me, for I have redeemed thee".[2] Here the forgiveness is not the redemption, but the necessary prelude to it: Yahweh has put away the past, as He removes a cloud from the sky; He will now use His kinsman's right and restore Israel to her land. Throughout the whole usage of *ga'al*, as of the parallel term, *padhah*, there is actual and concrete application to a definite situation, there is some bondage or deprivation or oppression from which deliverance is given. This is well illustrated in the picturesque descriptions of Psalm cvii., which begins, "Let the redeemed of Yahweh thank Him"—the redeemed being the gathered exiles who are pictured as lost travellers, prisoners, sick men, storm-tossed sailors. We are not concerned with the price of the divine redemption, corresponding to the seventeen shekels paid by Jeremiah to Hanamel; there has been far too much shekel theology in the Christian Church. The true emphasis is seen in such words as those of Isa. lii. 3: "Ye were sold for nought; and ye shall be redeemed (*ga'al*) without money."

We have studied in some detail the two chief terms for "redemption" in the Old Testament, in order to give more precision to the whole Biblical idea, for a similar metaphor underlies the New Testament terms (see § 3). But the whole conception is, of course, much wider than the use of these terms. It is, in fact, co-extensive with the history of Israel, as interpreted by the highest religion of Israel. That history is conceived as redemptive, from the Exodus out of Egypt, with which the history of the nation began, down to coins of the last Jewish rebellion (Bar Kokhbah's) in 132–5 A.D., which bear the inscription "The redemption of Israel". There is no

[1] Isa. xliii. 1.  [2] Isa. xliv. 22.

Q

exaggeration in what Davidson has said: "Behind the people's national life lay the consciousness of redemption as much as it lies behind the life of the Christian."[1]

The core of this consciousness was the faith in the divine covenant which bound Yahweh to Israel. "Covenant" is not a happy rendering of the Hebrew word "berith", as it suggests the legalized "contract", for which we should look to the Roman rather than to the Hebrew type of religion. A "covenant" in the Hebrew sense is a ceremony which establishes or expresses some "binding" relation.[2] But when God enters into a covenant, this relation is necessarily the expression of His grace, and springs from the initiative of His own nature and purpose. This holds of the covenant of Sinai,[3] where Yahweh states His requirements of Israel, receives her pledge, and then enters into the bond of shared sacrificial blood (blood sprinkled on altar and on people) which establishes and confirms His "kinship" with Israel. The conception of the covenant which underlies the Book of Deuteronomy[4] extends the terms of the covenant made at Sinai in ethical demand along prophetic lines and, in particular, emphasizes the divine grace in the election of Israel: "Yahweh did not set His love upon you, nor choose you, because ye were more in number than any people; for ye were the fewest of all peoples: but because Yahweh loveth you."[5] In the third great expression of the covenant-relation, that of the Priestly Code of the fifth century B.C., the majesty of God is safeguarded by the emphasis on the divine promises, to Abraham and onwards; there is no need of any ceremony to ratify these, and in fact the

---

[1] Art. "God" in Hastings's *Dictionary of the Bible*, II, p. 202.
[2] E.g. Abraham and Abimelech, Gen. xxi. 22 ff.; Jonathan and David, 1 Sam. xviii. 3, 4; xx. 8: xxiii. 17, 18; Ahab and Benhadad, 1 Kings xx. 29–34.
[3] Exod. xxiv. 3–8 (E).
[4] Especially seen in Deut. xxvi. 17–18.     [5] Deut. vii. 7, 8.

whole sacrificial ritual may be held to supply the ceremonial side of the covenant. In this, man obeys the divine ordinances, and God generously accepts the offerings which remove the barriers due to man's ignorance and sin. The post-exilic sacrificial system, in fact, may be regarded as a multiplied renewal of the covenantal relation.

In all these expressions of the covenantal idea, therefore, we must think of a redeemer-God who acts through history and in individual lives, because of what He is and of His freely assumed relation to His people. That relation can be abused by disobedience, and men may presume upon it with tragic results to themselves. But it is such that God cannot give up His people, and again and again forgives and restores.[1] This is not because He is in any way dependent on them, but because of that quality in Him which the Hebrew calls *hesed*, an untranslatable term, to which neither "loving-kindness" nor "mercy" does justice. It is the loyalty of love which binds a man to help his fellow in difficulties,[2] and binds God to redeem Israel out of all her afflictions.

The Old Testament idea of redemption, then, lays emphasis on the divine initiative, comprehends within itself the deliverance from material as well as from spiritual perils and constraints, and deals primarily with Israel as a people, though growingly concerned with the relation of the individual to God, within that social solidarity. The statement of the idea in the religion of Israel is concerned with the result rather than with the process. Whatever elements may be included in the final result, through the demand for moral or ritual obedience, the final emphasis is on the divine grace. If anyone hesitates about this, in view of the elaborate ritual of the Priestly Code, he does well to consider the Book of Psalms as its accompaniment

---

[1] Cf. e.g. Hos. xi. 8, 9.
[2] Cf. the cognate Arabic *hashada* meaning "to gather in order to help".

and higher interpretation. Or if he thinks of passages
which seem to lay undue stress on human merit and point
to a self-complacency[1] which ill accords with the characteristic humility of the best Christian piety, let him put
alongside of them those far more numerous passages which
contrast the majesty of God and the littleness of man,
though God is yet mindful of him, and visits him as a
Redeemer.[2]

§ 3. *Redemption in the New Testament.* In the New
Testament, the words "redeem" or "redemption" occur
twenty-two times in the Authorized Version and "ransom"
three times, translating Greek words of two groups, viz.
those connected with the verbs *lutroō* and *agorazō*. These
continue the metaphor already studied in the Old Testament, *lutroō* denoting primarily the ransom paid for the
emancipation of a slave, and the more general *agorazō*
denoting "purchase in the market". The former is best
illustrated from the Greek inscriptions[3] which record the
liberation of a slave through payment to his owner in the
name of the god of a temple. This gives point to St. Paul's
admonition to stand fast in the freedom with which Christ
has set us free, and not to fall back into slavery, and to
remember that we are bought with a price.[4]

The noun *lutron* occurs in the words of Jesus, "The Son
of man came . . . to give his life a ransom for many."[5]
The context emphasizes the life of service to others, and

---

[1] E.g. Neh. v. 19: Ps. xviii. 20 ff.

[2] Isa. ii. 10, 11; Job xlii. 5, 6; Isa. lxiii. 9; Ps. viii. 4.

[3] Cf. Deissmann, *Light from the Ancient East*, p. 327, who cites a Delphic
inscription of 200 B.C.: "Apollo the Pythian bought from Sósibius of
Amphissa, for freedom, a female slave, whose name is Nicaea, by race a
Roman, with a price (*timé*) of three minae of silver and a half-mina.
Former seller according to the law: Eumnastus of Amphissa. The price
he hath received. The purchase, however, Nicaea hath committed unto
Apollo for freedom."

[4] Gal. v. 1; 1 Cor. vi. 20, vii. 23 (*agorazō*).

[5] Mark x. 45 = Matt. xx. 28.

the many who profit are here contrasted with the one who serves, without any suggestion of theological arithmetic.[1] The preposition *anti* means simply "for",[2] and no theory of substitution ought to be extracted from it. The emphasis falls on the death as the culminating act of service, without specifying the particular manner in which it secures the emancipation of "many". Similarly Christ is said to have become our "redemption" (*apolutrōsis*).[3]

We get more precise information as to the character of the redemption wrought by Christ's death in the classical statement of Romans iii. 24, 25: "Being justified freely by his grace through the redemption that is in Christ Jesus, whom God set forth to be propitiatory (R.V. mar.), through faith, by his blood." Here the explanation of the ransom is found in the originally quite distinct conception of sacrifice.[4] The blood of Christ removes the barrier which hindered man from approaching God, according to the established and universally accepted necessity for sacrifice. We have here, then, the blending of two distinct metaphors to explain the redemptive work of Christ. In fact, the term "justified" introduces a third originally distinct range of ideas, viz. those drawn from forensic usage; the "righteous" (justified) person is one on whom the judge has passed the verdict of acquittal. The blending of "ransom" and "sacrifice" is seen also in the Petrine passage,[5] which describes the redemption as wrought by the offering of the "precious blood" of Christ, set in contrast with the mere

[1] Cf. also Mark xiv. 24 "shed for many" and Isa. liii. 11 (the probable source of both). Note also 1 Tim. ii. 6 "for all", where the stronger equivalent, *antilutron*, occurs.

[2] As e.g. in Matt. xvii. 27.

[3] 1 Cor. i. 30. The general use of "redemption" in relation to Israel and Jerusalem (Luke i. 68, ii. 38, xxiv. 21) need not concern us; it is drawn from the Old Testament, e.g. Ps. cxi. 9. In Acts vii. 35, Moses is called a "redeemer" (*lutrotes*) (A.V. and R.V. "deliverer"); in Heb. xi. 35 the *apolutrōsis* is "deliverance" from physical torture.

[4] Cf. Eph. i. 7.                               [5] 1 Pet. i. 18, 19.

money payment of silver and gold in an ordinary ransom.
On the other hand the Epistle to the Hebrews contrasts
the "eternal redemption" wrought by Christ through His
blood with that of the imperfect offering of the blood of
goats and calves.[1]

We get another angle of approach to the meaning of
"redemption" when we turn to those passages which
indicate from what state of bondage the Christian is
ransomed. It is "worthlessness", "lawlessness", "sin",
"trespass", "transgression".[2] All these rightly suggest a
moral and spiritual change in the believer, but we are not
warranted in confining ourselves to that "subjective" view
of the emancipation. The ransom and the sacrifice and
the verdict of acquittal as wrought by the blood of Christ
all suggest something objective, something in fact from
which this subjective change springs, as in the great Old
Testament pattern, Isa. liii, where the sufferings of
Israel are conceived as an *asham* or guilt-offering through
which the other nations can approach God, though they
are *also* actually moved to penitence by the very spectacle
of the sufferings, in the light of God's vindication of His
Servant.

Other instances of the term "redemption" point to its
completion in the future parousia of Christ, and illustrate
its more general use, without any stress on the underlying
metaphor. That day of redemption is near at hand; it
marks the full acquisition of the inheritance already
partially possessed; it will bring a "spiritual" body to
match more adequately the redeemed spirit.[3]

The other term (*agorazō, exagorazō*) is frequently used in
the New Testament in the sense of "buy", without soteriological reference, but in a few instances it supplements the

[1] Heb. ix. 12 (*aiōnian lutrōsin*).
[2] 1 Pet. i. 18; Tit. ii. 14; Col. i. 14; Eph. i. 7; Heb. ix. 15. On this
aspect of redemption, see further § 4 "Redemption from what?"
[3] Eph. i. 14; Luke xxi. 28; Eph. iv. 30; Rom. viii. 23.

use of *lutron*, etc. Thus St. Paul bases appeals both for chastity and for the spirituality of religion on the reminder "Ye were bought with a price", the contexts showing that the emancipation of a slave is still in view.[1] The purchase is said elsewhere to be by the blood of Christ.[2]

In the Epistle to the Galatians the purchase is said to be unto the adoption of sons—the slave becomes a son— and also to be "from the curse of the law",[3] Christ Himself becoming a "curse" for us. This is one of the clearest indications that St. Paul conceived the death of Christ as both substitutionary and penal,[4] its parallel being that of 2 Cor. v. 21, where the Sinless is said to be made sin in our behalf, that we might obtain acquittal and become actually righteous. The general "curse" resting on all the dis- obedient (that is on all Jews and all Gentiles), is expressed in Deut. xxvii. 26: "Cursed be he that confirmeth not the words of this law to do them." The particular "curse" resting on Christ is that of Deut. xxi. 23, "he that is hanged is accursed of God" (whether as a criminal or as bringing peril to the community by the exposure of the corpse). The particular curse historically manifested in the Cross of Christ vicariously replaces the general curse resting on all men and warrants its removal. The cogency of this argument depends partly on the "actuality" underlying prophetic symbolism[5] as initiating or liberating a divine activity. Christ *actually* bears a part of the universal curse (in its consequences) and thus enables God graciously to remove it altogether.

In this survey of the two chief terms for "redemption"

---

[1] 1 Cor. vi. 20, vii. 23, cf. 2 Peter ii. 1; the figurative use in Eph. v. 16, Col. iv. 5 ("redeeming the time" i.e. from the bondage of evil) also keeps up the idea of the metaphor of emancipation from slavery.

[2] Rev. v. 9; cf. xiv. 3, 4.

[3] Gal. iii. 13, iv. 5.

[4] Cf. Lietzmann, *ad loc.*

[5] An "actuality" not unrelated to that of sacrifice itself; see Chapter XIII, § 2.

in the stricter sense, we have seen the "objective" emphasis;
Christ has done something to "redeem" the believer,
prior to any influence of His work on the believer. We
can test this by surveying the much wider terms,
"salvation" and "save". There are one hundred and
fifty-one instances of the Greek equivalents in the New
Testament, forty-five of the noun (*sōteria*) and one hundred
and six of the verb (*sōzō*). These can be classified as
follows:—

(1) Deliverance, in the fundamental and most general
sense . . . . . . . . . .    6
(2) Deliverance from disease or demon-possession  .   16
(3) Deliverance from physical death  .  .  .  .   25
(4) The universality of this deliverance, especially its
extension from Jew to Gentile  .  .  .  .   15
(5) The reference of this deliverance to God or Christ
as its source  .  .  .  .  .  .  .  .   23
(6) The experiential content of the deliverance (faith
and conduct)  .  .  .  .  .  .  .  .   33
(7) The eschatological completion of the deliverance  .   33

———
151

From such a classification, several features at once
emerge. The first is the wide extension of usage, covering
much which would not occur to us as part of the religious
connotation of the term. The first three classes (a third
of the whole) denote deliverance, as from captivity,[1] from
disease or demon-possession,[2] or from physical death.[3]
Even if we include "faith-healing" in our present conception of the scope of the Christian religion, it is clear that
the range of the New Testament idea of "salvation" is
much wider than our own. Salvation meant deliverance
from any kind of ill, and the specific faith of the Christian
increased the intensity, without limiting the extensity, of

[1] Phil. i. 19.
[2] Matt. ix. 21; Luke viii. 36.                    [3] Matt. viii. 25.

the general experience of being "saved", by whatever means.[1]

In the second place, more than one-fifth of the instances (thirty-three) have a more or less definite eschatological reference, the future being sharply contrasted with the present, as in 1 Peter i. 5: "a salvation ready to be revealed in the last time", or involved in the present, as in Mark x. 26, where "saved" is parallel to "enter into the kingdom of God". This reminds us that the idea of "salvation" for the Christians of those days was centred in a future consummation, and not, as so often with us, in a new present character.[2] The modern emphasis tends to fall on salvation from the power of moral evil in present experience. The New Testament, without, of course, denying or excluding this element as an accompaniment or even a condition of salvation, finds its centre of gravity in a cosmic event. Christian work and love are reckoned amongst "the things that accompany salvation".[3]

In the third place, the reference to God or Christ in twenty-three instances reminds us that "save" implies a "Saviour", rather than a moral development. We are apt to dwell on the first part only of St. Paul's words: "Work out your own salvation with fear and trembling, for it is God which worketh in you both to will and to work, for His good pleasure".[4] If the divine side of the experience of salvation is thus emphasized, even when the appeal is directly practical, we can judge of the underlying emphasis in such words as those of Eph. ii. 5, "by grace have ye

[1] We may compare the Old Testament here, noting the change of emphasis from the material to the spiritual.

[2] Note the significance of Rom. xiii. 11: "Now is our salvation nearer than when we believed".

[3] Heb. vi. 9: the Greek phrase stands "for what has a bearing upon, or is connected with; here, for what pertains to and therefore promotes *sōteria*" (Moffatt, *International Critical Commentary*, p. 83).

[4] Phil. ii. 12, 13.

been saved."[1]    The whole idea is much more that of a
divine act, and much less that of a moral process, than the
modern mind is ready to believe, and it is, as we have
seen, a divine act which finds its consummation and
completion in a cosmic event.    Even when we consider the
Johannine emphasis on a present judgment, the salvation
is correlated with the judgment, as in the words: "God
sent not the Son into the world to judge the world; but
that the world should be saved through Him".[2]    Christ
has become to all that obey Him causative (*aitios*) of
eternal salvation.[3]    The emphasis on His "name", the
only saving name,[4] suggests the emphasis on an objective
work, even in the undeveloped theology of the earliest
Church.    In the more developed theology of Eph. i. 13, 14,
we note the sequence of hearing the word, responding to
it with faith, and being "sealed" by the Spirit, with a view
to the final and complete "redemption".    All this "gospel
of your salvation" is wrought "in Christ", viz. in that
sphere of mystical union with Him which is perhaps the
most characteristic feature of the Pauline conception of
salvation.    Another sequence, that of Romans v. 8-10,
gives us the best epitome of the Pauline conception
of salvation, here traced step by step: "The proof of
God's own love for us is in the fact that Christ died for us
whilst we were still sinners.    Much more, then, now that
we are justified by His blood, we shall be saved by Him
from the wrath.    For if, being enemies, we were reconciled
to God by the death of His Son, much more, having been
reconciled, we shall be saved by His life."

This history of man's salvation begins with the love of
God, springing from His own nature, spontaneous and
undeserved by us.    The proof of it is seen in the second

---

[1] The perfect participle is employed, denoting a completed act—on
God's part.
[2] John iii. 17.        [3] Heb. v. 9.        [4] E.g. Acts iv. 12.

step, the grace of Christ in His death for us sinners. This great objective fact is wholly independent of us or of our attitude to it. The third step is that of justification, the acquittal of the sinner through the (forensically) substituted bloodshedding of Christ. The fourth and last step here named is that of salvation, which is specifically connected with the *life* of Christ as justification was with His death. St. Paul's argument is that we were justified being sinners—then how much more, when we have actually been brought into this mystical union with the life of Christ and bear the fruit of the Spirit, how much more may we be sure that this life of His which lives in us will save us at the last judgment!

From such passages it is apparent that any adequate study of the New Testament conception of redemption would involve detailed examination, not only of the more general term "salvation", but also of many closely related and relevant terms, such as "faith", "justification" and "parousia" (the final manifestation of Christ). But, even from what has been already shown, we can claim that the New Testament redemption is strongly eschatological, though essentially marked by present moral and spiritual "accompaniments", that it is inseparably linked to the saving work of Christ, more especially that of His crucifixion and resurrection, that it includes deliverance from all that is alien to man's well-being and promotes "life" in the fullest sense. In fact the favourite antithesis to "salvation" is "death" or "destruction".

§ 4. *Redemption from what?* In the previous section, we have seen that the death of Christ is conceived in the New Testament as redemptive and as saving man from a number of evils to which he is exposed. The fact is common ground in all types of Christian experience, and there are various suggestions of the way in which this salvation was achieved by Christ. Thus we have had the three distinct metaphors of a ransom purchasing release from bondage, a sacrifice effecting reconciliation, a penal substitution securing acquittal. None of these, however, was worked out into a distinct and definite theory of the atonement, as is evident from the frequent blending of metaphors in a single statement.[1] Such blending of metaphors continued through the earlier centuries and continues even to-day, as when "redemption" and "sacrifice" are mistakenly used as if they necessarily implied penalty. But the first of the three outstanding metaphors to be worked out as a definite theory was that of "redemption" in the strict sense of "ransom". It is not possible or necessary here even to outline the history of the "ransom" doctrine.[2] From the time of Irenæus in the second century down to that of Bernard of Clairvaux in the twelfth, "the customary and orthodox statement of the doctrine of the Atonement"[3] was that of a ransom paid by Christ through His death to the devil. It was generally held[4] that man by his sin had put himself into the devil's power, and that this right of possession by the devil carried a just claim for compensation which God met by the ransom of His Son delivered into the devil's power on the Cross. Yet the bargain was a bad one for the devil, since the (concealed) divinity of Christ prevented the devil from holding Him captive. Such a theory is not Scriptural, but it is logical enough when once we take the ransom-metaphor literally and ask to whom was the ransom paid. It was not until Anselm, in the latter part of the eleventh century, criticized

---

[1] Cf. Rom. iii. 24, 25 where all these metaphors are involved.

[2] A convenient review will be found in L. W. Grensted's *A Short History of the Doctrine of the Atonement*, Chapter III; more fully in R. S. Franks's *A History of the Doctrine of the Work of Christ*, esp. I, pp. 56 f, 83 f., 110 f.

[3] Grensted, *op. cit.*, p. 56. This was, of course, often supplemented by sacrificial and other metaphors.

[4] Gregory of Nazianzus is the most notable exception; see Grensted, *op. cit.*, pp. 81, 82.

this doctrine of a ransom paid to the devil, in support of his own theory of a satisfaction of God's honour, that the devil-ransom theory ceased to hold men's thought, though we must not ignore the presence of other metaphors in the complex of atonement ideas amongst which that of "ransom" occurs as a prominent feature. It is, indeed, a highly significant fact that theologians have rarely, if ever, been content with a single line of thought in their attempts to frame a doctrine of atonement. In that fact there is an implicit confession that no single theory is adequate.

If truth could be guaranteed by mere length of tradition (here doubtless largely due to Augustine's endorsement) no doctrine of the Atonement would be more venerable than that of a ransom paid to the devil. However impossible it is for us to-day, we ought to recognize the measure of truth which secured its acceptance through so long a period. The doctrine did recognize the seriousness of sin, did confess that deliverance from it was not in man's power, and that such deliverance must spring from a positive act of God. The recognition also of a certain justice in the devil's claim to man (however crossed by the frequent idea of a divine deception of the devil) did also carry with it the acknowledgement of a "law of righteousness" as accepted by God. The doctrine developed and worked out from this metaphor is no cruder than that from penal substitution has often become.

It is clear that the kind of deliverance which we conceive Christ to have wrought will always be conditioned by our sense of what it is from which we are delivered. In the classical experience of the New Testament, as we have already seen, the expression of this varies with varying relations. There are the physical evils of suffering and death. There are the darkness of ignorance and the corruption of moral evil. There is the sense of bondage to some external power which seems to compel us to do what we would not, or the more specific form of this which makes it bondage to demonic powers or to Satan, the prince of evil. Finally there is the condemnation of the last judgment anticipated by the guilty conscience.[1] It will be seen that the believer is redeemed, partly from evils that threaten him from within his own personality, and partly from powers that menace him from without. The deliverance then consists partly in a change of attitude that will prevent the renewal of these evils through actual sinning, and partly in such overthrow or removal of the power exercised from without as shall remove all fear of it or of the consequences of past sin.

In such an analysis of the evils from which early believers felt that they were redeemed by Christ, there is evidently both a permanent and a transient element. The average man of to-day is still as conscious as ever of the general futility or bondage of much of his life, of the gap between what he knows to be "good" and of his own achievement of it. He is also aware of the intrinsic corruption of his own nature through certain courses of action. These things are undeniable; they are written large in the world's life and literature. But the average man is not usually ready to-day to use the New Testament terminology and to ascribe these evils to his own "sin"; even the religious man, who does make some use of that terminology, uses it often in a very perfunctory or conventional sense that robs it of much of its meaning. His "sin" (as apart from the "crimes" recognized by the law, and any social wrong visibly done to others) is more or less a private affair,

---

[1] For a comprehensive review of these evils see Professor Kilpatrick's article on "Salvation" in the *Encyclopaedia of Religion and Ethics*, XI, 125 ff., where he enumerates and illustrates the following:—

(1) darkness, (2) sin (as consciousness of condemnation), (3) human life (as loss of status), (4) corruption, (5) bondage, (6) fear of demons, (7) fear of death, (8) sensitiveness to suffering, (9) moral evil, (10) the doom of the world.

which he may or may not confess to God. He would prefer the peace of innocence, but since this is irretrievable he makes the best of a vaguely uneasy mind.

It is much the same with the sources of evil external to himself. They are there and not so very different from those of old, though they are differently named and analysed. The fear of the microbe that causes a disease replaces that of the demon which was once thought to cause it. The fear of poverty or social disaster is probably more acute, because of our more highly developed civilization and our "softer" ways of living.[1] The fear of suffering and death still haunts men, even though they trace these features of human life to the working of purely natural laws. The fear of a last judgment is probably rare to-day, since it seems possible to dismiss the great white throne as only a fragment of outworn mythology, like the very existence of Satan. But since such foreboding of judgment to come is the projection (whether true or false) of a guilty conscience into the unknown future, we can hardly expect to find it when the very consciousness of guilt is, as so often, wanting.

On the other hand there is probably as much recognition of moral evil by the majority of decent men as there ever was. It is true that much which was called sin in the Victorian age is no longer so condemned. Failure to observe the Lord's Day after the pattern of the Jewish Sabbath, novel-reading, card-playing, theatre-going, are no longer counted wrong by the ordinary Christian of to-day (whatever he may think of the increased laxity of marital relations, the irresponsibility of parents towards their children, the luxury and extravagance of the idle rich, the dishonesty of much large-scale finance). But,

Our "thirst for applause" is, according to Ruskin (*Sesame and Lilies*, § 3), "on the whole, the strongest impulsive influence of average humanity".

on the other hand, there is a far wider sense of social responsibility in general, and a severer condemnation of the evils wrought by some forms of industrialism, by the malnutrition and bad housing of the poor, by enforced unemployment and by war. There is as strong an antipathy and indignation amongst decent people against every form of tyranny, oppression of the weak, cruelty, as ever before, and one of the results of the large-scale barbarism of Nazi totalitarianism must surely be to increase this healthy antagonism to evil, and to make us even more aware of the lesser and sporadic forms of such evils. It is doubtful, therefore, whether on the whole there is less condemnation of moral evil than before. The more important question is as to the religious evaluation of this evil—a very different thing. That is what we ought to mean by "sin" in the strict sense of the term, for it is a religious, rather than a moral, term. In this sense, there is undoubtedly a decreased consciousness of *sin*; evils are condemned, in ourselves or in others, but their reference to the divine holiness is by no means adequately realized, even amongst those of us who are Christians. This inadequacy is doubtless partly due to the decline in dogmatic certainty and to the subjective tendencies which appear in various forms of humanism, as well as to the false conclusions drawn from Biblical criticism and the excuse for self-excuse found in popular theories of biological and social evolution.

Take, however, the really awakened conscience of a Christian. Any description of it must be more or less individualistic. Yet its elements, as distinct from its forms of expression and particular applications, are universal, since they spring from the permanent relation of the soul to God, as He is known in Jesus Christ. Such a man, relentlessly examining his own life, as no outside spectator of it can, will be first of all aware of particular and definite *sins*; indeed it may have been, as R. L. Stevenson suggested, "a killing sin" that first "stabbed (his) spirit broad awake". It may have been simply the consequences of such a sin that awoke his fears, for men are saved by fear as well as by love. But human personality is so constituted that an initial fear may pass into a deeper consciousness of what a particular sin has meant. It has robbed him of peace, the peace of unity within. It has affected the lives and happiness of others, even if the source of this effect was unknown to them. It has lowered for him the true dignity of human nature, revealing an inner weakness of which he is bitterly ashamed. It has reduced him to the slavery of a fixed habit from which he now seems powerless to escape. Something of all this finds utterance in the seventh chapter of the Epistle to the Romans, culminating in the cry, "O wretched man that I am! who shall deliver me from this body of death?"

But no man made conscious of his particular sins can detach them from his whole life and general attitude. To be conscious of sins means the beginning of the discovery within himself of a general state of sinfulness. The selfish act or habit has behind it the selfish spirit. The constant evasion of moral issues and of moral duties indicates a cowardice of the whole man. The encouragement or mere allowance of the unclean suggestion reveals to the man who is honest with himself that his inner man is a prey to lust, even though social restraints and decent conventions keep him outwardly a respectable member of society. He becomes aware also of all the opportunities for the good act which he has lost in his sinful blindness—the sins of omission as well as those of commission. He realizes his own utter unworthiness before the holy God, whom his sins and his sinfulness concern so deeply. As he enters into the experiential knowledge of the Christian Gospel of grace, his sins and his sinfulness acquire a new significance. They are set over against the background of that grace as

R

churlish ingratitude, the culpable neglect or the wilful rejection of the love of God in Christ. As he looks back over the inner story of his life, he is bound to cry again with Augustine, "Sero te amavi."[1]

A third discovery awaits him, if he is thoughtful enough and persistent enough to make it. As he looks back on the beginnings of a particular sin, he may be able to say, "If I had not encountered so-and-so, if I had not been exposed to that particular temptation, I might never have passed under the thraldom of this sin. If I had been differently brought up, if I had had a different parentage, I might have been a much better man." There is often partial truth in such thoughts, though never enough to give a real defence against the condemnation of conscience. It is true that we are all bound up in a great social complex, and no calculus can ever assign exactly how much of the guilt of sin is mine and how much another's, even in regard to any particular sin.[2] If any man is tempted to make this social solidarity an excuse for his own wrong-doing, let him remember also how his own wrong-doing, directly or indirectly, has added to the evil influences affecting others. When one is set off against the other, there is no room left for self-excuse. Each sinner has refunded something into the evil of social environment as well as drawn something from it.

This social solidarity in sins and sinfulness is a fact which cannot be ignored. It helps to explain the practical "universality" of sin, though there can never be an explanation which fully accounts for that which springs from a free choice. The doctrine of Original Sin, like that of a thorough-going evolutionary explanation of moral evil,

---

[1] "(Too) late have I loved thee"; *Confessions*, X, 27.

[2] The same truth holds of the work of grace in the human heart. No man knows how much is his own and how much is God's; they are too subtly intertwined for any human hand to disentangle.

proves too much and ultimately denies freedom.[1] But it is a fact, not to be ignored in any consideration of the doctrine of Redemption, that the solidarity of the race in sinfulness confronts God with a challenge of its own. Sin is not simply a private matter between the individual and God; it concerns the race and the whole course of the history of the race. If in that history the purpose of God is defeated, He cannot be finally triumphant, even though every individual life were redeemed. History surely has a meaning and value for God, apart from the units that contribute to it.[2] Whatever the present, the past has dishonoured God and *we* cannot redeem that past, though the Apostle urges us to redeem the present.[3] When we are considering such high themes, time itself must be viewed in its eternal meaning. The records of time cannot, from that high view-point, be simply expunged or ignored on the ground that they have, in spite of all their evil, issued in good. God must do something with history as the record of the past, both the history of the race and the history of the individual life which is so integrally a part of it. That history, let it be remembered, exists before God in appalling completeness, not as before us, in the flotsam and jetsam of chance record.

Our answer, therefore, to the question "Redemption from what?" is, broadly speaking, to assert a twofold need. On the one hand, each of us needs new power to live, that is, deliverance from all the evils that threaten us in actual living, whether from within or from without. On the other hand, though in closest relation with the inspiration and maintenance of this new power, we need, as a race and as the individual members of it, redemption from the burden of our guilt, which means our responsibility for the temporal defeat of the divine purpose. That is

---

[1] See Chapter IV, § 2.     [2] See Chapter IV, § 4.
[3] Eph. v. 16; Col. iv. 5.

why the penitent heart is always reaching out for something more than the *energies* of grace, working in the heart and life.   In the Cross of Christ, through many generations, men have found that something more, however difficult they have found its articulation to be.   The crude theories, based on metaphors which at most are but single facets of the jewels in the crown of divine truth, show the history of this attempt at articulation, and even the crudest of them has owed its temporary supremacy to the measure of truth within it.   That Christ has already won a victory over evil on the Cross,[1] all believers can feel; just what that victory means each will try to express in the way that has become most natural to him.   But the history of the doctrine warrants us in saying that the victory won and shared with the believer is not only a victory *within* him which imperfectly reflects and repeats that of Gethsemane and Calvary, but also a victory won *for* him, in a realm beyond his present experience, yet essential to the full redemption for which his heart longs.   Though we are compelled to study the relevant aspects of this redemption separately, we must not forget its unity, the unity of the white light of the Gospel of the glory of God in the face of Jesus Christ, which our prismatic thinking must needs break up into a band of colours, that "stains the white radiance of eternity".

[1] On this metaphor of a conflict in which Christ is victor, see Chapter XIII, § 1, "The Redeemer's Victory."

# CHAPTER XIII

## THE REDEMPTIVE SUFFERING

§ 1. *THE Redeemer's Victory.* In a book[1] which has exercised considerable influence, Professor Aulén of Lund has emphasized the actual victory won by Christ over sin and death as the basis of Atonement. He claims that this realistic conception underlies Pauline doctrine and is continued in Irenæus and the Greek Patristic writers in general, and that it is also dominant in Luther, though not in the later Reformation theologians. For this reason he calls it the "classic" type, as opposed to the "Latin" type represented by Anselm, and the "subjective" type represented by Abelard. The advantages of the "classic" approach to the work of Christ are, it is claimed, that this work is ascribed to a continuous activity of *God* in His grace, that it deals with sin as an objective power, that the work of Christ is directly continued by that of the Holy Spirit, that this view closely links the Incarnation with the Atonement, and that it does justice to the cost of Atonement to God.

These are laudable aims, with which we ought to have every sympathy, but the point is as to how far the so-called "classic" type as such attains them. We need not discuss the use of this rather question-begging epithet "classic", or the validity of Aulén's views as to where the emphasis falls for St. Paul and for Luther. There can be no doubt that the metaphor (for it *is* a metaphor) of a conflict

---

[1] *Christus Victor*, by Gustaf Aulén, translated by A. G. Hebert (S.P.C.K., 1931).

between good and evil in which the historic Christ actually wins the victory is a frequently used and useful way of depicting His work. But does it take us any further than, or even as far as, the other metaphors, which have perhaps much more claim to be called "classic"? God's victory won in Christ is rightly ascribed to the grace of God, but further analysis of this grace has (frankly) to accept "the tension between the Divine Love and the Divine Wrath"; "the Divine Love prevails over the Wrath, the Blessing overcomes the Curse, by the way of Divine self-oblation and sacrifice" (p. 171). This is to help out the metaphor of "victory" by other metaphors, and is not a theological "solution" at all. Nor does it tell us how much the Atonement costs God, since Aulén makes no use of Divine passibility (see § 4). It is by bringing together the *suffering* of Christ and the suffering of God that we may best hope to remove the reproach of transactionalism and to make Christ's work indeed God's.

Further, it is difficult to see, on Aulén's theory, how the work of Christ becomes available for believers in Him, except by way of moving them to win a like victory. Though he approaches his thesis through Irenæus, whose "recapitulation" doctrine does involve the ancient conception of "corporate personality" (see § 3), he makes no explicit use of it. Yet it is indispensable for the interpretation of both Pauline and much Patristic thought. Nor does he offer any modern equivalent to it. We seem to need here some conception of spiritual solidarity (see § 3) and some closer correlation of the victory of believers with that of Christ, such as might be found in the actuality of vicarious suffering as part of the whole social structure.

This points to the most fundamental criticism of Aulén's thesis, viz. the need for a deeper philosophy of history, to give background to the work of Christ, a clearer conception of the relation of time to eternity, and of the correlation of Christ's work, both in the Incarnation and the Cross and the Resurrection, with the eternal Personality of God. "Victory" is indeed a vivid and dramatic metaphor to describe Christ's work, but it depicts *result* rather than method and process. Nor ought Aulén to dismiss any attempt to go further into the eternal realities as "rationalization"; all attempts to understand truth, including his own, might be so treated.[1] We ought rather to ask whether a right understanding of the victory won by Christ over sin and death does not itself suggest a deeper view than his. It can be claimed that the ultimate victory consists in a suffering, at once human and divine, which, through the gracious attitude of the Sufferer, transforms the very consequences of evil, for time and for eternity, in the individual and in the race. If we were to try to suggest this in terms of Aulén's metaphor, it would be to say that Christ's victory includes and involves that change of attitude in His opponents which itself transforms, not only the evil will, but its effects, and that the inevitable suffering brought by sin is so shared by God with the penitent sinner as to remove its worst burden. But to say this is to expand a useful, though partial, metaphor far beyond its limits, and to show its inadequacy for a fuller doctrinal theory.

Simply as one among other metaphors, the conception has real value for devotional thought, though the figure of victory in the New Testament is explicitly used of the *believers* more often than of "the captain of their salvation made perfect through sufferings".[2] The victory which overcame the world is our faith.[3] It is when this mortal has put on immortality that death is swallowed up in victory; thanks be to God which giveth us the victory

[1] "Reason can be compared to the force of gravitation, the weakest of all natural forces, but in the end the creator of suns and stellar systems—those great societies of the Universe" (A. N. Whitehead, *Symbolism*, p. 82).

[2] Heb. ii. 10.

[3] 1 John v. 4.

through our Lord Jesus Christ.[1] The saints who stand
around the glassy sea and sing the song of Moses the
servant of God and of the Lamb are themselves described
as victorious[2] according to the frequent watchword of the
Apocalypse, "To him that overcometh."[3] It is by the
blood of the Lamb that they have overcome.[4] But it is
also said that the Lion who is a Lamb has been victorious,[5]
whilst the "called and chosen and faithful" who are with
Him shall share *His* victory.[6]

In the Synoptic Gospels, it was primarily the demons
over whom Jesus is represented as victorious,[7] those
demons who were the contemporary explanation of disease
and suffering.   In the Pauline Epistles, we catch glimpses
of "the principalities and powers and world-rulers of this
darkness, the spiritual hosts of wickedness in the heavenly
places".[8]  It is over these that Christ has triumphed in
His cosmic victory.[9]  But before we can give much reality
to a victory won by Christ over the demons or over Satan
their prince, we must decide how far we really believe in
them.   At any rate we cannot replace them by abstractions
such as "Law", "Sin", "Death" and still keep the former
reality of a *personal* conflict.   We are in fact thrown back
on those considerations that met us in asking the question,
"Redemption from what?" (Chap. XII, § 4).  If we
emphasize—as surely we must—the conflict of Christ with
moral evil, from the Temptation to Gethsemane and the
Cross, we must go deeper into the nature of things before
we can replace ancient demonology by more adequate
conceptions.   The evil is as real as ever, and the barbarians
of to-day may quite possibly lead us to take the devil

[1] 1 Cor. xv. 54, 57.
[2] Rev. xv. 2; cf Rom. xii. 21, 1 John ii. 13, 14, iv. 4.
[3] Rev. ii. 7, etc.
[4] Rev. xii. 11.                              [5] Rev. v. 5, 6.
[6] Rev. xvii. 14.                             [7] Matt. xii. 28.
[8] Eph. vi. 12.                               [9] Col. ii. 15.

and all his angels more seriously than we have been apt to do in modern times.

§ 2. *The Redeemer's Sacrifice.* We have taken "redemption", in its narrower and original sense of "ransoming", as the starting-point of our discussion, and this is justifiable, both on Biblical and historical grounds, and because of the intrinsic value of the metaphor to describe what the Cross of Christ has actually done for believers—to obtain for them a deliverance from the captivity of sin, and the burden of its guilt. But redemption in the wider sense rightly includes the use of other metaphors, and amongst them from the very beginning is that of sacrifice.

Here we must go back to the Old Testament, for that is the historical source of the New Testament usage, and the right interpretation of that usage is admittedly conditioned by the Old Testament meaning of sacrifice. Sacrifice is, of course, by no means peculiar to Israel, but it certainly received a characteristic development within Israel. The ancient nomadic sacrifices of the Semites were apparently of the type later known as the "peace-offering", a communion sacrifice, in which the blood of the victim was drained out on the sacred stone, whilst the offerer and his family group partook of the flesh. It was probably within Canaan, and from their Canaanite kinsfolk, that the Hebrews derived the "burnt-offering", to be interpreted as a simple gift to the deity. Around these two types of animal sacrifice, dominant in the pre-exilic period, other sacrifices, such as the "meal-offering" (of cereals), naturally gathered, and these offerings would acquire differing meanings, according to the intention of the offerers. The two chief forms of animal sacrifice, frequently combined, might be simply eucharistic, expressing gratitude for past favours, or petitionary, accompanied by the prayer for help in specific circumstances, or expiatory, to wipe out some offence to the deity, or propitiatory, as intended to change His attitude to the offerer. The prophets' criticism of contemporary sacrifices was not necessarily intended to do away with them altogether, but was more probably intended to check the abuse of them, by which they became the substitutes, instead of the accompaniments, expressions and encouragements, of true piety and right conduct.

But the prophets help us to understand the meaning of sacrifice for the Israelites in another and less familiar way. Every reader of the Old Testament will recall some of the acts of "prophetic symbolism", such as the wearing of a yoke or the breaking of pottery by Jeremiah, or Isaiah's walking about Jerusalem bare-foot and lightly-clad. These acts are more than dramatic expressions of what the prophet has otherwise said,[1] simply expressing bondage, destruction or captivity. Like the spoken word, they are instrumental acts, helping to bring about that which they signify. They are part of the divine activity, that part which the prophets initiate. They are an essential and operative feature of the prophet's contribution to the shaping of history. No doubt, if considered apart from the prophetic conception of God, they would be little more than forms of the symbolical magic which is so wide-spread amongst early and primitive races. As such, the prophets would themselves have condemned them, as surely as they condemned the merely *opus operatum* view of sacrifices. But, taken up into their faith in the living God of Israel, prophetic symbolism ceased to be magic and became religion; this was one of the means by which God worked His will and initiated His mighty acts.

We can interpret the Hebrew sacrifices in the same way, with the confidence that the Hebrew prophets might

---

[1] For the proof of what follows I must refer to *Old Testament Essays*, pp. 1–17 (1927; published by Griffin & Co.).

themselves have so interpreted them, had not the circumstances of their times called for a different emphasis. The sacrifices also were symbolic acts, actualized approaches to God, which initiated a new relation to Him for the group or the individual, when offered with the right intention. The communion-meal of the peace-offerings was a realistic act of fellowship with the deity on whose altar the victim's blood had been poured. The gift of the burnt-offering expressed and confirmed the loyal homage of the offerer to God. These acts were the acts of the offerer himself and continued to be so right down to the latest times, whatever elaboration of the ritual was developed by the priestly professionals, notably in regard to the later sin-offering. The lay offerer cut the throat of the animal victim that its blood might be given to God. The lay offerer laid his hands on the victim, not to transfer his sin to it, or to make it his substitute, but simply to claim it for his own and to say to God in unmistakable act, "This is mine, and I give it to Thee." The whole act of sacrifice thus initiated a new relation to God, affecting the past, present, or future.

Already, within the Old Testament, this widespread and familiar practice had led to the metaphorical use of the conception, as applied to the offering of human lives to God.[1] The most notable example of this is to be found in the idea of exiled Israel as the suffering Servant.[2] Here the sacrificial interpretation is unmistakable, and the Servant's suffering is explicitly made an *asham*, or "guilt-offering" (one of the post-exilic developments of sacrifice, emphasizing compensation). The Servant was not originally a Messianic figure, and it was one of the most notable and influential advances of New Testament

[1] This is possibly a renewal, on the higher level of spiritual relations, of the ancient practice of human sacrifice, long since abandoned by the Israelites.
[2] Isa. lii. 13–liii. 12.

theology beyond that of the Old Testament to set forth the idea of a Messiah whose sufferings could be regarded as a sacrifice.

The metaphor of sacrifice underlies our Lord's words at the Last Supper: "This is My blood of the covenant which is poured out for many."[1] The most natural explanation of the phraseology is that the fundamental covenant of Sinai is in view, spiritualized by the consciousness of that new and better covenant of which Jeremiah spoke, whilst the words "for many"[2] are a conscious echo of Isa. liii. 12: "he bare the sin of many." The covenant-sacrifice at Sinai was of the peace-offering type, the manipulation of the blood (dashed on both people and altar) effecting realistically (after the manner of prophetic symbolism) the blood-kinship alliance of Yahweh and Israel. On the higher level of a more spiritually conceived relation, Christ says that His blood (about to be poured out) will create a bond between the new Israel of His disciples and God, and that the cup of wine which the disciples now share is a prophetic symbol of that actual blood-shedding, an instrumental act which initiates the completion of the covenant by the death on Calvary, for it is Calvary anticipated in miniature.

St. Paul makes relatively little use of the metaphor of sacrifice, for his chief concern is with the very different forensic conception of a new "righteousness", and with the mystical complement or rather, content, of this in a faith-union with Christ. But it is significant that the sacrificial adjective "propitiatory" creeps into the dominantly forensic statement of Romans iii. 25.[3] Here, and

[1] So Mark xiv. 24. Matt. xxvi. 28 expands by the addition "unto remission of sins". St. Paul adds the adjective "new" to covenant, making more explicit the reference to the Jeremianic prophecy (1 Cor. xi. 25 cf. Jer. xxxi. 31–34), as does Luke (xxii. 20).

[2] Also similarly found in the "ransom" passage, see Chap. XII. § 3.

[3] It would not affect the reference to sacrifice, if this were rendered (as by C. H. Dodd, *The Bible and the Greeks*, p. 94) "expiatory".

all along the history of the doctrine of redemption, the metaphor of sacrifice shows its great adaptability and its fitness to combine with the use of conceptions springing from other metaphors. The most consistent and elaborate use of the metaphor of sacrifice is, of course, that to be found in the Epistle to the Hebrews (esp. viii.–x. 18), where Christ is the High Priest who offers His own death upon the Cross as an eternal sacrifice, securing an eternal redemption and cleansing the consciences of men, as the Jewish system could never do. Christ's offering (in obedience to the will of God) is complete and final. The rending of His flesh in this sacrifice was the rending of the veil which hid the heavenly sanctuary from human eyes. In worship we follow the new and living way which He has opened up into the presence of God by His sacrifice of Himself. He suffered on the Cross without the gate, just as the ancient sin-offering was burned without the camp.[1] So we may go forth from the old Israel with Him, bearing His reproach, remembering the better and eternal city, and offering through Him our sacrifice of praise and right doing.

In the Epistle to the Hebrews the sacrificial death of Christ is brought into relation with three different types of sacrifice in the Old Testament, viz. the covenant-offering, the sin-offering and the special offerings of the Day of Atonement. The references to the covenant-offering take the use of the blood in a covenant-sacrifice as an accepted datum of thought, just as is done in the covenant of the Lord's Supper. The interest of the writer is in the superiority of the new sacrifice to the older sacrifices; he is not concerned to give a philosophy of sacrifice, in order to show in what its necessity consists. In x. 11, 12 the daily offering of the old régime is contrasted with Christ's offering of a single sacrifice for sins for ever (cf.

---

[1] ix. 18–22, cf. x. 29, xii. 24, xiii. 20.

x. 18).  In ii. 17, Christ is said "to make propitiation for the sins of the people".[1]  This simply tells us the result of Christ's death, without anything definite as to the precise way by which that result is reached.  The central point of contact with the Old Testament ritual is found in the sacrifices of the Day of Atonement.  The main emphasis falls on the entrance of the high priest within the veil.  Christ entered once for all, taking with Him, not the blood of goats and oxen, but the blood of His own sacrifice consummated on earth (ix. 12).  He was able to do this—to die and yet to live with the blood of his own sacrifice still at His disposal—because of "eternal Spirit", because His nature made Him greater than death and enabled Him to go on living forever (ix. 14).  The sacrifice is not one of physical life alone, but neither is it of ethical obedience alone; it is both, in the unity of the Redeemer's personality.  By such a sacrifice, and its complement in the obedience of the believer, following the Pioneer and Consummator of his faith, the necessary reconciliation with God was wrought, and no further question needed to be asked.

Both in the New Testament and in the subsequent history of the doctrine of redemption the metaphor of sacrifice has held a prominent and permanent place down to our time, though the actual rites from which the metaphor was drawn have long ceased to be familiar scenes and must be searched for in the darker corners of the earth. The metaphor lends itself, even more easily than that of "ransoming", to combination with other theories.  Especially does it commend itself for the language of devotion, whether in prayer or hymn, either alone or blended into the whole complex of ideas drawn from different sources which may go to express the value of Christ's death upon the Cross for the believer.  Thus in the Consecration

---

[1] Cf. Luke xviii. 13 for the same verb.

Prayer of the Anglican Communion Service, He is said "to suffer death upon the Cross for our redemption; who made there (by his one oblation of himself once offered) a full, perfect and sufficient sacrifice, oblation and satisfaction, for the sins of the whole world". Here the student of the history of the doctrine will detect the three metaphors of ransoming, sacrifice and satisfaction—each pointing to a different theory, if it were worked out logically as, at one time or another, it has been. Again the first verse of "Rock of Ages" emphasizes the sacrificial efficacy of the cleansing power of the Cross, whilst the second verse turns to the very different forensic thought of the fulfilment of the law's demands.[1] In a comprehensive book called *The Fullness of Sacrifice*, Bishop Hicks has worked out the doctrine of the Atonement from the metaphor of sacrifice, as was well worth doing. He rightly claims that the metaphor in the New Testament must be explained by the practice in the Old Testament.[2] He further argues that Jewish sacrifice is realized in practice under "three main forms; the sin-offering, representing the idea of the surrendered life: the burnt-offering, that of the life dedicated and transformed; the peace-offering, that of the life bestowed and shared".[3] Now, whatever the devotional truth and value of these conceptions, they are an artificial systematization of the sacrifices named which does not correspond with their actual meaning in the history of Israel's religion. The emphasis of these conceptions on the life of the victim is drawn from the third type, the communion-meal of the peace-offering, and this is made (as in Robertson Smith's theory of sacrifice) to dominate the rest too ex-

[1] An interesting example of such combination may be seen in Milton's *Paradise Lost*, III, ll. 226 ff., where the figures of penalty, victory, sacrifice, satisfaction and ransom will all be found—"on Me let thine anger fall", "I shall rise victorious", "a sacrifice glad to be offered", "satisfy for man", "ransom'd with his own dear life".

[2] *Op. cit.*, p. 248.  [3] *Op. cit.*, p. 249.

clusively in a way that does not correspond with the true theology of the Old Testament and would not be accepted by its best exponents to-day. Hebrew sacrifices are too complex in origin to be explained by a single theory; if they had to be, the simple idea of a gift expressing homage is probably more fundamental in Hebrew thought, and anyhow, the attitude towards sacrifice in New Testament times was rather that of obedience to the ordinances of the Torah than of any conscious return to the nomadic "peace-offering". Further, the sin-offering was largely concerned with the removal of ritual offences by the peculiar manipulation of the blood and no more expresses the idea of the surrendered life than does the burnt-offering, whilst the burnt-offering is itself the completest form of gift to God and has no necessary suggestion of a life "dedicated and transformed"; it may be and often was simply an expression of gratitude for divine help in the past, or the ground of an appeal for divine help in the future.

If, however, we keep closer to the historical meaning of sacrifice in the Old Testament, and follow the suggestions of "prophetic symbolism" which we have seen to be closely allied with it, there are several reasons which we can give for the universality and permanence of the use of the metaphor. The death of Christ on the Cross was the costliest of gifts to His Father, and so far as we are one with Him by faith—a point to which we shall return later—it is *our* gift too, a gift we could never have made without Him. That gift by its intrinsic nature and value gives us confidence in approaching God. If it is indeed made our gift, how can God reject us who humbly approach Him in the company of the great Offerer of Himself? It is a gift which carries with it the promise and potency of all the gifts which we can hope to offer acceptably—for the whole life of the Offerer gives meaning to the death, and only as we are led to share that life can we claim to share in the offering of the death. So far as we do sincerely share in the offering, we are beginning in it "to present (our) bodies a living sacrifice, holy, acceptable to God, which is (our) reasonable worship".[1] Along such lines as these, the interpretation of Christ's death as a sacrifice will always be fruitful. But the metaphor does not in itself satisfy our thought, when we try to turn it into a theory; or rather, shall we say? the metaphor, true as far as it can take us, needs completion from a wider range of thought, and all the more because the practice from which the metaphor was drawn is no longer with us, to actualize the intensity of the spiritual meaning.

§ 3. *The Redeemer as Representative.* Every doctrine of redemption worthy of the name implies the "vicarious" principle of being or acting in another's stead, or on behalf of another. This principle is not, of course, to be identified with a particular form of redemptive theory, such as that of penal substitution. Any conception of the work of Christ which makes Him the effective representative of man in His redemptive work may also properly be called "vicarious". Such conceptions have found distinguished exponents, notably McLeod Campbell and Moberly, who would figure in any adequate historical review. But quite apart from the use made of "representation" by these writers, such as the *offering* of a perfect penitence on behalf of man (McLeod Campbell) or the *identification* of a perfect penitence with the imperfect penitence of man (Moberly), the term raises an important question for any constructive theory of the Atonement. This is as to the way in which Christ is related to man and men, so that these may benefit by what He has achieved. If the answer given is "by faith in Christ" this is not enough, for it leaves open the further question as to the rational grounds for this faith. If the

[1] Rom. xii. 1; this passage is more fully discussed in Chapter XIV, § 1.

S

reply to this is, "the human nature which Christ shares with us", we might still ask what constitutes Him the effective representative of man or men. Representation by sample does not in itself amount to executive representation. As Professor Grensted puts the point, "the only true manward theory is one which does not merely regard man as in some way rising to welcome the display of a nobler manhood, but which sees in Christ the reunion of man and God, the fulfilment of ideal humanity for and in each individual man who by faith puts on Christ."[1] His own suggestion is that "the way of union is through mysticism",[2] a view constantly recurring through the long history of the doctrine. We may clarify our ideas in relation to this matter by reference to "corporate personality", an ancient conception which figures largely in the Bible and in later theological developments as well as in the realm of law.[3] According to this conception, a larger or smaller group (nation, clan or family) could be treated as a unity, originally conceived as based upon the blood-tie and traced back to a common ancestor. The whole group could function through, or be seen in, any one of its members, as the early ideas of blood-revenge show; he was regarded realistically as the representative of the group, without any special delegation to the office. Thus, in early law, the individual could be punished for the faults of the group, or the group for those of the individual. Since this "corporate personality" was not confined to the living (as we may see, for example, amongst

[1] *A Short History of the Doctrine of the Atonement*, p. 372.
[2] *Op. cit.*, p. 371.
[3] Cf. "The Hebrew Conception of Corporate Personality" by H. Wheeler Robinson, in Beiheft 66 of the *Zeitschrift für die alttestamentliche Wissenschaft* (*Werden und Wesen des alten Testaments*, 1936); H. C. Dowdall, "Corporate Personality psychologically regarded as a System of Interests" (*Proceedings of the Aristotelian Society*, for Nov. 25, 1935), and "L'Anatomie d'un Corps Social, etc." (*Recueil d'Etudes en l'honneur d'Edouard Lambert*).

the Hebrews), but included the dead and the yet unborn, the group could be conceived as living for ever.

The theological importance of this conception may be seen in the Pauline contrast of Adam and Christ.[1] The sentence of death was passed upon all men because of the sin of their representative, Adam; equally, the gift of "life" was bestowed on all who are Christ's because of His "act of righteousness". In both instances, there is a formal conception of what we might loosely call "social solidarity", which is constituted for Adam's group by descent, and for Christ's group by the new relation of being "in Christ" by faith. This "mystical" relation may be called (for the Apostle) the inside of the external relation of corporate personality, by which Christ is the Head of the one Body (a further metaphor, which suggests how closely the unity of the group is conceived and how vital is the doctrine of the Holy Spirit to give reality to the mystical relation).

Further applications of the ancient and wide-spread conception of corporate personality may be seen in the Recapitulation doctrine of Irenæus, according to which Christ sums up the human race, and thus is able to "redeem" it by the realism of His saving acts, and again in the Augustinian doctrine of Original Sin, though the corporate unity of the race in Adam should not be confused with the transmission of sin by *concupiscentia*. But we certainly cannot simply transfer the ancient conception to a modern theology; our whole way of regarding life (since Rousseau) is far too individualistic. A modern conception of "social solidarity" is usually based on economic or moral ideas; it is a goal rather than a starting-point, as it was for ancient thought. But we still need some form of thought to be the protective shell for the kernel of faith-mysticism, in order that we may individually say of Christ, "He has won *my* victory; He was offered

[1] Rom. v. 12–21; 1 Cor. xv. 22, 45–49.

for *me*; He suffered in *my* stead", or, if that form be preferred, "on my behalf".

Dr. Vincent Taylor has recently stressed the idea of Christ as man's representative.[1] His analysis of the idea seems to me to show both its strength, and also, when taken alone, its weakness. He includes in the idea three elements: the obedience of Christ, His submission to the judgment of sin by God, and His perfect penitence for the sins of men (here following McLeod Campbell and Moberly, who have evidently exercised considerable influence upon him). But he recognizes the need for something more by passing from this conception to the supplementary one of sacrificial offering. His use of the Old Testament sacrifices (as mainly eucharistic and representative, and resting on the identification of the offerer with his offering) is much nearer the historic truth than that of Bishop Hicks.[2] But we need a rationale of sacrifice to make the conception cogent and satisfying as a doctrine of Atonement, however valuable it is to express religious devotion. It has already been suggested that such a rationale for the Old Testament sacrifices can be found in the actuality of the event, the accomplishment of a tiny fragment of history in the miniature world of the offerer. If this explanation be accepted, it is obviously applicable when the metaphor of sacrifice is applied to Christ. On His own supreme level, His life and His death bring something to pass which is admittedly the fulfilling of God's will. The focal event of the Cross has behind it, and therefore in it, the whole force of Christ's obedience and consecration to His Father's purpose. His offering in both life and death is therefore one of the highest worth to God. But the use of this rich metaphor of sacrifice does not answer our question—a

[1] In *Jesus and His Sacrifice* (1937), pp. 305 ff., and in *The Atonement in New Testament Teaching* (1940), pp. 254 ff., at greater length. See also Chap. VI of his latest book, *Forgiveness and Reconciliation*.

[2] See the previous section.

question of the intellect rather than of the faith which instinctively accepts its truth—as to how that sacrifice avails for each of us, how it is linked to us, whose own offerings to God are always imperfect.

Perhaps the best answer to this question lies along the line indicated in the latter part of Chap. XI, viz. in regarding Christ as linking the imperfect personality of man with the perfect personality of God (in the given conditions of earthly limitation). If He is indeed that to which our best and worthiest aspirations point from afar (and it is the intuitive assertion of Christian faith that He is), then He becomes man's only true representative by *intrinsic right*. Why should we not give full theological weight to this devotional fact? Why should we not find intellectual satisfaction (so far as that is possible when our limited and sin-handicapped understanding tries to deal with the mysteries of God) in this unique category of actuality? Christ is my representative in "all I could never be", simply by being Himself. Faith—my faith—is the condition of my entrance into the "corporate personality" of His Body, the Church of the Spirit. But whether I have faith or not, He is there and His perfect representation of me is waiting for me when I am ready to make use of it, in my approach to God. The actual confidence which He then gives me is the only and sufficient proof that He adequately represents me before God.

But if this line of thought warrants the conception of Christ as the representative of man, it is not yet adequate as a doctrine of redemption.[1] We must look more closely

---

[1] It is significant that Dr. Vincent Taylor should prefer the term "reconciliation" (*katallage*) to "redemption" (*apolutrōsis*); see p. 279 of *The Atonement in New Testament Teaching*. He says: "Redemption . . . is of more restricted content, since it concentrates attention more especially upon the thought of deliverance from evil and from sin." It is for that very reason that I have adopted it to denote the central theme of this book; it seems to me to avoid the ambiguity of "reconciliation", which can permit (though not when given the New Testament content of *katallage*) a "moral influence" theory of the Atonement.

into the work of Christ to find that, and, as I believe,
must carry back His suffering as man's Representative to
His suffering as God's.

§ 4. *The Divine Redemption.*　In the previous sections
of this chapter we have briefly reviewed some of the most
suggestive and helpful ways of regarding the Cross of
Christ, in which the Christian has constantly found the
fulcrum of God's redeeming work.　We have seen that
Christ appears as victorious over the moral evil which is
man's worst foe, as offering a sacrifice of perfect obedience
to His Father which man has failed to bring, and as man's
representative by the intrinsic right of a perfectly fulfilled
manhood.　But, however fruitful these lines of thought,
they do not seem to carry us far enough.　They each
emphasize an achievement in terms of humanity, without
sufficiently correlating it with the *divine* redemption of
man.　They are, moreover, apt to leave us with the
suggestion of a "transaction", less repellent, indeed, than
that of a crudely penal substitution, but still making
redemption external to God.　There is here real difficulty.
Can we meet it, as we tried to meet the related and underlying problem of the Person of Christ, by applying the
principle of the "inclusiveness" of personality?

On the Cross of Christ, Christian faith sees the God-man
bearing in suffering the sin of the world.　In the earlier
theology of the Church, however, it was assumed (because
of the Greek presuppositions on which that theology was
largely based) that God Himself is incapable of suffering.
Accordingly, it has been maintained by "orthodox"
theology that the human nature of Christ alone suffered,
whilst the divine appropriated the results of that suffering.
Thus von Hügel can speak of "genuine, indeed immense,
Suffering within one of the two natures of the one Person,
Christ . . . (God) has allowed real, direct Suffering to come

as close to Him, in the humanity of Christ, as, in the nature of things, Suffering could come".[1] But, as we have seen, this doctrine of two distinct natures in one Person, classically formulated at Chalcedon, states rather than solves the problem, and does not satisfy the unity of the Personality which we meet in the Gospels. It cannot, therefore, be made the basis of any adequate doctrine of the Atonement, for it leaves us with an unreconciled dualism.

If, however, we approach the suffering of the Cross along the line of that "inclusiveness" of personality already suggested, we can get nearer to a conception of the unity of the human and the divine in the work of redemption, and avoid disruption of the Personality of the Redeemer. The spiritual kinship of man and God rules out any *historical* difference between sinless humanity, and the divinity which accepts the limitations of that humanity, though the *doctrinal* recognition of the divine within the human is naturally of cardinal importance. This would point to the further belief that, within the limits of our humanity at this particular point of time, God Himself suffers on the Cross of the God-man.

We ought not to be deterred from saying this by the objection that it repeats the ancient heresy of Patripassianism, and would incur the scathing epigram of a Tertullian. The whole approach of modalistic Monarchianism to the Cross was very different from ours, moving from different presuppositions to different conclusions. "It is not an attempt to bring Christian doctrine into relation with an *a priori* view that passibility belongs to the divine nature."[2]

Given an historical and undogmatic exegesis, there ought to be no question that the Biblical picture of God

[1] "Suffering and God", in *Essays and Addresses*, Second Series, pp. 204, 209.

[2] J. K. Mozley, *The Impassibility of God*, p. 36. The context gives a useful survey of historical Patripassianism.

is of One who suffers, and that this picture cannot be dismissed as merely figurative.[1] In the Old Testament He is amply portrayed as afflicted in the afflictions of His people, moved to anger by their sin and to joy by their well-doing. He carries them as His burden, instead of being a burden to them, and He cannot finally abandon them, notwithstanding the sorrow they bring to Him. In the New Testament, the measure of His love is said to be His sacrificial gift of His Son, a gift costlier than any other to Himself. If God loves, He must know the sorrow that all love brings and the sacrifices which it entails, when the object of that love acts unworthily. If the suffering Christ is the true Revealer of God, if indeed we see the divine glory in the face of Jesus Christ, that glory must not be robbed of its redemptive intensity by making God impassible. No human love would be worthy of the name if it were incapable of suffering for love's sake. But if the highest levels of our humanity do not in some degree reveal God, what can we know of Him? We cannot think rightly of God as existing in Aristotelian detachment from the world. An unconcerned heaven above, whilst there is a sinful and suffering earth below, would be an impossible conception for the Christian. If there is joy in the presence of the angels of God over one sinner that repenteth, not less must there be sorrow over the sin that made the repentance necessary. Joy and sorrow (which is suffering) are the heavenly correlates of the earthly actualities of good and evil.[2]

Why, then, do some theologians still hesitate to say that God suffers? The objections raised are chiefly three— that suffering implies some kind of frustration, that any change in God brings Him out of the eternal into the

---

[1] For a fuller discussion of divine passibility than can here be given, reference can be made to my book, *Suffering, Human and Divine*, Chapter IX.

[2] See Part I, Chapter IV.

temporal order, and that a suffering God cannot be the Absolute which philosophy demands. In reply we may admit that suffering does mean for man some kind of frustration, some constraint imposed upon him by his finite nature or environment. But even man rises above such frustration when he willingly accepts the suffering in order to accomplish something worthy. Is it, then derogatory to God that, having limited Himself by the very creation of man endowed with some measure of freedom, He should face and accept the suffering which the working out of His own purpose brings? As for the argument that suffering brings God into the temporal order, we may properly answer that this order belongs to Him rather than He to it, and that we ought to think of the temporal process as taken up into the eternal purpose of God. The time-order which is inseparable from our experience and conception of a personality always developing cannot, of course, mean exactly the same thing for Him as for ourselves. But it must mean something, and something real. The process, whether in the individual or in the race, must have some place in the mind and heart of Him who has willed it, however difficult or impossible it may be for us to conceive the divine consciousness of a *process*. As for the suggestion that the God and Father of our Lord Jesus Christ cannot be identified with the Absolute of philosophy, we might fairly ask whether the conception of Absolute Being, without relations, has any religious value at all. The God in whom the Christian believes is the sole source of all being beyond Himself, but by the very fact of His creative activity in pursuit of His eternal and unchanging purpose He has necessarily limited Himself. Self-limitation is indeed the single and adequate answer to every form of objection to the passibility of God, for self-limitation may be a real fulfilment of personality, human or divine.

We may find support for the claim that God Himself
suffers through and for man in the fact of vicarious suffering,
writ so large on Nature and history.  Before we begin to
speculate on its significance, we can see that all life is
actually bound together, not man's alone, but that also
of the animal world beneath him.  Each individual form
of life must struggle in order to survive—or it would
cease to be.  But each depends on its social and economic
environment, for existence, sustenance, protection, education.  That universal interdependence constantly involves
suffering, and suffering for others.  At the lower stages of
life this is instinctive, but at the higher it becomes conscious
and even, in the full sense, voluntary.  There is no need
to illustrate this familiar truth, which belongs to the life-
pattern of us all, beginning with our birth out of travail.
But it is vicarious suffering that enters into the noblest
spiritual achievement, and the Cross of Christ, considered
simply as a fact of history, is its purest and highest instance.
But why should we stop there, and rob God of the highest
form of attainment which human life displays?  Ought we
not to expect that God will enter into this fellowship of
suffering which all His creatures share—not as they do, by
the sheer necessity of social relationship in its most
realistic forms, but by that higher compulsion of love
which is supremely His own?  Such divine self-sacrifice
is visible on the Cross of Christ, if that Cross is integrally
and inclusively related to God.  Then, and only then, is
the true spiritual continuity of the universe fully manifest.

If, however, no more than this were said, the argument
would justly be criticized as failing to supply any doctrine
of redemption that was more than "revelational".  The
Cross of Christ would be the symbol and manifestation of
the hidden suffering of God, by which man is moved to
penitence and inspired to believe that the God who suffers
through him and with him is thus declared to be ready to

forgive him.   But we have argued that something more is
needed to supply an adequate doctrine of redemption.   To
realize what this is, and how it is supplied, it is necessary
to recall previous references to sin and guilt.

We saw (Chapter XII, § 4) that man has a triple responsibility for sin, and therefore a triple form of guilt, which is
moral blameworthiness before God.   There are the particular sins which he has committed, the general sinfulness
of his nature, and his share in what was called the social
solidarity of sin.   Whatever change of personal attitude
may be brought about, as when genuine penitence brings
self-condemnation, and prevents the repetition of sins
already committed, his personal renunciation of his own
past does not cancel his responsibility for it, or for the
habits of the sinful nature which he has built up, habits
which make the present change of will so hard to carry
into effect.   Moreover, the effects of his sin on other lives
have largely passed beyond his control, just as the effects
of the sins of others upon himself have passed beyond
theirs.   In fact, we can never make an exact distribution
of responsibility, which means of guilt, and each of us
must be held to share in the guilt of the whole world.

By the very structure of the universe, by the creation of
a world meant to achieve the divine purpose, it is impossible
for sin to be the concern of man alone.   Sin, as a partial
or temporary defeat of the divine purpose, concerns God.
Just so far as we take seriously the achievement of moral
good as having value for God, so we must take seriously
the moral evil which conflicts with that purpose, and
brings suffering to God.   True, He is Himself responsible
for the *possibility* of moral evil, since He has given to man
freedom of moral choice, a freedom which does not belong
to the stars in their courses.   But man's own measure of
responsibility for the abuse of his freedom remains.   He
is guilty of bringing upon God the sorrow of a defeated

purpose, and the spiritual suffering entailed by the very existence of moral evil in a world which must constantly be sustained by God.

What will be the reaction of the holy God to the impact of this suffering? We may approach that highly important and much debated question by asking what is the first reaction of a good man to the evil which he encounters outside himself. Surely he will feel and show uncompromising antagonism to it. Whatever allowances he may make for the history and circumstances of the evil-doer, however humble he may be in remembering his own moral failures, he will react with a righteous indignation and a justifiable wrath. The good conscience, unless misled by sophistries and sentimentalities, will also demand some measure of retribution.[1] The punishment of the evil-doer may and rightly does include the aim of making him a better man by discipline, or of deterring others from imitating him. But these distinct aims must not obscure the moral truth that the evil which brings suffering on others shall not escape with immunity from suffering. The principle of retribution is part of the moral structure of the universe. The good citizen must be, on occasion, a minister of wrath and an executor of penalty. In an ordered society such responsibility is normally delegated to its properly appointed representatives—police, magistrates, judges— the evil being treated as crime against the social order, and the aspect of deterrence being usually uppermost. But the fundamental justification for penal law is desert, not philanthropy.[2]

If, then, there is a legitimate and indeed necessary place for "wrath" and the infliction of penalty in the

[1] On this whole question, see the able and convincing discussion of penalty in Edwyn Bevan's *Symbolism and Belief*, pp. 206–51. See also Dale, *The Atonement*, Chapter VIII.

[2] So Dale, *op. cit.*, pp. 375 f.: "He must deserve to be punished. or the law has no right to punish him."

attitude and conduct of good men, we must not eliminate these from our conception of the holy God. In fact, the recognition of divine wrath and retribution has been a constantly recurrent feature of the awakened conscience, and is not to be dismissed as mere anthropomorphism. If they do not belong to divine holiness, then we have no means of knowing what holiness really means. It is the healthy, not the morbid, conscience that recognizes suffering as the due penalty of sin. The connection between particular evil and particular suffering may not be easy to trace, or may not be traceable at all, save as the outcome of God's general control of the spheres of Nature, history and the individual consciousness. But however chary we ought to be of interpreting other people's misfortunes as penalties, we are on surer ground in judging ourselves. The guilty conscience will often accept suffering as penalty, whatever its precise cause, knowing with the certainty of an inner conviction that it is deserved. Indeed, it is often only through the experience of the consequences of evil-doing (including any suffering thus interpreted as penalty) that the consciousness is awakened to the heinousness of sin. Men can be saved by fear as well as by love, even though "perfect love casteth out fear".

We may claim, then, that one necessary feature in the reaction of divine holiness to human sin is properly expressed by the metaphor of divine "wrath", provided we eliminate all that is unworthy in the human wrath from which the metaphor is drawn. But this wrath of God is not the blind and automatic working of abstract law— always a fiction, since "law" is a conception, not an entity, till it finds expression through its instruments. The wrath of God is the wrath of divine *Personality* and does not exhaust the activity of that Personality. God is the Judge of all the earth, but He is more than that. This is why strictly penal theories of the Atonement fail to satisfy

us, not so much because they are untrue, as because they
are inadequate.  To be made worthy of God they must be
more or less supplemented by other aspects of His nature
and activity, and so gain in appeal only by losing their
logic.  God is Redeemer as well as Judge.  His reaction
to sin is to be found not only in the infliction of retributive
suffering (often largely obscured or even temporarily
evaded in the complexity of the physical order and of
social life), but also in that initiative of grace which
constitutes the Gospel.

The Gospel of divine redemption could never have been
reached by any *a priori* reasoning.  It springs from the
spontaneous activity of God, expressing His essential
nature and purpose.  It could be given to man only
through the divine initiative, because it is constituted by
that very initiative.  It must take historical form in order
to be both intelligible and effective.  More was needed
than a prophetic message in human speech, a Sermon on
the Mount.  Even for the prophetic consciousness, God's
speech was in His acts.  The mighty act of redemption
could not be simply a declaration of that which remained
unseen.  God must enter that temporal arena where sin
challenged Him, and win His victory there.  Yet this
must be part of a divine redemption in the eternal order,
for sin concerns both realms.  At the same time our
knowledge of God's dealing with sin must be drawn from
that part of it which He has made visible in history—the
Cross of Calvary.  Just as the visible part of the iceberg
reveals and is part of a greater submerged mass, so the
temporal handling of sin is part of the eternal which it
reveals, and Christ does in time what God is always doing
in eternity.[1]  Our only way of realizing the eternal reality
is to concentrate on the temporal actualization of it,

_____

Bushnell, in *The Vicarious Sacrifice*, has given repeated and eloquent
emphasis to this thought, which is not, of course, confined to him.

and to see God in Christ reconciling the world unto Himself.

Here the salient fact which most concerns us is the reaction of the God-man to the evil which men do to Him. We rightly feel indignation against that evil, so clearly set forth in the story of the Passion. We feel also, and again rightly, that an instant act of retribution, wrought by the "more than twelve legions of angels", would have been wholly just. Yet the most impressive fact of the Cross is the prayer of the Sufferer, "Father, forgive them, for they know not what they do." In that prayer, and in the whole attitude behind it, there is an actualization of divine grace in the given historical circumstances which constitutes effective revelation. The intuition of Christian faith acclaims it as most likest God, or rather, when once achieved and manifested, as the only reaction supremely divine. By it, Jesus is seen to transform His Cross from defeat to victory, and from shame to glory.

The term "transformation" is one of the two key-words of the doctrine of divine redemption as here outlined, the other being "actuality". The actuality of the Cross made it an inherent part (not simply an external revelation) of the suffering of God through the sin of man. Here, in one specific though supreme instance, we see God suffering in time as He suffers through our sin in eternity. His holiness could not conceivably have entered our world without suffering. But it was by no means inevitable that the suffering should have been borne as this was borne.[1] The bearing of it was grace, which is love in action. The result of that grace was the transformation of the event.

When we try to ascend from this to that reality of the Cross above, which is its necessary and eternal background

---

[1] Contrast the attitude of the Old Testament prophet who in many ways comes nearest to Jesus (e.g. Jer. xx. 12: "let me see thy vengeance on them").

and foundation, we have more need than ever to be very humble in our speculation. Here most of all our thought as well as our language will assuredly be inadequate, if it were only, as H. R. Mackintosh has said,[1] because we have not learnt to love enough to understand the divine love; "we see the Atonement so often through the frosted glass of our own lovelessness". We must keep clearly in view the differences, as well as the resemblances, when we climb by the ladder of analogy to the eternal realm.

In the first place, when we speak of the redemptive suffering of God apart from the Cross on earth, we are entering a wholly spiritual realm. The physical sufferings of the Cross had their own necessary place in the work of Christ, but even in Him they were wholly subordinated and made subsidiary to His spiritual sufferings. Now the *wholly* spiritual fact is very difficult for us to conceive, since we can know it here only under the forms and through the ministry of physical organisms anchored in time. But the spiritual fact is not less real, not less "objective", because of this. The difficulty lies in the kind of imagination we possess, which compels us to enshrine even the most spiritual insights of poetry in concrete forms. In the theology of redemption, the concrete imagery of poetry is replaced by the actualities of the Cross. The spiritual suffering of the Redeemer is our one safe guide into the heart of God.

In the second place, we must emphasize the theocentricity of redemption, as over against the Christocentricity, with which many forms of soteriological doctrine leave us.[2] We do not really exalt Christ by setting Him over against His Father in a quasi-duality (which easily becomes a real dualism), or by providing only a vague

---

[1] *Sermons*, pp. 176, 177.
[2] Erich Schaeder's *Theozentrische Theologie* (first edition in 1909) has not received sufficient attention in this country.

background of divine goodwill towards His work, whilst the exposition of salvation begins and ends with the Cross of earth. Redemption is God's work, since sin is God's concern. When the Psalmist confesses, "Against thee, and thee only, have I sinned," his confession urges a ground for forgiveness, since it lies in God's hands to deal with that which is, at last, only God's concern. To confront in this way the holiness of God is the hope as well as the despair of sinful man. The holiness of God, however terrible, has its own infinite resources, and all things are in His control. No doubt, it is necessary for us to picture Christ over against God in our devotional approach, and even in our theological analysis. But this duality cannot be made ultimate, without making a Christian doctrine of God impossible. Just as we were led to think of an "inclusive" Christology, so here we must always conceive the work of Christ as part of the whole work of God, and consider that work in its unity of result, as well as in its apparent duality of operation.

In the third place, we must think seriously of the guilt of man in relation to the holiness of God. In the high and holy place, as in the Cross below, sin makes its impact on holiness as suffering. Within the consciousness of God, sin cannot exist in any other form. The guilt of man actually consists in causing this suffering in the Holy One. Let us fix on this elemental truth, without any regard for the familiar metaphors, such as those of the judicial tribunal or of the feudal sovereignty of God. The law of righteousness itself belongs to the divine nature; as Dale has said, "In God, the law is *alive*; it reigns on His throne, sways His sceptre, is crowned with His glory."[1] Nor is there any court of appeal external to God before which His honour must be vindicated, however true it is, as is argued throughout this book, that there are deep under-

---

[1] *The Atonement*, p. 372.

T

lying necessities, in the very nature of the world which God has created, which have to be satisfied. The truth of retribution is not denied, if God Himself shares in the suffering which it entails. The sacrifice is not less but more if we carry it up from the seen to the unseen Cross, and believe that God so loved the world as to make His own sacrifice, and that He commends His own love toward us, in that while we were yet sinners Christ died for us.[1]

In the fourth place, we see the essential act of redemption in what God does with the suffering which springs from and measures man's guilt. By bearing it as He does He transforms the suffering, and therefore removes the guilt. The temporal consequences of sin may, and often do, continue to be borne by the sinner, but for the forgiven sinner these consequences also are transformed and are patiently accepted as discipline and no longer as penalty. But this truth belongs to another part of our theme (Chapter XIV) and here we are concerned only with the suffering borne by God through the sin of man. His loving acceptance of it transforms it into grace, and removes the final obstacle to forgiveness. The forgiven sinner looking into the face of God hears from Him the words of the Redeemer on earth, "Neither do I condemn thee; go thy way; from henceforth sin no more." Yet the words of God come not as a superficial and arbitrary discharge from condemnation; they are spoken by One who knows the cost of forgiveness in the suffering which the sin has brought upon Himself, as upon the crucified Redeemer.

In this eternal realm, the divine principle of transformation which was actualized on Calvary is extended to all human history, all history, both before and after Christ. The time-process, as we have seen again and again, must be taken up into ultimate reality, if human life has real

[1] John iii. 16; Rom. v. 8.

meaning and value for God. Yet the sequence of before and after, inseparable from our consciousness except for its occasional glimpses of timeless reality, must be translated into something beyond conception in the eternal consciousness of God. For Him, we may perhaps venture to say, the ultimate reality is the *meaning* of things. Even for us in our present consciousness there are prophecies of that truth. The real meaning of an event is the ultimate fact arising from that event. The meaning of all the events of an individual life is its ultimate biography. The meaning of all the events of history is, at last, the only thing that matters about history. When, therefore, we try to conceive our human history *sub specie aeternitatis*, the result should be not a panorama of events, but a statement of final meaning. Now, in the single life, we know how rich and strange can be the transformation of meaning. The event which we dreaded in prospect and resented in retrospect can eventually be changed from a curse to a blessing. Religious faith makes this miracle of transformation—"human nature's highest dower"—into an actual means of grace, by bringing every event within the providence of God. Part, and not the least important part, of His over-ruling providence is seen in the inspiration of a change of attitude to the irrevocable event, which gives it a new meaning, and so constitutes a new fact. That which is seen imperfectly and fitfully in our human experience may be reverently carried up into the eternal realm. However blotted the record of human history, however much of discord it has brought into the symphony of God's purpose, His way of dealing with it all transforms its meaning and constitutes the ultimate fact about it. The blot is worked into the finished design of the picture, the discord is resolved into an enriched harmony. The sin-marred world, viewed as a whole, is transformed into a realm of victorious and forgiving love. This transformation is in the deepest sense a redemption, for it ransoms history from its bondage to the irrevocable.   The world's value to God is not simply restored but immeasurably enhanced, and this not by any process of bookkeeping, but by the miracle of grace.   The whole world is redeemed, for its meaning is transformed.

In this way of interpreting the Cross of Christ, there can be no hint of "transactionalism" between Christ and God, as though God needed to be reconciled by the endurance of a penalty, the payment of a ransom, the offering of a sacrifice, on the part of Christ.   God Himself, suffering both in His Son and beyond the historical suffering of His Son, is the ultimate Redeemer.   But neither have we here a purely "subjective" doctrine of Atonement, as would be the case if the redemption consisted only in man's being moved to repentance by the spectacle of divine suffering. Whether in time or in eternity, the divine reaction to the suffering inflicted on God by sin is the most "objective" fact in the spiritual history of mankind.   It is wholly independent of man, and even of man's eventual response to it, in the sense that it precedes, and is not conditioned by this.   It is *there*, waiting for our penitent approach, the perpetual surprise of the awakened heart.   It carries its own evidence, as all that springs from God must do.   Its method and content are deeply rooted in the very nature of the spiritual order.   Yet its achievement is the fullest and most spontaneous liberation of the love of God, which is the essential characteristic of His Being and His purpose. None but God could so bear man's sin, and none but God could so transform its consequence of suffering.   "Where sin abounded, grace did abound more exceedingly."[1]   The superlatives of Christian thanksgiving find here their sufficient justification.   Whatever the individual outcome of human history, the eternal fact of the divine redemption

[1] Rom. v. 20.

has transformed its sorry tale into the glory of a new creation, with its new opportunity for man.

How is the doctrine of redemption here outlined to be related to the familiar doctrines of the Atonement based on the metaphors of ransom, sacrifice, satisfaction, penalty? These metaphors are firmly embedded in the vocabulary of devotion, and are constantly used even by those who would hesitate to work out the metaphors into an explicit theory. There should be no peril in this, if we know that they are necessarily metaphors, each capable of expressing some aspect of the truth. The "ransom" expresses the cost of the actuality of redemption wrought by Christ, and points upward to the eternal cost of the divine forgiveness. The "sacrifice" extends this thought by making the death of Christ an actual offering to God, something that has unique worth for Him, by which the penitent sinner is emboldened to approach Him, in the faith that this offering has become his own. The "satisfaction" of God's honour is still a true thought when we refer it to the redemption of history and the vindication of God's purpose seen in miniature on the Cross. The conception of a "penalty" to be endured is robbed of its obvious dangers when we stress the truth that it is God who endures it. What, in fact, we have been trying to do is not to deny these truths, but to get back behind them, as it were, into that eternal realm from which they draw their truth. If in that realm we are overwhelmed and humbled by the very nature of our attempt, this is what we ought to expect. But those who have once caught the vision of a deep reality of redemptive grace in God beyond any power of man's to comprehend in its fulness will be likely to use the metaphors of the Bible and of Christian devotion the more intelligently and profitably, because they realize that it is the mystery of God's transforming love which animates them all. His way is in the sea and His path in the great waters, and

His footsteps can only in part be known; yet if we do but touch the hem of His garment we shall feel the thrill of His power.

It is clear that the divine redemption wrought in this eternal realm must have its complementary application within the world of time, where redemption is necessarily a process, not a timeless reality. We started, as we always must, from the historical event of the Cross. We come back to that Cross from its basis in the eternal world, and we see it more clearly as the actual counterpart, an essential part indeed, of the whole redemptive work of God. It is this because it initiates, within the realm of history, the process of transformation in which the timeless reality consists. By the actuality of a divine transformation of the consequences of sin upon the Cross of Christ there are liberated the spiritual energies and influences which eventually transform men from being enemies into being friends and servants of God. Only when that process is completed in all who yield themselves to it will the full victory of God be won on earth, the victory over evil in human life which is the earthly replica of the heavenly victory. Or rather, let us say—since "replica" is a quite inadequate term to express that which time brings to eternity—only through the moral and spiritual transformation of men does the category of time work out that eternal reality on which it depends.

The more particular discussion of this process belongs to the next chapter,[1] but some aspects of it do concern us here, particularly the degree to which the redeemed may be regarded as co-operating (in their own dependent and derived manner) in the total work of redemption. The full significance of "cross-bearing", which Jesus made the one essential test of discipleship, is not to be seen merely

[1] XIV, "The Redeemed."

in its aspects of probation and service. It is also part of
the whole scheme of vicarious suffering by which men are
bound up in the bundle of life with God.[1] By it, men fill
up that which remains of the suffering of Christ for His
body's sake, which is the Church.[2] In that apostolic
intuition of a universal and far-reaching truth, we have
the most vital answer to the problem of human suffering.[3]
Apart from the discipline which suffering may bring, and
the service which suffering may render,[4] there is this great
thought to sustain the sufferer—that by it he may enter
into a fellowship with God possible in no other way. It
is a fellowship of insight and knowledge because it is a
fellowship of experience. The believer's humble participation in the work of Christ is not the least of his present
rewards. By bearing the cross with Him, he makes his
own tiny contribution to the actual redemption of the
world. Herein lies the most satisfying answer to the
challenge of the mystery of suffering. The suffering which
extends downwards to the whole creation groaning and
travailing together in pain until now also extends upwards
to God on His eternal throne. The practical solution of
the problem, as of most of the problems of life, consists
in looking upwards. Jesus said to His disciples, "Are ye
able to drink the cup that I drink?"[5] God said through
the lips of Jeremiah to the despondent Baruch, "That
which I have built am *I* breaking down, and that which I

[1] 1 Sam. xxv. 29.

[2] Col. i, 24. It is illuminating to link with this verse the thought of
those who suffered before Christ, "the long line of servants sent by the
Lord of the Vineyard to claim the fruits that were due (Mark xii. 1–5) in
whom our Lord sees the principle of victory-through-suffering which finds
its supreme exemplification in His own passion" (A. G. Hebert, *The Throne
of David*, p. 69).

[3] For fuller discussion of this, see *Suffering, Human and Divine*,
Chap. XI.

[4] In Isa. liii., the sufferings of Israel are interpreted as a sacrifice through
which the nations are both moved and *enabled* to approach God.

[5] Mark x. 38.

have planted am *I* plucking up . . . and seekest *thou* great things for thyself?"[1]

It is sometimes said, and not without justice, that the final test of a doctrine of the Atonement is in its capacity to be preached; can it be turned into the necessarily simple message of the evangelist? The conception here presented can meet that test. When the preacher points to the Cross of the God-man, he can proclaim as Gospel truth that God suffers in His eternal Being through every sin which man commits, even as we see Christ suffering on the Cross. He can declare that God wills to bear that suffering in His love for man, and by bearing it removes the guilt of man by transforming its uttermost consequence. To reject such love, whose only measure is the Cross of Christ, is to love darkness rather than light, to act as an ungrateful churl, and to deprive oneself of the very confidence which life so sorely needs. For "if God is for us, who can be against us?", what power, seen or unseen, "can separate us from the love of God, which is in Christ Jesus our Lord?"

[1] Jer. xlv. 4, 5; note the emphasis on the divine suffering caused by man's sin, which Baruch (like his master) is invited to share with God.

# CHAPTER XIV

## THE REDEEMED

§ 1. *THE Ideal Life.*[1]  In the most comprehensive survey of the Christian life which the New Testament affords—that of Romans xii.–xv. 13—the feature of supreme importance is the point at which it begins.  The life to be described is essentially a redeemed life, and from that characteristic both its dynamic and its peculiar and essential qualities are derived: "I appeal to you *by all the mercy of God* to dedicate your bodies as a living sacrifice, consecrated and acceptable to God; that is your cult, a spiritual rite."[2]  Behind this apostolic appeal is God's own approach in the Gospel of Christ, which the apostle has elaborated in the previous chapters.  The "brothers" who have responded to that divine appeal have been by their very response initiated into a redeemed life characterized by "righteousness, peace and joy", and sustained by the Holy Spirit,[3] the source of that renewal of the mind (xii. 2) which is essential to the life.  As the practical exhortations begin, so they fitly end:[4] "May the God [who is the source] of hope fill you with all joy and peace in your faith, so that you may overflow with hope, *in the power of the Holy Spirit.*"  Faith passes thus naturally into hope, because the consummation of faith in a completed

---

[1] This section is obviously much briefer than it ought to be, but I have discussed its chief points in greater detail in *The Christian Experience of the Holy Spirit.*

[2] So Moffatt (italics mine); but note that 'bodies' according to Hebrew psychology really means 'personalities'.

[3] xiv. 17; cf. Cc. vi–viii.          [4] xv. 13.

redemption is eschatological.  The redeemed life is therefore both retrospective and prospective; it looks before and after, though its "sweetest songs" are not "those that tell of saddest thought",[1] but of forgiveness and of fellowship with God.

The particular kind of life here described is specifically a corporate life, in which each member of that brotherhood which is the Body of Christ accepts his own ordained part a part which is vital and necessary, however limited in scope.  In this corporate consciousness, he is humble as to himself, and sympathetic towards the rest; he will serve them in love, and their joys and sorrows are his also.  So far as evil has to be encountered in his personal relations with others, he will overcome it by good (after the pattern of the Cross).  He will bring loyal obedience to the civic authorities whom God has set over him, whose sword-bearing is a ministry of God; he will not indulge in baser things; he will respect the consciences of those who may be honestly wrong in their judgment; he will transcend all racial differences, such as those of Jew and Gentile.

It is a familiar enough picture to those who have come under the influence of the New Testament, or of the institutions based upon it, but is it, even for the mass of "Christians", more than an unrealized ideal?  How many of us would dare to claim that its most intimate and searching principles are substantially true of ourselves?  Most of us, indeed, have sometimes encountered a man or woman for whom the claim might be made, and we have felt, dimly or clearly, the fascination and the power of such a character.  But probably most of those who bear the name "Christian" would hardly venture more than to agree with the conclusion reached by William James, after his study of "Saintliness".[2]  "Let us be saints,

[1] Shelley, "To a Skylark".
[2] In *The Varieties of Religious Experience*, Lectures XI–XV.

then, if we can, whether or not we succeed visibly and temporally. But in our Father's house are many mansions, and each of us must discover for himself the kind of religion and the amount of saintship which best comports with what he believes to be his powers and feels to be his truest mission and vocation".[1]

One thing ought to be clear—that we cannot hope to be good Christians in character and conduct without sharing in the essentials of the Christian faith. The redeemed life cannot be lived in anything like its fulness without experience of the Christian redemption. When the apostle Paul is warning Corinthian Christians against the temptation to sexual sin, his argument is twofold:[2] "you are temples of the Holy Spirit, and you were bought with a price." That lifts the struggle to a different level from any consideration of prudence or even of self-respect. It brings in the highest motives, the fact of redemption and the promise of "sanctification" in order to make the redeemed life an actuality. Similarly, when it is a question of right conduct towards a wrong-headed fellow-Christian, St. Paul points out that this man is "the brother for whose sake Christ died".[3] All the great classics of devotion, all the methods of practical discipline in the devout life, are ultimately the elaboration or systematization of this principle. They aim at getting mind and heart so concentrated on the fact of redemption[4] that the redeemed life may go on spontaneously from strength to strength in its spiritual pilgrimage, by the constant aid of the Holy Spirit.

The prose of theology cannot here replace the poetry of religion. If redemption is to become a sufficient motive, it must be felt as something full of the romance of a

[1] *Op. cit.*, p. 377.    [2] 1 Cor. vi. 18–20.
[3] 1 Cor. viii. 11.
[4] As in Ignatius Loyola's "Hic est meta laborum" of the contemplation of the Cross (*Exercitia Spiritualia*, p. 265 of 1696 ed.).

great love. It is the love of Christ which constrains the
Christian, the fact, not our analysis of it. David's warriors
at Bethlehem fight their way through the Philistine ranks
to bring him a draught of water from the familiar well,
for which he had vainly longed. The romance of their
daring stirs him to a fitting response: "he would not
drink thereof, but poured it out unto the Lord."[1] There
is a contagion in the realm of the Spirit, by which like
awakens like. That Christ died for all is the dynamic of
the obligation "that they which live should no longer live
unto themselves, but unto Him who for their sakes died
and rose again".[2]

It is this personal response which best displays the
psychological nature of Christian faith in the New Testament sense. It is primarily an act of will; the emphasis
on volition is characteristic of both human and divine
personality in the Bible. This is often concealed from
the English reader because of the literal translation
"heart", which suggests to us the emotional aspect of
consciousness. When Pharaoh's heart is hardened this
does not mean that he becomes callous to Israel's sufferings,
but that his *will* is "made strong"[3] not to release the
people. Similarly, St. Paul's psychological terms, though
Greek in form, usually have a Hebrew connotation,[4] and
we must emphasize the volitional reference in his use of
the term "heart", i.e. in the words "If thou shalt confess
with thy mouth Jesus as Lord, and shalt have faith in
thy heart that God raised Him from the dead, thou shalt
be saved."[5] Here the intellectual content of the faith is
explicitly brought out, but its essential feature is a
volitional response of the whole personality, the response

[1] 2 Sam. xxiii. 16.                              [2] 2 Cor. v. 15.
[3] So the Hebrew in Ex. iv. 21.
[4] Cf. "Hebrew Psychology in relation to Pauline Anthropology" in
*Mansfield College Essays.*
[5] Rom. x. 9.

of an indivisible unity, like Wordsworth's motionless cloud
in the sky:—

> "That heareth not the loud winds when they call:
> And moveth all together, if it move at all."[1]

As a sound comment on the Pauline conception of faith,
we may take Luther's classical definition:—

"Christian faith is not an idle quality or empty husk in
the heart, which may be in deadly sin (as they say) until
charity come and quicken it; but if it be true faith, it is a
sure trust and confidence of the heart, and a firm consent
whereby Christ is apprehended. So that ... Christ Himself
is present. ... Faith taketh hold of Christ and hath Him
present, and holdeth Him enclosed, as the ring doth the
precious stone."[2]

This "will to believe" is, however, no arbitrary act or
experimental venture. In modern phrase, it is a value-
judgment, which derives its inner (moral) compulsion
from the nature of divine grace as seen in Christ. We
can also call it an "intuition", for it is the direct
"looking into" the historical actuality of Christ which
penetrates through the human to the divine and reaches
Him who thus exercises His power over us. Such
faith may have its dim beginnings far away from its
ultimate goal; it may well be at first no more than that
struggle for faith which Robert Louis Stevenson has so
finely described:[3]—

> "still to battle and perish for a dream of good ...
> ... contend for the shade of a word
> and a thing not seen with the eyes:
> With the half of a broken hope for a pillow at night
> That somehow the right is the right."

[1] *Resolution and Independence*, XI.
[2] *Commentary on Galatians* on ii. 16; fo. 61, 62 of Vautroullier's (1575)
edition.
[3] *If this were Faith* ("Poems", p. 179 of 1922 ed.).

But, dim or clear, Christian faith is the personal response to the objective reality of the redemptive work of Jesus Christ. With such a faith, repentance and the peace and joy of forgiveness are indissolubly linked; in fact, these are different aspects or applications of the unity of faith, though they may not all be apparent together or be brought out in any systematic order. "Repentance" is properly that inner change of mind (*metanoia*) which may be called the negative side of faith. The intuition of a new value inevitably carries with it the application of a new standard to character and conscience. That which is incompatible with, or hostile to, the new value is condemned as evil and there is self-condemnation because of our responsibility for this evil.[1] The "change of mind" may be no more sudden than the gradual inflow of faith. But it may safely be said that repentance will deepen as faith in Christ deepens, because of the ever-growing vision of the new standard. That is why the sense of sinfulness is always deepest in the saints, though present in every Christian. The need for repentance stands in the forefront of the preaching of Jesus and His disciples,[2] and repentance before God is coupled indissolubly with faith in Jesus Christ.[3] Such repentance necessarily involves sorrow,[4] but it is a "godly sorrow" in the true line of life and salvation. It points forward, or rather, it is actually interwoven with the positive side of faith which is confident of forgiveness, because of the redemptive suffering of God. Here the full redemptive content of faith comes into action and becomes the basis of that "joy and peace in believing" which permeates the New Testament consciousness and gives to it its most characteristic features, lifting it to the mountain heights where the winds of the Spirit blow, to give health and strength to the redeemed life.

[1] Acts viii. 22; Heb. vi. 1.　　[2] Mark i. 15; Acts ii. 38.
[3] Acts xx. 21.　　[4] 2 Cor. vii. 9, 10.

Further, though the redeemed life is always individual in its response to Christ, it is always life in a new "corporate personality" or social solidarity. The most characteristic work of the Holy Spirit, on whom the whole Christian experience depends, is the creation of a new fellowship (*koinōnia*). The gifts and graces of the Christian life are all pointed towards mutual service; they are all created within, and primarily for, the Christian community, by the Holy Spirit (cf. "the fellowship of the Holy Spirit" in the Benediction). The Church is the outstanding expression of this ideal fellowship of the Spirit,[1] cherished amongst its members and outflowing towards "them that are without".

One of the tests of any doctrine of redemption is its adequacy to bring the believer into so close a relation to Christ that faith in Him is justified. In the New Testament, as we have seen, there is no difficulty about this, because prevalent conceptions of "corporate personality" with a long Old Testament and ethnic history[2] made perfectly natural the conception of Christ as representing or "recapitulating"[3] the community of believers. The social emphasis of the new faith was manifest from the beginning. The teaching of Jesus is dominated by the two conceptions of the Fatherhood and Kingly rule of God, both implying a community, whether of sons or subjects. The Epistle to the Hebrews (xii. 22f.) reminds the men of faith that they have already come to "the general assembly and Church of the firstborn who are enrolled in heaven".

[1] See more fully on this subject my book, *The Christian Experience of the Holy Spirit*, Chapter VI.

[2] Cf. "The Hebrew Conception of Corporate Personality" by H. Wheeler Robinson in Beiheft 66 of the *Zeitschrift für die alttestamentliche Wissenschaft* (1936); A. Causse, *Du Groupe Ethnique à la Communauté Religieuse* (1937); *The Individual in East and West*, ed. by E. R. Hughes (1937).

[3] Cf. Eph. i. 10 and the development of this idea in the theology of Irenaeus.

The unity of believers in Christ is so vital and actual that
it can be set forth under the Johannine figure of the Vine
and its branches (John xv), or under the Pauline figures
of a temple, with Christ as its cornerstone, a body with
Christ as its head, a bride whose husband is Christ.[1] But
the most explicit statement of corporate personality is the
Pauline contrast of Adam and Christ,[2] each the representative head of a group which is naturally conceived as
sharing in the life or status of its representative.[3]    Given
such a conception of corporate personality, as part of the
common stock of ideas, faith was the simple acceptance
of a relation already fully intelligible, and the way was
easy for one with so ardent a temperament as Paul's to be
conscious of a mystical union with Christ—"I have been
crucified with Christ; yet I live; (and yet) no longer I but
Christ liveth in me; and that life which I now live in the
flesh I live in faith, the faith which is in the Son of God,
who loved me and gave Himself up for me."[4]

The conception of corporate personality no longer
remains vital in modern civilization, characterized as this
is by a strong accentuation of individual life, though
there are approximations to it in the conception of the
nation or the Church.  But to these, for the most part,
at any rate, the accepted realism of the ancient idea
is lacking, and they are rather final constructions of
"ideology" than premises of faith.  The closest realistic
parallel might perhaps be found in the growing conception
of social solidarity, the recognition forced on us all in
modern times that none of us *can* live unto himself.[5]    It

[1] Eph. ii. 20, 21; i. 23; ii. 14–16; iv. 4, 12, 16; v. 23, 30, 25–27.
[2] Rom. v. 14 ff.; 1 Cor. xv. 20 ff., 45 ff.
[3] Cf. the "representative" theories of e.g. McLeod Campbell and
Moberly, to which reference was made in XIII. § 3.          [4] Gal. ii. 20.
[5] The original point of the phrase is "not unto self but unto Christ"
(Rom. xiv. 7 ff.), though the extension to mean, "not unto self but unto
my neighbour" is a true expression of the New Testament teaching (Matt.
xxv. 40, Rom. xiii. 8–10, 1 John iv. 20).

may well be that, in days to come, a still livelier and more widely spread recognition of this fact will become the basis not only of a new social and international order but also of a new and more living consciousness of what the Church essentially is. If that were to come about, faith would cease to seem (as it does to so many) an arbitrary opinion and an individual idiosyncrasy; it would be a perfectly natural expression of a social realism which all accepted. We might then cease to call faith-union with Christ "mystical", for it would correspond to the actuality of normal social relations. Such a basis is still far from existing to-day, but its very possibility, and its partial and imperfect beginnings, may confirm the believer in holding that he does actually share with his fellow-believers in the benefits of Christ, the Head of the Body, animated by the Holy Spirit. In such a Church-consciousness, the contrasting emphasis of the "evangelical" and "catholic" Christian would be blended, to the advantage of both.

The ethic of the redeemed life, so nurtured on the actuality of redemption, so controlled by the nature of that redemption, so sustained by the Holy Spirit through whom Christ is still within and amongst His followers, is, in a single phrase, the spirit of the Cross. The believer, in his own degree, bears the Cross with his Master, and bears it cheerfully and courageously, because he now sees life, past, present and future, in a new perspective. The transformed mind[1] transforms the world. The present penalties of sin, inevitable as its present consequences, are accepted as just desert, the sufferings to be encountered in the Christian path are transformed into valued discipline, the mystery of death becomes, for the Christian hope, the door of entrance into the fulfilment of life's best, the home of that music of which we hear but faint and fleeting

---

[1] Rom. xii. 2 (*metamorphousthe*).

U

echoes, and of that poetry of which we take but a few fragments to our hearts.[1]

§ 2. *The Kenosis of the Spirit.* In the account of the "redeemed" life which has just been given, the emphasis fell on that which is the foundation of the whole structure, viz. the redemptive work of Jesus Christ. The new life was described as the activity of a personal response to the grace of God actualized in Jesus Christ. But it is necessary to supplement what has been said by considering this redeemed life more directly as the sphere of divine activity, the work of the Holy Spirit continuing the work of Christ. There are many ways of doing this, but a very suggestive (and often neglected) one is to ask what it must mean for God to dwell as Spirit within the believer. This point of view is indicated when we speak of "The Kenosis of the Spirit". The phrase is meant to suggest that God as Holy Spirit enters into a relation to human nature which is comparable with that of the Incarnation of the Son of God at a particular point of human history.

As applied to the Person of Christ, the term "kenosis" is taken from St. Paul's description of His pre-existent glory, of which He "emptied Himself" ('*eauton* '*ekenōse*), that He might become the Redeemer of men by His death upon the Cross.[2] We are not here concerned with this "self-emptying" in regard to the Son of God (see Chap. XI), except to note that because of it, Jesus wins the new title "Lord", and universal adoration, after the pattern of

---

[1] Cf. J. B. Priestley's striking play, *Johnson over Jordan*, pp. 37, 91–92.

[2] Phil. ii. 7 ff. In *The Cross of the Servant*, pp. 73, 74, I have given my reasons for thinking that the phrase is derived from Isa. liii. 12. "He emptied himself to death" (cf. verse 7). In the Pauline echo of this original, three participial clauses occur in parenthesis to describe the self-humbling of the Son, before the completion of the phrase in verse 8 by the words "unto death". This view of the passage throws the emphasis, as elsewhere for St. Paul, on the death of Christ, rather than on the Incarnation, though this was a necessary condition of the Cross.

Isaiah liii.[1] The task now before us is to trace the continuity of the Spirit's work in completing the work of
Christ by what may properly be called a similar method
of "self-emptying".

When we speak of the presence and activity of the
Holy Spirit in the redeemed life, we ought to be as definite
and clear as to what we mean as when we speak
of the presence and activity of the Son of God in
the days of His flesh. The scope of the activity is, of
course, enormously increased, as is the variety of application. Every redeemed life becomes a new product and
illustration of it, and adds to its variety by the surrender
of the individual consciousness to the power and presence
of God. That is what we ought to mean by the power
and presence of the Holy Spirit—God Himself personally
present in all this variety of redeemed lives. It makes no
essential difference to our meaning (as we may see from
Romans viii. 9) whether we speak of the indwelling of the
Spirit of God or of the Spirit of Christ. For St. Paul, the
complete unity of divine activity is expressed by the
words: *"Through* Christ we have our access *in* one Spirit
*unto* the Father."[2] On the practical side, that is the most
important statement about the doctrine of the Holy
Trinity which the New Testament contains. The direct
and immediate contact with God is always through His
presence as Spirit. Only Spirit can touch spirit with that
inwardness and directness which Christian experience
demands. But this contact is itself "mediated" by the
historical personality of Jesus Christ, signalized as Son of
God from His resurrection.[3] All Christian experience is
through Christ, because it is based on His work as Redeemer, and permeated by the influence and quality of
that redemption. Through Him, then, we have our

---

[1] This is the underlying reference throughout Phil. ii. 5–11.
[2] Eph. ii. 18.                              [3] Rom. i. 4 (*'oristhentos*).

access to the hidden God, whose Fatherhood is revealed
in the open secret of the Gospel.   The Spirit of God covers
many other realms besides that of the redeemed life, but
here, as "Holy Spirit" *par excellence*, the personality of
Christ is taken up into the direct line of divine activity.
We may speak, then, of a Real Presence of God as known
in His Son, to be found in the life of every believer.   Do
we take seriously enough the stupendous implications of
this truth?   It is an overwhelming thing to say, "I live;
and yet no longer I, but Christ liveth in me."[1]  A missionary
in China once asked a Chinese scholar, who had read the
New Testament through several times, what struck him
most.   He answered that the most wonderful thing to
him was that a man could become a temple of the Holy
Spirit.   Pringle-Pattison has written of the doctrine of
the Trinity as being, when rightly understood, "the
profoundest and therefore the most intelligible, attempt
to express the indwelling of God in man",[2] and in another
place remarks, "If God is not thus active in the time-
process, bearing with His creatures the whole stress and
pain of it, the immanence of the Creative Spirit becomes
an numeaning phrase."[3]   In the New Testament this
Real Presence is personally conceived, just because it is
God who is present, and present through the Personality
of His Son.   It is Presence grieved by our sins, insulted
by wilful relapse, teaching patiently our infant lips to cry
Abba, and witnessing with our spirit that we are God's
children, helping our weakness and making intercession
for us.[4]   Such phrases would be equally true of the spiritual
sufferings of Jesus in the days of His flesh, just as we may
venture to transpose much of what is said of His spiritual
sufferings in to the sufferings of the Holy Spirit of God in us.

---

[1] Gal. ii. 20.                                 [2] *The Idea of God*, p. 410.
[3] *The Spirit* (ed. by B. H. Streeter), p. 18.
[4] Cf. Eph. iv. 30; Heb. x. 29; Rom. viii. 15 f., 26.

We still speak of crucifying Christ afresh by our sins, though what we really mean, in theological accuracy, is that we are crucifying the Holy Spirit. For, as Horace Bushnell forcibly expressed it, the Spirit "has His Gethsemane within us . . . if the sacrifices of the much-enduring, agonizing Spirit were acted before the senses in the manner of the incarnate life of Jesus, He would seem to make the world itself a kind of Calvary from age to age".[1]

God does not wait until man is perfect before making him in some way a partaker of the divine nature.[2] Just as it is true that while we were yet sinners Christ died for us, so is it true that while we are very unworthy Christians the sanctifying Spirit lives within us. In both ways, not in the first alone, the redeeming love of God is proved to us. The spiritual life of man, like the moral, is essentially the subtle interweaving of two elements, not yet brought into full harmony. Our moral problems are largely constituted by that warp of the body into which the shuttle of the soul must weave the weft of its higher nature. The redeemed life lifts the moral problems to a new level of meaning, and makes us conscious of dependence on something higher than ourselves for any success. This duality of individual life is seen on a larger scale in our social relations, economic, international and ecclesiastical. Even that New Testament Church which elicited some of St. Paul's most deeply spiritual utterances was the Church that desired to retain within its fellowship a man guilty of incest. It is this spirit of compromise within the Church which so often provides the first shock of dis-

[1] *The Vicarious Sacrifice*, pp. 43 , 47; see also the well-known passage in John Masefield's "The Everlasting Mercy", where the Quaker evangelist says to Saul Kane the profligate, "every dirty word you say Is one more flint upon His way, Another thorn about His head."

[2] This phrase, found in 2 Peter i. 4, means (as Bigg says, *ad loc.*) "very much the same as St. Paul's 'fellowship of (the) Spirit'."

illusionment to the young believer, as it serves to provoke the most pointed criticism of the outsider.

Yet, in spite of our sins, the Holy Spirit does not abandon us. He remains to reinforce the voice of conscience, to awaken the slumbering spark of higher aspiration into a clear flame, to bear with us the shame of our broken vow and frequent fall. In this continued fellowship, there is a deeper humiliation for God the Holy Spirit than ever came to God the Son. For Jesus Christ, the enemies were without, not within, and the body was a holy temple for the indwelling Spirit. But in "Mansoul" there are always traitors within the gate, and God must accept an unholy temple for His abiding—till He can transform it into holiness. *This* kenosis of the Spirit is therefore even deeper in its self-emptying than the kenosis of the Son, whilst continuing His redemptive work.

Even apart from human sin, there is always a divine self-limitation in the very conditions of human life, its finite nature, its progress by error,[1] the limits and imperfections of our vocabulary in which even the highest realities must find expression.[2] The Spirit speaks our language, just as Jesus spoke Aramaic. There can be no spiritual communication in a vacuum. There is always some medium, even though the fellowship mediated may be called "immediate" in comparison with more external media.[3] The texture of our truest thoughts about God must be woven out of earthly stuff, however heavenly the pattern of divine grace shown by it. The whisper of the Spirit must come to *our* ears, the impulse of the Spirit must fall upon *our* wills, and it is *our* minds that have always to recognize and interpret the divine event that has befallen us. We shall be taught humility and saved from fanaticism, if we realize more clearly *this* kenosis of

[1] See Chapter II.     [2] See Chapter III.
[3] See Chapter VI.

the Spirit also, which indeed goes back to the divine creation of human spirits, and is seen all along the line of human history. At one point in that history, the Holy Spirit claims a unique and supreme place for His work through the Personality of our Lord Jesus Christ. But there is a far wider activity of the Spirit, which would, if we could conceive it clearly, bring all existence into unity, and show us the divine self-emptying from the foundation of the world. Through this long and patient kenosis, God has carried the burden of all humanity, the humanity which it is His purpose to redeem. The believer is simply entering into a new and greatly deepened experience through Christ of what God has been doing all the time by His "prevenient" grace.

If, then, the Spirit of God continues to sustain and indwell a world that is so inadequate or contradictory to His holy nature, we have a redemptive kenosis that is worthy to be ranked with that of the Incarnation and the Cross, a kenosis that is, in fact, ultimately the expression of the same redemptive grace of God. We are confirmed in our interpretation of the Cross as actualizing in time the sufferings of the Eternal God through and for mankind. Every redeemed life which is transformed into the pattern of the Redeemer—for that, at the last, is the goal of salvation—is a new product of the Holy Spirit, at the cost of long patience and grievous pain. Every sin into which the believer may fall is not simply a set-back in moral development, it is a hurt to God. I have heard it said that this doctrine of the Christian life makes it too hard and terrible to be lived. So it would be, if God were holy in wrath and not also holy in love. Not till we realize that the worst aspect of our sin is the wrong and hurt we do to God by it—not its consequences to ourselves or to others, grievous as they may be—shall we know the magnitude and depth of the divine grace.

One other aspect of this great theme must not be forgotten, forming another parallel to the work of Jesus. The kenosis of the Spirit means the concealment of God, so that it may often be hard to recognize His presence and activity within us or around us. If He dwells in some degree even with the sinner, and identifies Himself so closely even with the imperfect saint, then the same thing will happen as befell Jesus, the friend of publicans and sinners. The divine is in disguise, and no official mark of an external and independent authority can ultimately decide for us that the divine is there. There is a moral as well as a theological challenge in this, both in regard to Christ and in regard to the Holy Spirit. They must both be recognized by the intrinsic qualities that are theirs. They must speak with their own authority. The note of authority is indeed the one infallible mark of the divine—not the authority of the sergeant-major, or of the totalitarian dictator, but that of an inner compulsion which goes deeper and carries further, because it awakens that love which is the only fulfilling of the law. We must not, therefore, because we humbly claim a place amongst the redeemed, expect a revelation of duty that will occasion no conflict of loyalties, an illumination of truth that demands no diligent search amid perplexity, a holy peace that needs no constant guarding, if it is to guard us.[1] The veritable signs of God's presence are intermingled with many other things. We walk with a stranger on the road to truth, and all the evidence of identity given to us may be the heart that burns within. We know the clash of duties and the hesitancy as to which is God's choice for us. We discover that the fellowship of the Church is a very imperfect thing, and far from the beauty of the bride of Christ for which we had looked. If we are ever tempted to wonder whether good is after

[1] Phil. iv. 7.

all not divine but human, let us meet that challenge by thinking of the divine kenosis, through which the very question has become possible. The heavenly treasure is indeed stored in earthen vessels, but its intrinsic worth is proved, "by the manifestation of the truth."[1]

§ 3. *Personality and the Life Beyond.*[2] The Theban Sphinx asked "What is life?" and made death the penalty of ignorance. Her riddle would have been shrewder and subtler had she asked "What is death?", but then she would have condemned herself, for not even a Sphinx could have answered it. Of all facts of human life, death is unique in this—that no hypothesis about it can be proved or disproved by experiment, though the experience of it will be universal. It is because of this paradox that our speculations abound, for none can give an authoritative denial to the wildest dreams or the most sentimental trivialities. Death still remains

> "The Shadow cloak'd from head to foot,
> Who keeps the keys of all the creeds."

Is there a door behind that Shadow which any of the keys will unlock, a door through which we pass beyond the Shadow into the dawn of a new day? Or is the Shadow that of an impenetrable rock, where man's only discovery will be that

> "—every mother's son
> Travails with a skeleton?"

Even then, we might elect to take refuge in the reflection with which Cicero closes his discussion of old age: "If I am mistaken in believing that the souls of men are immortal, I am content to be mistaken, nor do I wish to

---

[1] 2 Cor. iv. 2.

[2] On the whole subject, there are two excellent recent books, viz. John Baillie's *And the Life Everlasting* (1934) and A. E. Taylor's *The Christian Hope of Immortality* (1938).

have wrested from me, whilst I live, the mistake that cheers me. If dead (as certain negligible philosophers deem), I shall feel nothing, nor do I fear to have my mistake laughed at by dead philosophers."

We cannot cross-examine death, and learn whether its "truth" is the whole truth and nothing but the truth. But we can hear and weigh the testimony of life—the life that death so challenges. For countless generations men have analysed this "life" into a solid body and a shadow-soul, or some such wraith-like form. When the vital functions of the body cease—which is the dictionary definition of death—the poor wraith pursues its pitiful path in other realms. But its "life" is not worth the living, as the Greek Hades and the Hebrew Sheol abundantly prove; how could it be when the initial analysis has assumed that the body is the predominant partner, whilst he who "sleeps" can do no more than dream? Far more of this primitive animism than we usually recognize survives into our own times; it still colours—or rather robs of colour—our thought of the life beyond death, as it still influences our funeral customs. If such a life is to have either cogency or value, it must have more, not less, reality than this life; it must be worth while, because it is rooted and grounded in the best that is ours already; it must be the continued and progressive life of a personality of whose reality we are already convinced. That personality is much too intimately linked with our present body for the animistic conception to be true. Nobody knows what the exact relation is, but the evidence suggests that body and soul are rather brother and sister from the same womb than arbitrary business partners. But even this metaphor is inadequate to express the unity of the body's service to the soul, and the soul's influence upon the body. Professor Pringle-Pattison, who held and defended a Christian faith in immortality, did not hesitate to say,

"Let us, then, finally dismiss this idea of the substantial soul as some sort of supernatural mechanism to hold the conscious experiences together, and if we must indulge our imagination with the picture of some bearer of the conscious life, let us be satisfied with the body, in which that life is certainly rooted in a very real sense."[1] He finds it sufficient to think of "the living body as the embodied soul",[2] on the lines of Aristotle, and this seems a more satisfactory conception than, e.g. Professor McDougall's defence of animism. Similarly the Hebrew idea of personality involves all the members of the body, apart from which the "soul" has no individual existence. The Hebrew conceived man not as a trichotomy nor as a dichotomy, but as an animated body, as against the Platonic idea of an incarnate soul. Such a view of the unity of personality, body and soul, need not mean for us that consciousness is merely a function of the body, and must necessarily cease to be with it. The reality of consciousness is not dependent on our explanation of it. There is no scientific explanation of the fact of consciousness, and there can be no scientific disproof of its continuance after the body has served its purpose. If we resolutely put aside the animistic prejudice that the body is more "real" than the soul, which begs the question, there is no ground at all for saying that the physical fact or combination of facts which we call death can affect the supraphysical reality of consciousness. If it is said that man is merely a machine, let him who says it produce any other machine that *knows itself to be a machine*. No man, in short, is a consistent materialist in life; why should he become one in regard to death? We may go further than this, on the basis of organic evolution itself. If we follow the story of man's ascent from his remotest origins, we find a succession of differing factors which make for survival

---

[1] *The Idea of Immortality*, p. 103.      [2] Ibid., p. 92.

in the earlier forms of life—"assimilation, sexual reproduction, muscular force, cunning or mind";[1] "the method
of Organic Evolution has been one throughout—that of
selection; what has changed is the criterion of selection. . . .
At first it was power of food-assimilation, then advance in
methods of reproduction, thereafter physical force, then
cunning or mind, and with the appearance of man the
criterion has become increasingly a moral one."[2]  But if
human personality is the costly product of so long a line
of struggle and travail, and if new qualities are emerging
in him that detach themselves more and more from the
physical conditions of earlier life, is it not reasonable, in a
rational universe, to suppose that this costly product of
human personality is not flung away at the moment of
physical death, when it has had time to shew only the
promise and potency of new development? Such an
argument involves faith that the universe *is* rational, but
that assumption we make in all our living.

It is perhaps not so much from without as from within
that the reality of personality, and therefore its life beyond
death may seem to be challenged to-day. The psychological analysis of consciousness, reinforced by the study of
anthropology, seems to trace much in us that we call
"moral" or "spiritual" to earlier stages of our own conscious
or sub-conscious life or that of the race. The result is
that many to-day are tempted to ask whether the self
(as well as the alleged realities to which it attaches itself
in morality or religion) is not an illusion. Does not its
natural history disprove its spiritual nature? This is, of
course, only another form of the Victorian dilemma as to
science and religion, raised by the evolutionary origin of
man. But how can "origins" disprove "values"? It is
with the ultimate values of personality that the issue lies,

---

[1] J. Y. Simpson, *Man and the Attainment of Immortality*, p. 228.
[2] *Op. cit.*, p. 275.

not with our analysis of them, true or false. The true source of personality is in God and the discovery that it had sub-personal stages, whether physical or psychical, would in no way disprove this ultimate source.

However difficult it may be to define personality, there would be general agreement as to its salient features. "The Person is aware of and takes interest in Past, Present, and Future; is self-determined in approximately as great a degree as externally determined; and is consequently a centre of continuous conscious and deliberate activity."[1] "Personality itself is a social category."[2] "The union of individuality and universality in a single manifestation forms the cardinal point in personality."[3] Those three statements describe personality in its individual, social and religious relation. One quality of personality which underlies all these relations ought to be specially named (for it intimately concerns our subject), and that is the nature of its unity. "The unity of the Mind or Soul is of quite a different kind from that of the Body. . . . The Body as a material system is included within a vaster material system. The other parts of this system are external to it and excluded by it. On the other hand, the Mind or Soul connects itself with what we may figuratively call its environment not by *excluding* it from, but by *including it within* the unity of its own experience."[4] Thus personality is here and now creating its own world, gathering into its unity all that it may need. If we once reach the conviction that personality is undestroyed by physical death, then we have already in personality the content of a life beyond death, or the beginnings of such a content. For, as philosophical writers often remind us, personality is "an achievement which would be impossible apart from

---

[1] Temple, *The Nature of Personality*, p. 22.
[2] Sorley, *Moral Values and the Idea of God*, p. 130.
[3] Inge, *Personal Idealism and Mysticism*, p. 103.
[4] C. C. J. Webb, *Divine Personality and Human Life*, p. 272 f.

a principle of unity operative from the very beginning of what can be called personal life at all".[1]

In the light of what has been said about personality, we ought to be prepared for the assertion that religion is always the middle term between it and the life beyond. If personality is something in process of achievement by inclusion of values within itself from that larger world of persons to which it belongs, then it is committed of necessity to some kind of religious faith as the basis of that essential fellowship. This inference can be historically confirmed. We owe our Western ideas of a life beyond death largely to two sources—the Hebrew doctrine of a resurrection and the Greek idea of the immortality of the soul. Along both lines the faith was created by the discovery of a religious fellowship, not by the mere elaboration of the ghostly existence in Hades or Sheol. The truth is that religion has very little concern with mere survival, any more than it has with the actual length of a man's life. As the *Wisdom of Solomon* reminds us, "honourable old age is not that which standeth in length of time, nor is its measure given by number of years " (iv. 8). F. W. H. Myers tells us of a remark made to him by Ruskin, " 'Ah, my friend!' he answered once when I spoke of life to come, 'if you could only give me fifty years longer of this life on earth, I would ask for nothing more!' And half that season was granted to him, and all in vain; for what Tithonus may tread for ever unweary the 'gleaming halls of Morn'?"[2] The real weakness of the spiritualism which Myers defended is not so much that its evidence is defective, as that the contents of its professed revelations have no religious or moral value, or none that does not seem a ghostly copy of our own ideas. But the Hebrew faith in life beyond death began not with the Witch of Endor, but with the sense of fellowship with God that

[1] *Op. cit.*, p. 224.  [2] *Fragments*, p. 91.

shewed itself alike in the Messianic hope of a resurrection to life on this earth,[1] and in the sense of the covenant-love of God which breaks through the clouds of the seventy-third psalm:—

"Whom have I (to care for) in heaven?
  and possessing thee I have pleasure in nothing upon earth.
Though my flesh and my heart should have wasted away,
  God would for ever be the rock of my heart and my portion."[2]

That is not yet a doctrine of immortality. But it comes very near to it, by experience of something untouched by the thought, and untouchable by the fact, of death, by experience, that is, of the fellowship with God which is the essence of religion. It was the same amongst the Greeks. Their doctrine of immortality was not a development of the dim life in Hades, but a positive declaration of new religious faith. This faith grew up in connection with the mystery religions, especially the Orphic cult from the sixth century B.C., and from them passed to its noble expression in Plato. "The underlying idea, the whole aim of the ritual, is the identification of the worshipper with the god. . . . That which is capable of union with the god must be itself of divine origin, and may be expected to pass after death to its native sphere."[3] Historically, therefore, our faith in a real life beyond death has been cradled in religion, would not indeed have been begotten without it, and history suggests that this faith will always depend on the nurture and inspiration of religion for any real quality it possesses. Such a faith at its best will not be over-curious about the details of the life beyond; it has already learnt something of the standards of eternity. Its final argument will always be the love of God, the divine nature which it has learnt to know in present fellowship

[1] Isa. xxvi. 19.   [2] Verses 25, 26, Cheyne's translation.
[3] Pringle-Pattison, *op. cit.*, p. 24.

with Him. The surrender of faith which underlies this fellowship in its Christian form is not the loss of individuality by absorption into an ocean; it is felt to be the fuller realization of the true self. To such a faith, built on such an experience, the resurrection of Jesus Christ is the final proof—not in the sense of being an isolated miracle, but as an example and prophecy of the working of a law of life that is universal. As H. R. Mackintosh put it, "The experience of Jesus was a test case, and like every test case, it fixed a principle."[1]

Let us think, then, of the body as the scaffolding of the soul, first to be reared, essential to its creation, and already dimly showing something of the proportions of the building that shall be, yet doomed to fall without loss when its poles and planks have served their turn. If we wish to translate the metaphor into philosophic language, we may borrow von Hügel's words, which summarize his profound study of *Eternal Life*: "The sense, then, of Eternal Life requires, for its normal, general, and deepest development, *Duration*, history; Space, institutions; Material Stimulations, and symbols, something sacramental; and Transcendence, a movement away from all and every culture and civilization, to the Cross, to asceticism, to interior nakedness and the Beyond" (pp. 392–93).

In this world there is often the irrational survival of trifles, as when the archæologist finds drawn on the marble of the Forum the lines with which some Roman idler played backgammon or draughts. The life beyond has no room for such trifles, though it garners their spiritual harvest. As Emerson says, "this homely game of life we play, covers, under what seem foolish details, principles that astonish. The child amidst his baubles, is learning the action of light, motion, gravity, muscular force; and in the game of human life, love, fear, justice, appetite, man,

[1] *Immortality and the Future*, p. 178.

and God, interact."[1]    This is a realm where one illustration
may be worth many arguments.    When Cardinal Newman
died, he wore by his own desire a silk handkerchief which
had been left at his door more than thirty years previously
by a poor stranger, with a message of respect.    The
handkerchief remained in this world, yet surely it was the
sacramental sign of something that passed with him into
the life beyond.

   Let us hold fast to the conviction that it is personality
with which we are concerned, the whole personality (as
the Jewish-Christian doctrine of the resurrection of the
body implies) that has discovered its true self and its
abiding reality in the fellowship of men and of God, and
is the home of all that is of supreme value to Him.    That
has both a negative and a positive side.    Negatively, it
re-echoes the teaching of Christ, and puts the emphasis
where He put it.    One searching word of His challenges
a whole host of our speculations about the life beyond:
"in the resurrection they neither marry, nor are given in
marriage, but are as angels in heaven."[2]    If the most
intimate tie of physical relationship is broken, so far as its
present form is concerned, how much more shall we have
left behind the poles and planks of all other structures
that belong to our present order!    The eschatologies
which men have so laboriously constructed are not without
their value, though they belong better to Dante than to
Aquinas.    They are the necessary symbols of thought, as,
in differing degrees, all must admit.    But directly they
become more than this, we are reading the eternal in the
light of the temporal—we are staring down on the lights
of the fair, forgetful of the starry sky above us.    The one
reality that gives continuity with the world beyond is
personality, and the positive side of this truth underlies
that other word of Christ's: "Whosoever shall lose his

---

[1] *Lecture to Divinity Students.*                    [2] Matt. xxii. 30.

X

life for my sake and the gospel's shall save it." A man may lose all yet gain all, and the explanation of the great paradox is that, as Bourget said, "nothing is lost when we make an offering of it." The law of transformation is fundamental to spiritual life, the life of personality.

It is necessary to consider this law in relation to the doctrine of the Holy Spirit, which is essential to our subject. That doctrine ought to include the "natural" as well as the "spiritual" creation, the creation of personality within the first Adam as well as the second. The Spirit of God transforms the temporal into the spiritual, and creates a soul out of a body, as it creates a spirit out of a soul, a new centre or nucleus for its own activities.[1] The real existence of that new centre is in the Spirit, not in the flesh. The spiritual wealth of the man of clay is not really kept in an earthen vessel, which crumbles to pieces in due course; it is already, as Jesus said, in heaven. But the Spirit that created this wealth by transformation from things temporal can be trusted to refund the wealth, of which it is the trustee, for the changed needs and conditions of life beyond death. The gifts and graces of the spiritual life are to be transformed (as Paul argued in connection with his doctrine of a spiritual body) into new manifestations. In other words, the content of the life beyond must be thought out in terms of the Spirit-transformed life here, and as in the first acquisition, so in the re-transformation, "we receive but what we give". If we apply this principle to the life beyond death, we shall see how it simplifies the problems men raise, without leaving us with bare and abstract solutions. In particular, we may confidently hold that the maintenance of a true Christian *individuality* by the Spirit in this life points to the retention of the individual values of personality in the

[1] The conventional terms are here employed, without acceptance of them as affording an adequate psychology.

life beyond death. Men grow not poorer but richer in God, and even a transformed self must still be a self.

What kind of life beyond death is Christian faith to expect? The answer is in terms of all that Christian personality knows already in fellowship with God—in the widest and deepest sense—through the Spirit of Christ, a fellowship which does not sacrifice individuality, though transfiguring it. We think first of the ethical values, measured in terms of the ethics of the Cross—the ministry to others like that of spirits sent forth to minister to the future heirs of salvation, the ministry that we render so imperfectly here, but whose nobler amplitude we see already in Jesus. We conceive such a ministry as necessary in the world beyond—wherever, indeed, spirits are at many different stages of progress; we cannot tell how much such a ministry covers in our present experience, and whether the "guardian angel" does not stand for some deep truth of present experience. But the doctrine of the Spirit does not confine itself to right social relations, however fundamental they must be in our present stage of development. We think of what the vision of beauty means to the artist, the majesty of ordered sound to the musician, the intellectual interests of the scientist and of the philosopher; what infinite possibilities of "spiritual" life in all these realms are opened up in richer perspective and with wider horizons, through some ampler experience of fellowship with God in whom all these values are unified! One of the most un-Christian things Amiel ever wrote was that "latent genius is only a presumption. All which can be must come into being, and all that does not come into being was naught." Browning's familiar lines supply the Christian truth: "All I could never be, all men ignored in me, This I was worth to God." This is not said to suggest the hackneyed doctrine of a compensatory heaven. These present failures of ours do not make heaven necessary in order to vindicate God. Heaven is not God's vindication so much as His realization.

We must not shut our eyes to the fact that even the best of men have gone but a little way along this path, and that most of us at death are simply not yet fit for the rarefied air of the heavenly Himalayas. The actual experience of death, or rather of passing into new spiritual conditions, may have vast consequences and unknown powers of revelation. Yet it is difficult to see why the mere event of dying, which has nothing whatever to do with the essential values of personality, should miraculously turn sinners into saints. To hold fast to personality is to hold fast to moral continuity, and there can be nothing artificial and arbitrary in the ways of God with men. Death may indeed reveal to us the meaning of personality as we have never before seen it, just as the building first stands revealed when the scaffolding is removed. Yet that which is revealed has been slowly created; the "catastrophes" of spiritual experience, like those of the natural order, are long prepared, and have their hidden and gradual history before their dramatic disclosure. Moreover, we simply cannot think at all of personality as arrested and fixed into something wholly static at death. All personality short of God must be progressive personality, for it is finite life lived within the infinite. The progress of personality must depend on discipline, and discipline is always painful at some point or other. There is no necessity to call this development, which all will need, "Purgatory", because that term is apt to bring with it ideas which are unnecessary, and from our present standpoint may seem erroneous. The doctrine of Purgatory fixes the destiny of man at physical death, and usually makes his purgatorial suffering penal or retributive in the first place; does not Newman, in the *Dream of Gerontius*, plunge the soul into "penal" waters? But we cannot make the accident or incident of physical death the crucial point in the history of the creation of personality, nor is the conception of God as a Judge the highest we cherish. His relation to human personality can never be expressed simply in terms of so much suffering for so much sin. Sin must always bring suffering, for it robs personality of its inheritance in God, and there are undoubtedly crises of man's history when he makes either a true choice or a great refusal. But we have no sufficient ground for asserting that the final decision is always made at the present stage of our development; indeed, we all realize that many men on earth have never had a fair opportunity of making it. The New Testament itself recognizes this with its conception of "the spirits in prison" to whom Christ preached. On the other hand, if we realize the true meaning of eternal life, as something that is as truly "here" as it ever will be "there", a new note of urgency will come into the preaching of the Gospel, a note that is greatly needed to-day, when the prayer of "Maranatha"—"Our Lord, come ! "—means so little to most of us in its older form. If every moment of time has its eternal meaning, then, as Newman taught, we stand already before the judgment seat of God, and rehearse in succession that which will be summarized beyond time.

But what of the fate of those who fail to realize their personality in God? In the past, such questions have been too prominent in Christian thought and doctrine. There is something unhealthy in being over-much concerned with hell, when man's proper business is with heaven. When we curiously enquire into the fate of other men, we ought to hear a divine voice saying, "What is that to thee? follow thou me." The very mystery of the life beyond may serve as a moral and religious touchstone.

As a further warning, there is the marked difference of judgment amongst Christian men when they do speculate.

Their minds have usually run in some one of three lines of thought. They have believed in what is called "the larger hope"—the final restoration of all men through the victorious love of God; or in the everlasting suffering of the finally impenitent, as a just retribution for sin; or in "conditional" immortality, so that those only continue to live who are united with God through Christ, and the others are annihilated or cease to be. For each of these speculations a case can be made on grounds both of Scripture and of reason, and all of them are unsatisfactory, though a revised form of conditional immortality can make the best case for itself.[1] Perhaps the reason that the speculations fail is intrinsic to the subject. We are here in presence of the solemn mystery of human freedom, the strange and unique power of personality to seek and find its own realization. We cannot successfully introduce any dogma which contradicts that fact of experience. We cannot do it, in regard to the past, by an Augustinian dogma of Original Sin or by an evolutionary theory of the origin of sin, either of which makes sin inevitable and necessary—for then it ceases to be sin. But neither can we do it in regard to the future by asserting that all men will or will not turn to God; how do we know what use personality will make of its freedom under entirely new conditions? We do not know just where personality begins, either in the race or in the individual; how can we dogmatize about the manner of its ending? We cannot to-day look down with Jonathan Edwards[2] on the torments

[1] "Conditional immortality", so far as it makes eternal life a positive attainment in Christ, does not imply a divine failure in regard to those who do not attain it. The possibility is bound up with the gift of human freedom, by which God has necessarily limited Himself. If, according to His purpose, the right use of freedom is necessary for the attainment of eternal life, then the wrong use of freedom, *if permanent*, must forfeit it.

[2] This idea is not confined to Edwards, though he is the best known exponent of it; see E. Bevan, *Symbolism and Belief*, p. 237, note, where he shows that it belongs to Aquinas and "Catholic" doctrine.

of the damned in hell, and find in that sight a new source of joy for the saints in heaven; for that sight would rob us of faith in a God of love, a God who conquered by the Cross, and not by the methods of the crucifiers.

May it not be that the most Christian teaching is to say that we do not know, and that in the very nature of personality we cannot know, what the negative of personality is? Our concern is with the positive truth that we live in God, and only in God, and that without Him there is no life worth living. Our very ignorance may be the condition of the present challenge of God. He may be calling us to consider the inner realities of sin and grace, rather than their possible dramatic setting. He may have swept away the mists on which we saw ourselves reflected, that a land of far distances might be apparent. It is enough for us to know that as men may already enter into some experience of heaven whilst on earth, through their present fellowship with God, so they may know the meaning of hell through the lack of Him, in baffled and unsatisfied desire, in the anguish of unavailing remorse, in the horrible realization of their own uncleanness, cowardice, and selfishness. It is enough for the Christian preacher to be able to declare to such a man, even though he be a Judas crying, "I have sinned in that I have betrayed innocent blood", that he is already so far in the path of him who cried "God be merciful to me a sinner", and found acceptance. Let us be quite sure that God sees more good in men than we do, even though the sins hidden from our eyes are not hidden from His.

The fundamental question in this realm of personality and the life beyond is not about others, but about ourselves. How much of the eternal life is already ours?

That question finds its sufficient comment in the imaginations of a modern novelist and of a modern dramatist. The first[1] has pictured one who seeks entrance into the happiness of heaven because he has known so much of the suffering of earth, and he is told, "Heaven hath no happiness but that men bring." The second[2] gives as the reply to the anxious question, "What shall I find there?" the answer, "I do not know what things have illuminated your mind and touched your heart."

[1] I. Bacheller, *Darrel of the Blessed Isles*, p. 162.
[2] J. B. Priestley, *Johnson over Jordan*, p. 77.

# INDEX

## (A) NAMES

AARON, 205
Abelard, 245
Achan, 26
Acton, Lord, 6 n., 21, 28
Aeschylus, 41 n.
Ames, E. S., 11 n.
Amiel, 307
Amos, 101
Andrae, T., 102
Andrews, H. T., 213 n.
Anselm, 245
Apollinarius, 206
Apollo, 137
Apollonius of Tyana, 54
Aquinas, 31, 52 n., 186
Aristotle, 299
Arius, 206
Arnold, Matthew, XXV, 124 f.
Aton, 27, 127
Augustine, St., XXX, 96, 217, 242
Aulén, 245 ff.

BACHELLER, I., 312
Bacon, Lord, XXXI
Baikie, J., 127 n.
Baillie, J., 95 n., 297 n.
Bar Kokhbah, 199 n., 225
Barnett, L. D., 34 n.
Barth, K. (see also "Barthianism"), 95 n., 165 n.
Beethoven, 45, 47
Berdyaev, N., XLIII
Bergson, H., 75
Bethune-Baker, J. F., 207 n.
Bevan, E., 32 n., 51, 55, 114 n., 135 n., 173, 175, 200 n., 211, 268 n., 310 n.
Bigg, C., 205 n.
Blake, W., 147
Boehme, J., 81
Bourget, P., 306
Bousset, W., 203 n.
Brabant, F. H., XLVI
Bradley, A. C., XXXII n., 57

Bradley, J. H., 30 n.
Breasted, J. H., XXXVI n., 127 n.
Brown, W., 132 n.
Browning, R., XXXIV n., 20, 26, 31, 45, 61, 307
Brunner, E., 95 n., 165 n.
Buddha, 174
Bunyan, 62 f.
Burnet, J., 207
Bushnell, H., 19, 270 n., 293
Butler, Bishop, 8

CALVIN, 96, 190
Campbell, McLeod, 257, 260, 288 n.
Casson, S., 74
Caventou, 44
Chrysostom, 137 n.
Cicero, 297
Coleridge, 124, 134, 152
Collingwood, R. G., 21 n.
Constantine, 128
Cumont, F., 128 ff.
Cybele, 107
Cyrus, 223

DALAI LAMA, 116
Dale, R. W., 268 n., 273
Dante, 47, 49 f.
D'Arcy, M. C., 186
David, 284
Davidson, A. B., 226
Dayananda Sarasvati, 33
Deissmann, A., 228 n.
Denney, J., 84
Descartes, 9
Dewey, J., 155
Dhorme, P., 220 n.
Diocletian, 128 f.
Dodd, C. H., XLIV, 252 n.
Doughty, C. M., 132
Dowdall, H. C., 258 n.
Driver and Neubauer, 199 n.
Duhm, B., 203, 212

313

EDWARDS, J., 310 f.
Elijah, 101
Emanuel, A. L., 108
Emerson, 304 f.

FARNELL. L. R., 127
Farquhar, J. N., 33 n.
Fisher, H. A. L., XLI n.
Fox, George, 29
France, Anatole, 176
Franks, R. S., 236

GALEN, 143
Galloway, G., 111
Gardner, E. A., 137 n.
"Geddes, Jenny", 60
Goethe, 159
Gregory of Nazianzus, 236 n.
Gregory VII., XXXI
Grellet, S., 32
Grensted, L. W., 213 n., 236 n., 258

HACKMANN, H., 117 n.
Hanamel, 223 f.
Hananiah, 145 f.
Harnack, A., 81 n.
Harrison, M., 64
Hebert, A. G., 279 n.
Hegel, 111, 175
Henry IV (of Germany), XXXI
Heraclitus, 205
Herrmann, W., 81
Heschel, A., 150 n.
Hicks, F. C. N., 255, 260
Hocking, W. E., 157
Hölscher, G., 143
Holl, K., 174
Hooke, S. H., 120 n.
Hosea, 146
Housman, A. E., 297
Hügel, Baron von, 4, 9 n., 12 n., 14 n., 15 n., 102, 110, 262, 304
Huxley, Julian, 75 n.

IKHNATON, 127
Indra, 126
Inge, W. R., 4, 9, 206, 301
Irenaeus, 245, 259, 287 n.
Isaiah, 101
Ishtar-Tammuz, 120

JAMES, W., 14, 177 n., 282
Jeans, J., 41 n.
Jephthah, 25
Jeremiah, 33, 101, 146, 153, 166, 203, 224
Jonathan, Targum of, 199

Joshua, XLIII
Julian, 129
Justin, 197

KEATS, 110
Keller, Helen, 45
Kennett, R. H., 222 n.
Kilpatrick, T. B., 238 n.
Klausner, J., 199 n.
Krishna, 34, 161

LAMBORN, E. A. G., XXXVI
Lamech, 26
Lessing, 21, 81, 170, 175
Licinius, 128 f.
Lietzmann, H., 197 n.
Lotze, H., XXVIII n., 150
Loyola, Ignatius, 283 n.
Lucretius, XXV
Lull, Ramón, 6 n.
Luther, 189, 245

MACDONELL, A. A., 132 n.
Mackintosh, H. R., 55, 272, 304
Macmurray, J., XXVIII n.
Macnicol, N., 127 n.
McDougall, W., 299
Magna Mater, 129, 204 n.
Marett, R. R., 104
Markandeya, 34
Masefield, J., 293 n.
Matthews, W. R., 11 n., 37 n., 77, 211
Maximus of Tyre, 32
Ménégoz, E., 50 f.
Mill, J. S., 35, 126
Milton, 71 n., 255 n.
Moberly, R. C., 257, 260, 288 n.
Moffatt, J., 152 n., 281
Morgan, Lloyd, 8 n.
Morley, J., 24
Moses, 25, 97, 162
Moulton and Milligan, 43
Moulton, J. H., 129 n.
Mozley, J. K., 263
Muhammad, XXXVII, 25, 27, 97, 101 f., 162, 164, 169, 174
Murray, Gilbert, 22 n.
Myers, F. W. H., 134 n., 145 n., 302

NEWMAN, J. H., XXXIII, 4 n., 97, 175, 305, 308

ORIGEN, 40, 152, 204, 207 n.
Osiris, 27, 126
Otto, R., 131

PARKES, H. W., 137
Pascal, 166
Paul, St. (*see also under* "Scripture References"), 55, 173 ff., 189, 212
Payne, E. A., 204 n.
Pelletier, 44
Phillips, Claude, 46
Philo, 205
Philostratus, 54
Plato, 33, 41, 303
Poe, E. A., XXXIII n.
Porteous, N. W., 150 n.
Priestley, J. B., 290 n., 312
Pringle-Pattison, A. S., 207, 292, 298 f., 303
Prometheus, 162

QUINTILIAN, 187

RA, 127
Radloff, W., 135 f.
Revon, M., 128
Ritschl, A., 9
Ritschl, O., 179
Robinson, John, 25
Robertson, F. W., 31
Rohde, E., 135
Rose, H. J., 137
Rothenstein, J., XLI n.
Rousseau, 168, 259
Ruskin, J., 239 n., 302

SABATIER, A., 50, 101 n., 107
Sadhu Sundar Singh, 147 f., 201
Samuel, 116
Santayana, G., XXXIII n., 110
Schaeder, E., 272 n.
Schleiermacher, 29
Selbie, W. B., 134
Shakespeare, 30, 43, 46, 57 f., 71
Shelley, 47 f., 282
Shipley, A. E., 44
Siebeck, H., 111
Simpson, J. Y., 300
Sistine Madonna, 47
Skinner, J., 139, 146 f., 151
Slessor, Mary, 23
Smith, W. Robertson, 255
Socrates, 174

Söderblom, N., 92 n., 130 n., 166
Sorley, W. R., 68, 301
Spinoza, 32
Stevenson, R. L., 240, 285
Strack-Billerbeck, 199 n.
Stout, G. F., 22
Sullivan, J. W. N., 45
Sutherland, J., 53
Swedenborg, 80 f.

TAINE, H. A., XLI
Taylor, A. E., 38, 67 n., 68 f., 77, 104 f., 178 f., 297 n.
Taylor, Vincent, 260, 261 n.
Temple, W., 212 n., 301
Tennant, F. R., XXVIII n.
Tennyson, 297
Teresa, St., 109
Tertullian, 263
Traherne, T., XXIX
Trevelyan, G. M., XLI n.
Troeltsch, E., 92
Tufts, J. H., 155

URBAN, W. M., 41 n., 51

VARUNA, 127
Vaughan, H., 125

WARD, J., XXXIX n., 9 n., 41 n.
Webb, C. C. J., 15, 301
Wellhausen, J., 156
Wells, H. G., 75 n.
Wesley, J., 23
Westermarck, E., 67
Whitehead, A. N., 44, 162
Williams, N. P., 65 n.
Windelband, W., 207
Winkler, R., 16
Wittgenstein, 35
Wobbermin, G., 16 n.
Wood, H. G., XLVI, 178 n.
Wordsworth, 103, 124 f., 126, 285
Woolman, J., 55, 147 f.

YUAN CHWANG, 28

ZARATHUSHTRA (Zoroaster), 97, 101, 112, 129, 161, 174

## (*B*) SCRIPTURE REFERENCES

*(Page references are in bold face)*

Genesis i. 71; ii. 7, 141; iv. 23 f., 26; xv. 5, 133; xx. 3, 6, 133; xxi. 22 ff., 226; xxii, 221; xxviii, 12, 133; xxxvii. 5–10, 133; xli. 1–15, 133.

Exodus iv. 21, 284; xiii. 12, 13, 221; xxi. 8, 221; xxi. 24, 26; xxi. 30, 220; xxii. 29, 221; xxiv. 3–8, 226; xxx. 12, 220; xxxiv. 20, 221.

Leviticus, 99; xxv. 29, 223; xxv. 48 f., 223.

Numbers xii. 6, 133; xii, 6 f., 146; xxxv. 31 f., 220.

Deuteronomy vii. 8, 222, 226; xiii, 151; xiii. 1–3, 133; xix. 6, 224; xxi. 23, 231; xxvi. 17 f., 226.

Ruth iv. 1–11, 224.

1 Samuel ix. 8, 116; xii. 3, 220; xiv. 24 ff., 221; xviii. 3 f., 226; xx. 8, 226; xxiii. 17 f., 226; xxv. 29, 279; xxviii. 6, 15, 133.

2 Samuel xxiii. 16, 284.

1 Kings xviii. 42 ff., 101; xx. 29–34, 226.

Nehemiah v. 8, 220; v. 19, 228.

Job xix. 25, 224; xx. 8, 133; xxviii. 12–14, 73; xxxiii. 24, 221; xxxiii. 28, 222; xxxvi. 18, 220; xxxviii. ff., 71; xlii. 5 f., 228.

Psalms, 99; viii. 4, 228; xv., 17; xviii. 20 ff., 228; xxiv, 17; xlix. 7, 222; xlix. 8, 221; lxxiii. 25 f., 303; civ. 27 ff., 121; cvii, 225; cxi. 9, 229; cxxx. 8, 223; cxxxvi. 24, 220.

Proverbs, vi. 35, 221; viii. 99, 206; viii. 22 ff., 71; xiii. 8, 221; xxi. 18, 221.

Ecclesiastes v. 3, 7, 133.

Isaiah ii. 10 f., 228; v., 149; xxvi. 19, 303; xxviii. 23–29, 120; xxix. 7 f., 133; xxix. 10, 149; xxxv. 10, 220; xliii. 1, 225; xliii. 3, 221, 223; xliv. 22, 225; xlv. 5, 186; li. 10, 220; lii. 3, 225; liii, 198, 230, 279; liii. 11, 229; liii. 12, 290; lxiii. 9, 228.

Jeremiah viii. 21, 149; xiv. 14, 151; xv. 19, 149, 153; xx. 7, 33; xx. 12, 271; xxiii. 7 f., 89; xxiii. 9 ff., 151; xxiii. 28, 133; xxxi. 3, 211; xxxi. 10 f., 222; xxxi. 11, 220; xxxi. 31 f., 252; xxxi. 35–37, 120; xxxii. 7 f., 224; xxxii. 8, 145; xlii. 7, 144; xlv. 4 f., 280.

Daniel ii. 1 ff., 133.

Hosea ii. 21 f., 121; xi. 8f., 227; xiii. 14, 220.

Joel ii. 28, 133.

Amos v. 12, 220.

Zechariah iv. 1, 145.

Matthew i. 20, 133; ii. 12 ff., 133; v. 38 f., 26; vii. 11, 50; viii. 25, 232; ix. 21, 232; xi. 25 ff., 216; xii. 28, 248; xii. 39 ff., 116; xvii. 27, 229; xx. 28, 228; xxii. 30, 305; xxv. 40, 288; xxvi. 28, 252; xxvi. 39, 116.

Mark i. 11, 203; i. 15, 286; viii. 12, 116; ix. 7, 203; ix. 43 f., 143; x. 26, 233; x. 38, 279; x. 45, 228; xii. 1–5, 279; xiv. 24, 229, 252; xiv. 61 f., 198.

Luke i. 68, 229; ii. 38, 229; viii. 36, 232; x. 21 ff., 216; xi. 13, 50; xi. 29 ff., 116; xviii. 13, 254; xxi. 28, 230; xxiv. 21, 229; xxiv. 39, 43, 83.

John iii. 16, 274; iii. 17, 234; vii. 37, 101; xv. 288.

Acts i. 9 f., 200; i. 26, 116; ii. 4, 8, 138; ii. 38, 286; iii. 15 ff., 186, 198; iii. 21, 200; iv. 12, 234; vii. 35, 229; viii. 22, 286; ix. 10, 133; x. 10, 133; xvii. 28, 107; xx. 21, 286; xxv. 19, 173.

Romans i. 3 f., 198; i. 4, 291; iii. 24 f., 229, 252; v. 8 ff., 234, 274; v. 12–21, 259; v. 14 ff., 288; v. 20, 276; vi–viii, 281; vii. 24, 241; viii. 2, 123; viii. 9, 291; viii. 15 f., 212, 292; viii. 23, 230; viii. 26, 292; ix. 3, 6; x. 9, 100, 284; xii. 2, 289; xii–xv. 13, 257, 281; xii. 21, 248; xiii. 8–10, 288; xiii. 11, 233; xiv. 7 ff., 288.

1 Corinthians i. 22, 197; i. 30, 229; ii. 10, 55; vi. 18–20, 283; vi. 20, 228, 231; vii. 23, 228, 231; viii. 11, 283; xi. 19, 30; xi. 25, 252; xii. 12 ff., 143; xiv. 13 ff., 138; xiv. 18, 144; xiv. 19, 138;

xv, **212;** xv. 8, **198;** xv. 20, **83;** xv. 20 ff., **288;** xv. 22, **259;** xv. 35 ff., **83;** xv. 35–50, **123;** xv. 45 ff., **259, 288;** xv. 54, 57, **248.**

2 Corinthians i. 22, **55;** ii. 14, xlvii; iv. 2, **297;** v. 5, **55;** v. 15, **284;** v. 20, **189;** v. 21, **231;** vii. 1, **212;** vii. 9 f., **286;** xii. 2–4, **136;** xiii. 14, 16.

Galatians i. 15 f., **198;** ii. 16, **285;** ii. 20, **288,** 292; iii. 13, **231;** iv. 4, **214;** iv. 5, **231;** v. 1, **228;** v. 11, **197.**

Ephesians i. 7, **229** f.; i. 10, **287;** i. 13 f., **234;** i. 14, **55, 230;** i. 23, **288;** ii. 5, **233;** ii. 14–16, **288;** ii. 18, **16, 204, 291;** ii. 20 f., **288;** iii. 14 f., **50;** iv. 4, 12, 16, **288;** iv. 30, **230,** 292; v. 16, **231, 243;** v. 25–27, **288;** vi. 12, **248.**

Philippians i. 19, **232;** ii. 5–11, **291;** ii. 7 f., **290;** ii. 12 f., **233;** iv. 7, **296.**

Colossians i. 14, **230;** i. 16 ff., **206;** i. 24, **279;** ii. 15, **248;** iv. 5, **231, 243.**

1 Timothy ii. 5, **97;** ii. 6, **229.**

Titus ii. 14, **230.**

Hebrews ii. 10, **247;** ii. 17, **254;** v. 9, **234;** vi. 1, **286;** vi. 9, **233;** viii. 6, **97;** viii–x. 18, **253;** ix. 12, **230, 254;** ix. 14, **254;** ix. 15, **97, 230;** ix. 18–22, **253;** x. 11 f., **253;** x. 29, **253,** 292; xi. 35, **229;** xii. 22 f., **287;** xii. 24, **97, 253;** xiii. 20, **253.**

1 Peter i. 5, **233;** i. 18 f., **229** f.

2 Peter i. 4, **293;** i. 21, **144;** ii. 1, **231.**

1 John ii. 13 f., **248;** iii. 2, **55;** iv. 4, **248;** iv. 16, 6; iv. 20, **288;** v. 4, **247.**

Revelation ii. 7, **248;** v. 5 f., **248;** v. 9, **231;** xii. 11, **248;** xiv. 3 f., **231;** xv. 2, **248;** xvii. 14, **248.**

1 Esdras iv. 41, xlii.

2 (4) Esdras xiii. 1 ff., **198.**

Wisdom of Solomon, iv. 8, **302;** vii, **206.**

Ecclesiasticus xxiv, **206;** xxxi. 1 f. (R.V. xxxiv. 1 f.), **133.**

Enoch, xlvi. 1 ff., **198.**

Psalms of Solomon, xvii. 23 ff., **198.**

## (*C*) SUBJECTS

(*See also* "Contents," pp. xiii ff. *and* "Argument," pp. xvii ff.)

Actuality, XXX ff., 35, 53, 59, 61, 68, 155 f., 166 ff., 182 ff., 187 f., 270

*Agapé*, 43

*Agorazo*, 228, 230 f.

Analogy, 51 f.

Anthropomorphism, 155

Apollinarianism, 218

Architecture, XXXV f., 47

Art, XXXIII, 46 f., 187

Ascension, 200

*Asham*, 230, 251

Astrology, 119

Atonement (*see also* "Cross of Christ"), 55, 188, 219, 236, 272; metaphors of, 277; preaching of, 280

Atonement, Day of, 254

Authority, 6 f., 86, 170 ff., 179 ff.; of Church, XXXIX; of Word of God, 191; intrinsic, XXXVIII, 73, 192 f.

Baalim, 101, 120

Barthianism (see also "Barth"), 3, 17 n., 95 n., 165, 211 n.

Bhakti, 161

Biology, 44, 75 f.

Blood, 252, 256

Body and Soul, 82, 293, 298 f.

Buddhism, 28, 116, 161

Burnt-offering, 255 f.

Calvinism, 96, 180

Catholicism, XXXVIII, XL, 31, 96

Chalcedon, Creed of, 29, 207, 263

Christ (*see also* "Jesus"), actuality of, 213; in relation to Godhead, 201 f.; Person of, 210 f., 214, 216 f.; pre-existence of, 202 f.; priesthood of, 253; resurrection of, 80, 83, 123, 173 f., 304; supremacy of, XLVI, 107 f.; as Redeemer, 64, Cc. XI–XIII; victory of, 244, 245 ff.

Church, 82, 282, 287 f.

Consciousness,"diffused," 143; subliminal, 134, 142

Consecration Prayer, 254 f.

Contingency (*see also* "History"), 78

Corporate personality, 149 f., 246, 258 ff., 282, 287 f.

Covenant, 226 f.

Cross of Christ, 59, 162, 197 f., 231, 244, 262 ff., 270 ff.

Cross-bearing, 278 f.

Cult, of Israel, 99; in relation to faith, 102; survivals in, 101

DEATH, 298

Delphic Oracle, 137

Demons, 135 f., 232, 248

Divination, 115–118

Docetism, 30, 218

Dreams, 131 ff.

EVIL, actuality of, 68 f.

FAITH, 18, 186; in relation to conduct, 283; evangelical, 184 f.; intuitional, 166, 285; subjective aspect, 173; volitional, 284

Faith-healing, 232

Faith-mysticism, 234, 258, 288

Fall, 65

"Father" symbol (*see also* "Trinity") 50

Fellowship with God, 69, 279, 303

Freedom (*see also* "Responsibility"), XXVI f., XXIX, 66, 267

Friends, Society of, 109

*Ga'al*, 220, 223 ff.

Gnosticism, XXIX, 31

God, activity of, XXIX, 77 f., 159 f.; as "given", 9; as hidden, 78, 172, 296; initiative of, XLV and Ch. V; knowledge of, XXVII f.; 17 f.; Personality of, 14, 217; self-limitation of, 76, 187, 294

Godhead, 201, 217 f.

God-man, 207 ff.

Good, actuality of, 68 f.

Gospel, characterized, 174

Grace, 77, 276, 295

Group and individual (*see also* "Corporate personality"), 26

Guilt, 243, 267, 273 f.

HEAVEN, 52 and Ch. XIV. § 3.

Hegelianism, 36

*Hesed*, 227

Heresy, 29 f.

Hinduism, 33, 112, 127

History, axioms of, XXVI; contingency of, XLIV, 170; creative, XXIX, XXXVII; goal of, XLIII, 175; meaning of, 44 and Intro.; philosophy of, 71, 176; needing redemption, XLVIII, 71 f., 243; as revelation, 99 and Cc. IX, X; unity of, 169; worth of, 70

Holiness and sin, 268

"Hope, larger", 310

Hypostasis, 99, 205 f.

IDOLATRY, 32, 107, 164

Ignorance, 38

Images, 32

Immanence, 125, 292

Immortality, conditional, 310; religious basis of, 302 f.

Incarnation, XLVI, 9 f., 15, 17, 81, 110, 181, 217, 263

Incubation, 132

Individuality, 26, 301, 306

Inspiration (*see also* "Prophetic consciousness"), 143

Islam, 101, 112, 159, 166

Israel, history of, 87 ff.

JESUS (*see also* "Christ"), actuality of, 183; life of, 83 f., 191; supremacy of, 178, 192; teaching of, 81, 85, 164, 171

Justification, 235

KENOSIS, 9 f., 217, 290 ff.

Kinship of God and man, 15, 52 f., 164 f., 210 f.

*Kopher*, 220

Kur'an, 25, 97

LANGUAGE, difficulties in use of, 54; psychology of, 41 f.; symbolism of, Ch. III

*Lex talionis*, 26
"Liberalism" in theology, 4 n., 6, 81
Life, challenge of, 296; Christian, 281 ff.; duality of, 293; eternal, 304, 307; illusiveness of, 31 f.
Logos, 205 ff.
Lord's Supper, 252
*Lutroō*, 228 f.

*Mana*, 115, 119
Manichaeism, 30
*Maya*, 33 f.
Meaning, XL, 275
Media, physical, 114 ff.; psychical, 131 ff.; variety of, 89, 98 ff.
Mediation (*see* Part II, *passim*), 5, 89, 96, 108; O.T. types of, 98
Messiah, suffering, 197–199
Miracle, 121 ff.
Mithraism, 103, 128 ff.
Monarchianism, 263
Morality, compulsive element in, 153; origins of, XXXVI f., 67; in relation to religion, 19, 27
Music, XXXIII ff., 45, 47, 52
Mysticism (*see also* "Faith"), 6, 80 f., 108 ff.
Mythology, 33

*Nabi* (*see also* "Prophetic consciousness"), 90, 138
Natural and supernatural, 48, 79
Nature, divine activity in, 79; "laws" of, 121 ff.; miracle, 118 ff.; order of, 119 f.; revelation through, 98, 120 f.; value for God, 70 f.
Nature-religions, 111 f.
Nature and spirit, 130
Nature-worship, 126 ff.
Nicaea, Creed of, 206
Numinous, 131

OLD TESTAMENT, unity in variety, 88
Orphism, 303

*Padhah*, 220 f.
Pantheism, 128
*Parousia*, 230, 235
Parsees, 161
Passibility of God, 246, 262 ff.; objections to, 264 ff.
Patripassianism, 263
Peace-offering, 255
Pelagianism, 30

Penalty, 277
Penitence, "vicarious", 257
Personality, characterized, 310; in relation to Christology, 207 ff.; continuity of, 305; Hebrew ideas of, 299; inclusive, 168, 263; as basis of values, 73
Poetry, 40, 47 f., 53, 110
Potentiality, 59 f., 307
Prophecy, true and false, 151
Prophets, 162 ff.
Prophetic consciousness, 90, 98, 112 f., 138 ff., 143 ff., 164
Prophetic symbolism, XXXII, 156, 250, 256
Propitiation, 252
Protestantism, XL, 179 f.
Psycho-therapy, 132 f., 134
Psychology of the Hebrews, 140 ff.
Punishment, everlasting, 310
Purgatory, 308
Purpose of God, 74 ff., 188

RANSOM, 219, 277; from the devil, 236 f.
"Reality", tests of, 12 f.
"Recapitulation" doctrine, 259
Reconciliation, 261 n.
Redemption, 76 f., 214 and Part III, *passim*; the metaphor, 219; in the O.T., 88 f., 220 f., 225; from what? 230, 235 ff.
Relativity, 85, 107
Religion, philosophy of, 113 and Intro.
Religions, classification of, 111
Repentance, 241, 267, 286, 311
Representation, 257; by intrinsic right, 261
Responsibility, moral, 62 ff., 118; Ch. IV § 2.
Resurrection, 62, 302; of Christ, *s.v.* "Christ"
Revelation, 79, 86, 177 ff., 180 ff., and Cc. IX, X
Righteousness, 252

SABELLIANISM, 218
Sacraments, XXXII, 104 ff.
Sacrifice, of Christ, 249 ff., 277; covenant, 252 f.; meaning of, 251, 256, 260 f.; in O.T., 249 ff.; use of metaphor, 254; value of metaphor, 255
Saintliness, 282 f.
Salvation, 232 ff., 238 n.
Sanctification, 283

Satan, 68, 236 f.
Servant of Yahweh, 99, 199, 251
Shaman, 115, 135 f.
Shinto, 128
Signs, 116
Sin, evolutionary theory of, 310; Original, 259, 310; universality of, 64
Sin-offering, 254
Sinfulness, 241
Social solidarity, 242 f., 259, 288 f.
Son of God, 203 ff.
*Soteria*, 232
Space-metaphor, 200
Sphinx, 297
Spirit, inclusiveness of, 215
Spirit of God, kenosis of, 82, 290 ff.; Personality of, 291; as presence of God, 185, 292; suffering, 292 f., 295
Spirit, Holy, 10, 55, 105, 281, 283, 287
Stoicism, 205
Subject and object, XXXIX f., 124 f., 173
Suffering, divine (*see also* "Passibility of God"), 263
Suffering in Nature, 266
Supernatural, *see* "Natural and supernatural"
Survival of death, 302
Symbolic acts (*see also* "Prophetic symbolism"), 40
Symbolic magic, 40, 117, 250
Symbolism of thought, 9 and Ch. III § 3

Symbolo-fideism, 50 f.

*Testimonium spiritus sancti internum*, 190
Theocentricity, 272 f.
Thought, and act, 57; and life, 42
Time, process, XLVI; metaphor, 200 f.
Time and eternity, XLII ff., 169, 171, 181, 265, 278, 305
Tongues, gift of, 137, 144
Torah, 97, 99, 256
Transactionalism, 262, 276
Transformation, XLI, 193, 271, 274 f., 306
Trinity, Holy (*see also* "Godhead"), 204, 292
Truth, absolute and relative, 21, 37; hidden, 19 f., 21, 31, 296

UNIVERSALISM and particularism, 91 f.

VALUE-JUDGMENTS, 153, 285
Values, XXXV, 8, 13, 154
Veda, 101, 159
Vocabulary, adequacy of, 48 ff.

WILL, 58, 69, 186 f.
"Will to believe", 285
Word of God, 189 f.
Worship, 100 f., 103
Worth, intrinsic, 152, 176
Wrath of God, 268 ff.